THE UNFOLDING MESSAGE OF THE BIBLE

THE HARMONY AND UNITY OF THE SCRIPTURES

by

G. CAMPBELL MORGAN

London,
PICKERING & INGLIS
1961

Hope. Inspiration. Trust.

WE'RE SOCIAL! FOLLOW US FOR NEW TITLES AND DEALS:
FACEBOOK.COM/CROSSREACHPUBLICATIONS
@CROSSREACHPUB

AVAILABLE IN PAPERBACK AND EBOOK EDITIONS
PLEASE GO ONLINE FOR MORE GREAT TITLES
AVAILABLE THROUGH CROSSREACH PUBLICATIONS.
AND IF YOU ENJOYED THIS BOOK PLEASE CONSIDER LEAVING A
REVIEW ON AMAZON. THAT HELPS US OUT A LOT. THANKS.

CONTENTS

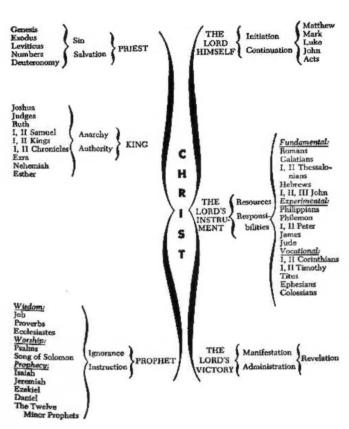

THE HARMONY OF THE TESTAMENTS

The Old Testament: The Need	The New Testament: The Supply

Genesis, Exodus, Leviticus, Numbers, Deuteronomy } Sin / Salvation } PRIEST

Joshua, Judges, Ruth, I, II Samuel, I, II Kings, I, II Chronicles, Ezra, Nehemiah, Esther } Anarchy / Authority } KING

Wisdom: Job, Proverbs, Ecclesiastes *Worship:* Psalms, Song of Solomon *Prophecy:* Isaiah, Jeremiah, Ezekiel, Daniel, The Twelve Minor Prophets } Ignorance / Instruction } PROPHET

CHRIST

THE LORD HIMSELF } Initiation / Continuation } Matthew, Mark, Luke, John, Acts

THE LORD'S INSTRUMENT } Resources / Responsibilities } *Fundamental:* Romans, Galatians, I, II Thessalonians, Hebrews, I, II, III John *Experimental:* Philippians, Philemon, I, II Peter, James, Jude *Vocational:* I, II Corinthians, I, II Timothy, Titus, Ephesians, Colossians

THE LORD'S VICTORY } Manifestation / Administration } Revelation

INTRODUCTION

In most of his books, Dr. Morgan is a teacher and the reader a student; in this book, the scene and the relationship are different. This is a fireside chat, and the most informal of all his writings. It is as though the reader were invited into the home of the renowned and beloved scholar to sit before the fire and just talk about the Scriptures. It is as intimate as that. Here is completely new and previously unpublished material, and a new look at the warm and glowing personality of this master of the Word.

Originally, he called it "The Harmony of the Scriptures," but we felt that such a title might indicate that it was another of those "Harmonies" which run the Gospels in parallel columns, for the purposes of comparison. This is not a comparison, but a weaving together. The Bible is indeed a library of sixty-six books, each of which must be studied separately if we are to understand it. But we must also understand that the books are chapters in a long, connected story—the story of a community, and a record of divine government—and that, as Dr. Morgan has it, "It is concerning... Christ, and the history of that Lord, that the Bible is one."

This is the divine, interwoven tapestry of the Word, as God gave it warp and woof, described by one who sees the golden thread of one increasing purpose and unfolding message running through it all. It is G. Campbell Morgan at his informal and inspiring best.

The Publishers

GENERAL CONSPECTUS

Bible teachers insist upon the fact that the Bible is a library, and that is an important fact to know and to remember. We have sixty-six books, as we find them in our Bible, bound together, written over a period of 1,500 years, mostly in Hebrew and Greek and some small portions in Aramaic. But it is a library, and that must be insisted upon again and again when studying the Bible.

But while that is perfectly true, these books form a whole in a simple and yet very remarkable way. This series of studies is intended to show that wholeness: that although we treat the Bible as a library and advise students desiring to begin the study of it to take a book at a time, it is certainly true that we shall far more intelligently study any part of the Bible in proportion as we have some conception of its entirety, a view of the wholeness of it. That unity is what we are attempting to show.

I wonder how many are familiar with those wonderful lines of George Herbert. I have written them in the beginning of a number of Bibles at one time or another, because they do so express my feeling in the matter. He said about the Bible:

> Oh! that I knew how all thy lights combine,
> And the configuration of thy glory,
> Seeing not only how each verse doth shine,
> But all the constellations of the story.

In this first Lecture I propose to take a general conspectus. I shall first describe some of the terms that may be used, and then take a broad outlook at the whole of the library.

Our theme is the harmony of the divine library. What is harmony? The dictionary definition of harmony is "a fitting together of parts so as to form a connected whole." It is agreement in relationship. That is harmony.

If a musician were lecturing on harmony he would go much more into detail in the matter from the musical standpoint. If my friend, Frank Salisbury, the artist, were lecturing on harmony, he would go more fully into it from the standpoint of colors and artistry. But it is all there. It is a fitting together of the parts so as to form a connected whole; how it agrees in relationship, and the relationship of all its varied parts.

The harmony of the Scriptures is the harmony of the Testaments, Old and New. I but refresh your memory when I say we get our word testament from the Latin, and the Latin word *testamentum* means a witness. It has much wider meanings in use, but a testament is a witness. I take my Greek New Testament and find that the word means practically, if not always, a testament as a witness that constitutes an agreement.

We do not find that word Testament used about the Scriptures anywhere in the Bible except perhaps at one place; and it may be open to question, though I think it cannot finally be so. It is used when Paul, writing to the Corinthians, spoke of the reading of the Old Testament. Using the Authorized Version it reads exactly like that: "The reading of the Old Testament." The Revised Version has changed the word to "covenant," "the reading of the Covenant." Of course, it is the word our Lord made use of when He said, "This is the new covenant in my blood." I am only dealing with the word now, not with its placing there. But testament means a witness, and a witness that constitutes the principles of a covenant.

So we take the Old Testament and the New. In the Old Testament we have the Hebrew Scriptures. I do not mean that they belong to the Hebrew nation alone, for they belong also to us. One cannot read the New Testament without reference to the Old. We can start at the very beginning of our New Testament and read, "The book of the generation of Jesus Christ, the son of David, the son of Abraham." Suppose we had never read that before! We should say at once, What is this about Abraham and David? We have to go back to the Old Testament before we can begin the New.

Or if we take the second book in the New Testament, how does it open? "The beginning of the gospel of Jesus Christ, the Son of God. Even as it is written in Isaiah the prophet." Written where? In Isaiah. But we do not need the Old Testament! Don't we? Go back and look at Isaiah. So we might go all through the books. When I refer to them as the Hebrew Scriptures, I mean they were the Scriptures of the devout Hebrew.

Then the New Testament consists of the Christian Scriptures. By that I do not mean to say that the Old Testament is not for the Christians. I have been trying to show how necessary the Old Testament is, but we never finish in the Old Testament, if we are Christians. We always finish in the New Testament. But we must go back to the Old to find out all the things which are fulfilled in the New.

What is meant by "conspectus"? The word means a "comprehensive survey." Here is the Bible. It is a library of sixty-six books. We begin at the beginning, and read right through to the end. I am not saying it is the best way, though I am certain it is a profitable thing to do, especially for the young people, if they have never done it before.

I want to suggest two things as to broad outlook. First, that this Bible contains two great movements beginning in Genesis and ending in Revelation. I will name them, and then say a word or two about each. First, there is a history of a community, not a full one, not complete, not of the whole race, but of all the really essential things in human nature and human life. And it is a history. It is not an interpretation for psychology alone. It tells a story and there is a movement of continuity followed all through the story.

In the second place, it is a record of divine government. I am content to make these two statements and leave them. Taking the Bible in its entirety, it is first the history of humanity, and all the way a record of divine government. These are the two great movements that constitute the wholeness of the library.

It is the history of a community. If we begin to ponder dates we will in all likelihood be confused. It is not easy to deal with dating. In the Old Version we find on page after page a date, and the earliest date there at the commencement of everything is 4004 B.C., and the latest date at the end of the Apocalypse is A.D. 96. These are the dates with which we were familiar in childhood. Everyone knows that they were Ussher's dates.

An old friend of mine, Martin Anstey, produced with great labor and care an exact and remarkable volume that was a chronology of the Bible. When it was published it was out of the reach of the majority of people, but it has been a book of great value. Before Martin Anstey did his work he resolutely consulted the text itself, and every reference was tabulated. It was a tremendous piece of work. Another friend of mine, Philip Mauro, saw Anstey's book and condensed it into a small volume called The Chronology of the Bible, and in that will be found in the briefest form all the salient points of the dating found within the Bible. This is technical, but it is important. This Book is a history of humanity. It begins with the origin of the human race. How did this humanity come to be? What were its origins? It then records the fact of a disaster, a failure. (I am not afraid of the old word, a "fall.") And from that moment it proceeds, first of all, to trace the early chapters in the history of the race; then a moment when a man Abraham is called out from the rest, from whom a nation sprang. Then a nation under Moses, and it goes straight on, all the way through as far as history is concerned, right on to Malachi. I do not mean to say that the prophets are to be treated as history, but we cannot study them without considering the background of history behind them. It *is* the consolidated history" of a nation that came from a man—God's people, chosen, created for a very clear and definite purpose. Then the historic sequence shows a gap of about 400 years. No reference is made to it in the Bible at all.

Now take the New Testament and we find the same running history. The Son of God is seen as the Son of Man, and resulting from His presence in the world is the record of the creation and the growth of a new race of human beings. And so it runs on. We begin at the beginning with origins, and the account of failure. We look on and watch the process of the whole race seen for a little while, as a man comes and a nation is formed, and we look upon that nation. We watch that nation through into the New Testament, and there we have another disaster, the element of failure of the nation to fulfill its purpose, as manifested in the crucifixion of the Son of God. But there when the darkness is deepest, light springs, and immediately we see a newborn race, all human but different. And the process marches on until we come to the Acts, where we have glimpses of that new nation at the beginning, in all its initial movements, and the story is never finished, because it could not be finished. It has been running on ever since. But the Bible illustrates this new period and this new race. It is history; it is history right through.

Take the Psalms, or the Prophets; they are all set against a background of history. It is an historic sequence, and we cannot break in upon that historic sequence without doing some violence to the perfect message of the Bible delivered to the human race. But that is only one element. The other is this. It is a record of divine government from the very beginning to the end. I will not trace that but summarize; and I do so by turning to one of the ancient prophets, Jeremiah. Hear the words again in this connection. In the midst of his ministry, Jeremiah said: "A glorious throne on high from the beginning is the place of our sanctuary." The beginning! That is how the Bible opens. "In the beginning God created... Jeremiah says, "From the beginning was the glorious throne of God on high." Our Version says, "set on high." That word "set" is not in the Hebrew. Of course I am not objecting to its insertion, but in some ways it rather spoils it. It does not say it is set there as if by a time limit, and a beginning. It is "on high from the beginning." If we would know what Jeremiah meant, turn from Genesis to John. "In the beginning was the Word, and the Word was with God, and the Word was God." A glorious throne on high from the beginning (and mark the wonderful declaration) is the place of our safety, of our sanctuary.

When we come to the start of the Book we find God governing, but not governing by giving laws. He is not governing by uttering commandments. He is governing in communion. That is the meaning of the marvelous statement in the third chapter of Genesis, when the Lord God walked "in the garden in the cool of the day," as the Old Version puts it. Very pleasant, that "cool." But why they rendered *ruach* as "cool" there, I could never understand. He walked in the garden "in the wind of the day." That is a little better. It does mean "wind," but it is far more accurately translated "spirit." "The Lord God walked in the garden in the spirit of the day." The first man walked in fellowship with Him, and God governed by communion. We can say He uttered a law, if we like so to do, but He did it as He talked to him in the spirit of the day, as He told him his liberty was limited. We know the story. Throughout, God is always there, always on the throne, always governing.

Then came a catastrophe, a definite rebellion against that very government. From that moment on God is governing, shall I say, mediatorially; not as He did at first by direct communion, but through means and methods and persons and messengers and voices—God governing through prophets, through singers, always making known His will to humanity. I wonder as I look around me today why so many people want to get rid of the Old Testament with its revelation of human failure. It is the same story still running on, from the standpoint of human history. It is a long continuation, blunders, and disasters and appalling failure. But God is governing all the way through. Governing! That is the Bible. Go outside the Bible, and we may call that in question. But we shall find as we go through, that this method of government—and I want to say this carefully because my very words may be misunderstood—was that of an accommodation, not to principle, but to meet human necessity resulting from human failure.

I can take an illustration of the proceeding to which I have referred. The monarchy was an accommodation to meet human weakness; as the Temple was an accommodation to meet human weakness. So it has been all through, even the great prophetic utterances were an accommodation of God in which by symbols and sentences, here a little, there a little, He was talking to people who had been chosen, but who rebelled against obeying God. It is always God governing. That is the Old Testament.

Then we come into the New Testament and what do we find? Here I am going to summarize by two quotations. My first is from Paul in the Galatian Letter when he said, "When the fullness of the time came, God sent forth his Son." That was in Genesis—"In the beginning." In Mark—"the fullness of the time." It is a great phrase. Ponder it. We say it was a long time: but at the right time, at the right moment, in the fullness of the time, He sent forth His Son.

I am sure that could be illustrated by a consideration of world conditions, and certainly in this Hebrew nation. In the fullness of the time! The fullness of the time was when the whole world, Jew and Gentile, was bankrupt—in the fullness of the time He sent forth His Son. That is one quotation.

The other one is often used but I think too often the greatness of it is missed. I am referring to something James wrote in his Epistle when in a figure of speech he applied to God: "The husbandman waiteth for the precious fruit of the earth." That is the story of God's governing still. He is governing, He is waiting, and He is patient. Don't imagine that the long-suffering of God means anything other than the waiting for the fullness of time, as the Bible shows all the way through. That is one method of looking at it. Human history and divine government. I pray you remember, that the Christ with which the Bible deals was revealed as the Christ of the Cross. That is true in the Old Testament and in the New. Take up the New Testament and look at Matthew, Mark, Luke and John. It is one story in each case, and the one story is perfect because of the absolute harmony in these four Gospel narratives. Matthew, Mark, Luke and John give more space to describing, or referring to the death of Jesus than anything else. They take a great deal more space dealing with His death than with His teaching, or any department of His human life. That is the central thing. Whether we have the King in Matthew, it is the cross which is the throne; or the servant in Mark, it is the cross which is the chain that bound Him. Whether we have the Perfect Man in Luke, it is the cross that manifests His ultimate perfection. Whether it be God manifest in the flesh in John, it is the cross wherein His glory shines finally forth. That is the New Testament.

Or to go back to the Old Testament, that great line is running through it all. If I were asked what is the greatest story in all the Old Testament, I should say it is the story of the Passover, and that the Passover was the very foundation of the national life. Read the prophets, and see how constantly they were reminding the people that they had been redeemed, redeemed from Egypt. There is that thought underlying it all, running through. What is the supreme, the most glorious height reached by any prophet of any age among all those in our Bible? If we take time to think, we shall say the fifty-third chapter of Isaiah. It is the unveiling in the Old Testament of the coming of Christ, the vision of the Son of God.

Or turn to the poetry with all its figurative wonder, all its expressions of human vision in differing circumstances before God. What is the greatest theme of it? Psalm 22, "My God, my God, why hast thou forsaken me?" It brings us to the very presence prophetically of the cross itself. All the literature of the Old Testament leads to Christ. Nothing is finished. History is not finished. Prophecy is not finished. Poetry is not finished, until we reach Christ Himself, in the New Testament. All the Old Testament is centered in Him, all the New Testament is circling round Him. This is a library, but it is a great continuous history of humanity, and the account of divine government, and at the center of everything is Christ and His cross. All the high hopes, the highest aspirations of desire and expectation lead us on until we stand confronting Him on Calvary's cross; and in all the expositions and interpretations of the Apostles in the New Testaments, the evangelists tell the story of His earthly career and His triumphant death, and it is Christ and His cross. The whole Bible is unified there.

We may summarize it by quoting the four lines with which Myers' great poem "Saint Paul" begins and ends. Who does not love that poem? Paul is the spokesman. I feel as if the Bible is speaking to me, I hear it from Genesis to Revelation. What does it say? Just this:

Christ! I am Christ's and let the name suffice you;
Aye, for me, too, it greatly hath sufficed.

* * *

Christ is the end, for Christ was the beginning;
Christ the beginning, for the end is Christ.

That is the harmony of the Testaments. We have the first song after man has fallen; the song, as it seems to me, which God whispered into the heart of a mother, in which He says that her seed shall bruise the serpent's head. And that initial solo of the divine heart runs on with decades of longing through the ages, and it is running on still; and one day we shall listen to the ultimate anthem, "The Kingdom of the world is become the Kingdom of our Lord and of His Christ."

It is concerning that Christ, and the history of that Lord, that the Bible is one.

PART I

THE PENTATEUCH: THE SIGH FOR THE PRIEST

1. GENESIS

How many people have read the Book of Genesis? I do not mean study it. I have been studying it for sixty years and I do not know it yet. Its heights and depths are beyond me and that is the glory of the Bible. It may exhaust you, but you can never exhaust it.

In a general conspectus of the whole Book as a human library, we saw that we could really summarize the entire content of the Bible by saying that there is the revelation in the Old Testament of human need, and in the New Testament the revelation of the divine supply which meets that need. In the Old Testament we have, in the first five books, the beginnings of the human need, I mean by that, there is the consciousness of movement in these first five books, and then—to use a figure of speech—when we bend over them and listen, we hear the sigh for the priest, humanity's need for a priest. In the next group of books, principally historic, we have the cry for a king, humanity's need of a king. And in all the rest, whether poetry or prophecy, more correctly we find the quest for a prophet.

THE PENTATEUCH
"After the law of a carnal commandment"—Hebrews 7:16

THE PENTATEUCH: THE SIGH FOR THE PRIEST	THE NEED		
	Genesis The Reason: Man		*Exodus* The Preparation: God
	I. The Nature of Man Offspring of God Kingdom of God		I. A Separated Nation Created by God Constituted by God
	II. The Fall of Man Rebellion against God Exclusion from God		II. A Ritual Suggestion Exclusion Admission
	III. The Ruin of Man Family Society Race		III. A Guiding God Present Reigning
	THE ILLUSTRATION		
	Leviticus The Functions		
	I. Approach Offerings Priests		
	II. Access Governed Holy		
	III. Apprehension Feasts Signs		
	THE FAILURE		
	Numbers The Weakness: Man		*Deuteronomy* The Promise: God
	I. Ignorance of God Of His Wisdom Of His Power		I. The Purpose Retrospect (4:40) Resume (26:19)
	II. Triumph of Doubt The Enemies The Decision		II. The Plea Warnings (28:68) Covenant (30:20)
	III. Aaron Murmured Against Moses Sinned with Moses Died		III. The Promise Song (32:3) Blessing (33:29)

That is the Old Testament literature. Only let it at once be said that we hear the sigh for the priest, but cannot find the priest. We hear the cry for the king, but the king is not found. We are supremely moved by the quest for the prophet, but the prophet is not there. There are gleams and intimations and promises and movements toward priest and king and prophet, but he is not in the Old Testament. When we turn to the New, we meet Him at once.

Of these first five books in which we hear the sigh for the priest, we begin with Genesis. Let no one imagine we are going to do anything like examine Genesis, except in its atmosphere, its broad movement, its great facts that stand clearly revealed as we watch. To summarize: In the beginning, in Genesis you discover the reason for the need for the priest. Why does man need a priest? Genesis reveals that the need is wholly in man, not in God. In the divine intention and purpose, in the divine ideal, there was no need of a priest to stand between man and God. The necessity has arisen through man.

Turn to the Book of Genesis. We must take some little time with the arresting opening. When I speak of the opening I mean the first chapter, and the first twenty-five verses. These verses contain what may properly be called the opening of the Book. Take the very first sentence—how often we have thought about it, how often we have considered it. It may be said to be a cosmic sentence. First of all, it is an inclusive declaration. "In the beginning God created the heavens and the earth." That is inclusive, it is cosmic. But if you are really thinking when you utter that sentence, you are arrested by the fact that the earth is mentioned. Why mention such a small thing as our earth?

Let me describe a visit I paid to the Great Observatory in California. I sat down with a little company, under the guidance of an old man who had been there for nearly fifty years, studying the heavens. And when he had helped us to get a glimpse through his telescope, drawing our attention here and there until we were amazed, the old man looked at all of us, but speaking directly to me he said, "If you care to have it, I will give you a scientifically accurate description of this earth" I said, "Of course I would care to have it. What is it?" He said, "This is a scientifically accurate description of the earth: The earth is next to nothing." Next to nothing! There are some clever people that say the very smallness of the earth proves our Bible to be wrong, that a little tiny thing like this earth can never be seen of the great things of heaven. I am not arguing with them. Some people think that bulk is the evidence of greatness, but it is not.

Pause for a moment and look at Genesis 1:1, leaving out the reference to the earth. "In the beginning God created the heavens." That phrase, "the heavens," is an inclusive one, and it is "the heavens" not "heaven." The Hebrew word used in that way is always in the plural, and used in that way it refers to what we would speak of as the whole universe. So in that opening phrase God is put behind all the universe in this one cosmic sentence, this wonderful sentence at the opening of the Bible. There are certain explanations and references in subsequent literature, but here is the one complete sentence which gives you Biblical cosmogony: "In the beginning God created the heavens." Yes, "and the earth." As you read these twenty-five verses you will find reference is made to the heavens as a firmament, but this merely means extent, the great expanse. Another word you could use correctly is "space." I have been very interested, though I have not been able to follow it very fully, in a saying of Sir James Jeans that the whole of space is limited. That is very interesting. But I know it is limited. How, I know not, but I do know, for I know God has created, therefore there is some sort of limit to space.

And then you will find this remarkable fact in these twenty-five verses, that in these heavens there are luminaries referred to, the sun and the moon. They are only referred to in relation to the earth. We are told nothing else about the sun or the moon except the relation they bear to the earth. So here we are in the presence of cosmic things in the cosmic sentence, in this phrase, this marvelous little sentence. It is as though the writer of this record—Moses, as I verily believe— seems to dismiss the whole vast fact. He has referred to the earth, the sun and the moon in cosmic relation to the earth, and then sweeps the whole vast fact into this simple statement, "He made the stars also." Have you ever sat down, almost stupefied, in the presence of that? The simplicity and modesty of the language—nothing can explain that. "He made the stars also."

You may have heard of Heptarchus who attempted to catalogue all the stars ever made, and in his catalogue he said, "There are thousands of them." Now scientists today tell us that, if we took the time, even with the naked eye we can count up to 2,000! They tell me that is the extent of the possibility of vision of the human eye. But with the aid of telescopes and reflectors, it was Ptolemy long ago who peered into the vastness of space and said, "There are millions of them." And when Herschel turned his great reflector on to the heavens he made this announcement, "They cannot be numbered." That is the last word of scientific investigators of the heavens. Is it not interesting that all this should be said by scientists, and we are thankful for all they have done, but they are all ante-dated by our Bible. Jeremiah said what Herschel said long before the time of Herschel: "The host of heaven cannot be numbered." That is the ultimate finding of science. "In the beginning God created the heavens."

"And the earth." Now why is that said in a great cosmic sentence? Is it not enough to say "the heavens"? The earth is included. This earth of ours is just one in this cosmic sentence—why name it? Simply because directly you have said "earth" you have set the scene of drama of the Bible. The Bible is not about the sun, the Bible is not about the moon, the Bible is not about the stars, save to recognize and refer to them. But in this literature the scene of all its activity is this earth on which we are living. Now these opening twenty-five verses begin with God and they end with man. No trace of wrong here, no trace of failure, no trace of sin. It is Genesis, the beginnings. I repeat my word, that cosmic sentence takes in all the universe, that supremely strange universe of the earth, on which we are living today. So it opens. It begins with God, and in the opening the last thing is man, in verse 26, "Let us make man in our image, after our likeness." If you take these twenty-five verses, and run over in the same field into the second chapter, you will find man is presented. That is how the writer, Moses, opens all the records of Genesis. I go beyond that: all the records, the historic records of the Bible, deal with God and man in their relationship with each other. It is the great subject of the divine library.

Genesis deals first with the nature of man. It follows with the fall of man, as separating between man and God, and it reveals clearly the consequent ruin of humanity, and so the need for a priest is revealed. What does this chapter tell us about man? It is the old theme which is still being discussed today everywhere. What is man? What is man? It was the thing that possessed the psalmist in the olden days. You remember that poem exquisitely written, when he was perhaps on some mountain height in Palestine, lifting his eyes toward those very heavens; "When I consider thy heavens, the work of thy fingers, the sun and the moon which thou ordaineth, what is man?" That was the question. Of course his question did not end there, but he had seen something in man that had created wonder! "What is man that thou visiteth him, or the son of man that thou art mindful of him?" So the psalmist had seen, and had been overwhelmed by the majesty of the heavens, and impressed with the comparative likeness of man. Yet there was something about man. God visiteth him. Something about the sons of men. God had to do with them. Man dealing with God, God having to do with man.

What is man? What is man? Here we have the Biblical account of man, told in the simplest way. First of all the Biblical account declares that man is a distinct divine creation. Or shall I say, summarizing in the word of the Greek poets that which Paul quoted, "Man is the offspring of God." And that means what I already have said, a distinct divine creation, an infinite thing of mystery. How we have considered it, and how its full and uttermost meaning has baffled us! He is in the image of God, and in the likeness of God, whatever that may mean. A statement like this makes the great fact of the incarnation possible, understandable, believable. When you tell me that the idea of man thus is derogatory to the dignity of God, I say that statement is derogatory to the dignity of man. Man was made in the image and likeness of God. And incidentally, this account tells us that there are two elements merged in that being, not an angel, but a new being in the universe according to this record, a new created being altogether, and two elements merge in that being's personality. What are they roughly? Dust and Deity. God formed man of the dust of the ground. He fashioned man and breathed into his breathing places. The Old Version had "nostrils," for the translators apparently thought we only breathe through the nostrils. But this is a far more profound statement than that. You are breathing through your hands, through every part of your body. And this is the statement: "God breathed into his breathing places" when He created him, formed him of dust and breathed "life"? No, plural if you please. He breathed "lives," the intensive Hebrew plural showing that in man there are different elements of this one life. It is a divine life, a mystery. This man is a kin of the restoration of order concerning which the first chapter tells us. This man is a mingling of dust and Deity.

Still with the nature of man: It reveals man's supreme capacity. What is man's supreme capacity? What was he made for? To have dominion! He was to have dominion over all things in creation lower than himself, and always under the authority of God. Has it ever occurred to you that that infinite and ever-present capacity in human life accounts for all our wars and all our strife? It is the persistence of that capacity, I should rather say. What is the matter? All these men want to fight, they want to master, to dominate, to rule. It is the inherent capacity in man. And in the economy of God, that capacity was given to him that it might be exercised—a divine authority.

And still looking at these things primeval, there is no presence of wrong yet, none whatever in the story. He has divine capacity, he has dominion, he has opportunity. And what is the opportunity? Perfect environment: placed in a garden. It is tempting to stop with these things. How much might be said! I remember Joseph Parker saying this more than forty years ago—"They tell me that man is to be saved by environment. That heresy," said Dr. Parker, "was smashed into a thousand atoms long ago when God put him in perfect environment in the Garden of Eden, and he turned it into a pigsty." Perfectly true! He was in perfect environment. "And the Lord God planted a garden," which does not mean He laid it out like an Italian garden with borders and walks and all sorts of things. He planted it. I dare take that word and express it in another way. He packed it with potentiality. And all human history in all respects, all its buildings, have come out of a garden. Every bit of London has come out of a garden. It is all there. And He put man in the garden in perfect environment. What had he to do? Dress it and keep it. He was to dress it and cultivate it, and bring out its hidden potentialities in cooperation with God. And mark this: Here is the first adumbration of danger in the universe of man. He was to keep it, to guard it. There he was in perfect surroundings. God took that one man by the hand, the offspring of God, to be of the Kingdom of God. Go on to the second chapter at verse 16: "The Lord commanded the man that he might eat of the trees of the garden, except… That is the first place in the Bible that the word "command" in any form occurs. God's law covered all. He delivers the whole thing to man, but under terms of restriction; he may eat of the fruit of the trees, but there is a restriction. God put into the garden one tree, and marked it out and made it the sacramental symbol of man's restriction, made it to mark the limits of his liberty. I am still dealing with the first phrase. It is so important that I tarry with it. The Lord God, who has given to man his greatness, has given the word of command where the limitation of his liberty is clearly marked, and the sacramental symbol of that limitation is a tree, and it is there. There is no need for mediation. There is no proof of sin, no necessity for any to stand between man and God. He made men to have firsthand dealing with Him. You know it well. You have seen God walking in the garden in the spirit of the day. Communion! Communion with Him, talking with Him, and man listening to God. Until the Church and the world return to that conception of God and man, there is no hope for us. I do not care what other hypotheses you have about man and whence he came. I care nothing about them. They all break down. But this is the great flaming picture.

And I want to emphasize the fact that there is no need for a priest.

Now, read Chapter 3: "Now the serpent… That is the beginning of the account of the fall. Yes, I resolutely adhere to the old theological word—there is no other. You can say failure if you like, breakdown, missing the mark. There is no better word than the fall of man. What was it? Rebellion against the rule of God. Man is seen listening to a voice which slanders God. Man is then seen yielding to certain desires, and here we have an act of disobedience. That word does not sound as tragic as it ought to. But Paul knew how tragic it was. He used the word which is accurately translated so in our language. "As by one man's disobedience many were made sinners." And that fair and wondrous being, in the image and likeness of God, has listened to a voice that slanders God, and has yielded to desires and sought to satisfy them, outside the restriction which God placed upon him. And by that very act he is excluded. The nexus of communion is broken; it is broken by man, not by God. We sometimes sing: "My God is reconciled, His pardoning voice I hear." It is very beautiful and there is a sense in which it is true. But you will bear in mind, when we get into our New Testament we see God, not being reconciled to man, but man being reconciled to God. God has never turned His back upon man. Man turned his back upon God, and therefore—let a man speak with bated breath and reverence—there was none other that God could do but exclude him. I repeat my phrase. The nexus, the communicating link of communion is broken. God's communion did not cease, but man's communion did, and immediately.

In that second picture we stand in the presence of the revealed need for mediation. It was a long time, yes, centuries before Job in his agony cried out for one upon whom to place his sins, someone who should mediate and bring together and heal the rupture and restore the nexus. That is what humanity needs. It needs it today. No, this is not an old story, this is not a worn-out theme. And God forgive any man who calls it folklore. It is a revelation of the abiding facts of human nature.

I do not propose to go any further save summarize. From that moment follow through the book, and you will see the portrait in strange and wonderful clarity of the ruin of the race resulting from that rebellion against God. And proceeding in sequence, all the rest of the book reveals all the conditions resulting from that one fact of rebellion. Breakdown in the family—it is there just outside the garden. A man's home broken because of the failure on the part of his first-born. His mother called him in glad exultation, on the basis of the promise that was whispered into her heart by God, "Cain, I have gotten, I have obtained him." And then the awful catastrophe! So awful that she named her second boy "Abel," "Vanity." The breakup of the family! The story continues. There is a breakup of social relationships. We can go all through the book, and see the racial failure of humanity. What is the reason for it all? Man has excluded God, and therefore, by the stem, strange necessities of the case, God has excluded man from His fellowship.

This picture of the race emphasizes the need for a priest, for a mediator. I want to repeat what I have already said, and to repeat it quietly and solemnly: The reason why a priest, the mediator, was needed is found not in God but in man. As we have read the book we have seen that the dark story is not without light; though in Chapter 3 there began this terrible story with the words, "Now the serpent…" Follow over and come to Chapter 12. How does it begin? "Now Jehovah…" There are the dividing lines in some senses. "Now the serpent," and the result "Now Jehovah." And Jehovah is seen acting, and acting in Old Testament history toward the supplying of man's need. Man is excluded, but he is not abandoned. Nevertheless, his failure is persistent. If ever he is to be restored something must happen, someone must come, someone—I repeat again in the language of Job—who will lay his hand upon God and upon man and bring them together.

The sigh for the priest moans through Genesis.

2. EXODUS

Now, bearing in mind that the need for the priest is wholly in man, not in God, we come to consider Exodus. Let me say inclusively that Exodus is a revelation of the activity of God in which He began preparation for the complete supply of the need created by man. It is an account of the beginnings of that activity of God in which He was making preparation for the fullness of times, in which the priest should appear in human history. The priest is the great echo in the heart of God. It existed from the foundation of the world, for it was before the foundation of the world that the Lamb was slain in the purpose of God. Here we see the historic movement of that, and again I say, in the divine preparation. And here, if I insisted, as I did insist, that in Genesis everything was of man, here everything is of God.

You saw what man had done: created a need. What God is doing is moving toward the supply. The last words in the Book of Genesis are these: "a coffin in Egypt" That is how Genesis ends. And when you come to the Book of Exodus you read, "Now… It is equally correct to translate the Hebrew word "and" instead of "now." And the history is running on. There had been history before, but it ends with the bones of Joseph left in Egypt in a coffin. A very subtle ending! And then you come to Exodus, and Exodus historically begins exactly where Genesis leaves off. Now what do we find? Summarizing the Book of Exodus (of course, details are impossible and unnecessary for our purpose) what do you find? First, a separate nation; secondly, a ritual suggested, and all through a guiding God. Don't misunderstand that. There is no end to the things to be said yet. Even before this revelation, the need is perfectly clear, but that is what we have. God is revealing the scene of the beginnings of the great movement that culminated in Christ. I know we are apt to think that the ways of God are slow, but that is the vulgarity of our finite minds; and the terrible attempt we make to compass the divine activity into the little span of our own earthly career and life. But if the ways of God seem slow, I want to say here and now, the slowness is absolutely necessary by the conditions.

Oh, why does not God wind up all this turmoil today and get it done with? If you take your New Testament you will find why He does not. And one word tells the story. Look it up for yourselves. Get your context: "long-suffering"—the long-suffering of God.

Here we are centuries before Christ and the fulfillment, and we have these three things in the book. First of all the creation of a separate nation, and then the description of a whole ritual full of suggestion for that separate people, and all the way through God Himself seems active. Now look at this story with your Bible as to this particular nation. First of all, it is a nation brought into liberty from bondage. There was a beginning that Genesis gives you, the man Abraham; God's vantage ground was a man. And Genesis gives you his son, and his son's son, and his sons son's son. You see them continuing and at the end going down into Egypt. They spent 400 years there; 400 years until by the overruling of God they were segregated and it was impossible for them to form contaminating alliances with surrounding peoples. And the stress and the strain of those 400 years in their history stiffened their fiber and prepared them for what is to follow. So Genesis.

Now the moment you get into Exodus, you find that these people were not a nation yet, they were a mass. I think I will use a most objectionable word and grasp it from any improper meaning—they were a mob, a mob of slaves. And the hour is come when God leads them out, and He bases their national life upon the fact that He has redeemed them from slavery and set them free, released them, brought them into liberty, broken the chains, ended the oppression, brought them—and here I am quoting—"unto Himself." And the great initial Feast of the national life was, and is, the Passover in which they celebrated their deliverance from bondage. There followed the crossing of the Red Sea, and if you want really to understand the crossing of the Red Sea, you can read the narrative; and then read the Song of Thanksgiving on the other side, and you will see how perfect and glorious a victory it was.

Now here they are on the other side of the sea, a people separated, not yet conscious of nationality, not yet to be described as a nation, but a people unified by the suffering and the terror of the past 400 years, and unified in a further way by the delivering act of God. And so you find them on the other side of the sea. And then the book gives you the history of the first three months of their journeyings, and I would like to stop with that. We found them at Marah, and we found God giving all the resources of Elim, and then come into the shadow of the wilderness of Sinai, barren and difficult, and there they began murmuring. And God answered their murmuring by providing bread from heaven, until they found themselves at Rephidim; and there once again they murmured and God answered them by providing water from a rock. Then they touched the territory of a foe,

and they were at war for the first time. I did not say what I would like to have said: when He brought them out of Egypt He did not lead them straight, but led them by a crooked way. He told them to turn back and encamp at Pi-hahiroth, and He told them to do it lest they had to face war before they were ready. And the war came when Amalek came, and there was a tremendous victory for this people over Amalek, victory that called forth from them a name for their God, Jehovah-nissi, the Lord our Banner.

They came to the beginning of their national life, and if you read carefully the account of that time, you may see the purpose of that national life. What is it? "I bore you on eagles' wings, I brought you unto myself" "Ye shall be unto me a kingdom of priests." You see the movement; this nation was created to be kings and priests.

Now the priest is a mediator always. What were the priests supposed to do? And here we are straight up against the real meaning of that national life. God has redeemed them and brought this people across the sea, and through the wilderness so that He might have a people for Himself to the exclusion of all other people on earth. Of course, it has often enough been said that this is the heresy that cursed them in the end. They came to forget that God meant them for a kingdom of priests, and intended from that nation first of all that there should be someone to mediate between humanity and Himself. A kingdom of priests—and in that you have the foundation of the national life. Your minds are leaping the centuries, and naturally running on to the New Testament, and inevitably you remember that there is an apostolic writer who wrote by the Holy Spirit the theme of the Church of God as a kingdom of priests, the fulfillment of the original ideal for a separate nation; not separate nor segmented in order to be a pet, but in order to be a pattern; not separated in order that God might forget the rest, but that God might reach the rest through the revelation this people would make of Himself.

Then come the laws—I am not tarrying with them now as you have them in Exodus, because we shall deal with them fully when we come to Leviticus—laws pertaining to the life of a nation created for that purpose. And the great matchless love song of the heavenly places was sounding in the heart of God. "God so loved the *world*" that He created this nation, this nation that would lead all in the purpose of His will by the counsels of His might to the complete fulfillment of their need, to be priests.

I am not staying in these laws any further than to say that we are arrested and held by the fact that at the heart of this national life is a religious system, a ritual. I do not like to say religion was at its heart, because religion in the true sense is a word that some people object to. They say they do not like us talking about religion. That is all nonsense. Religion *is* religion, and it is in the whole of these laws and in these general discourses. Religion is at the heart of the national life. It permeated all the national life and into the heart of everything, and in order that the triumph of that nation might fulfill its function of what God meant it to be, you have these matchless sentences.

Go to the scene of the camp in the wilderness; look at the whole camp. You get the instruction here about the Tabernacle. Everything began under instruction. We want to begin that way. If you look at it you see the encampment with the outer circle and the tribes arranged symmetrically under their banners, some west, some east, some north and some south. You need to get the picture of the camp in your minds. You may have maps or plans in your Bibles. Now go inside the camp, and you come to the Levites, and it was their business to attend to the ritual and ceremonial to which we are now coming.

Tread softly and reverently and pass beyond the circle of the Levites, and you find yourselves in a court. It is the outer court of worship. In that outer court you will find a priest, an altar and a laver. Reverently press a little closer in and you will enter into the sanctuary itself. Enter in, and you will find it is divided into two; the first is the Holy Place with the golden candle sticks and the table and the shewbread, a golden altar and incense at the very entry. And then you pass inside and you are in the inner place, the Holy of Holies. What is there? There is the Ark, with a lid, a cover, always to be considered as part and yet not separate from the Ark itself. The proper name of it was a Propitiatory, and as you look you see the cherubim and their wings spread over it at each end of the Ark. And you have seen something strange, something—I do not like to use the word but I could use it—weird, mystic. And there is a light, the Shekinah. Now can we see this as little children: a picture of a camp, this nation with its twelve tribes pitched under their banners according to the description and order by divine arrangement. Then turn to the actual place of worship. The Levites served in that actual place, that Court, that Holy Place. Then the Holy of Holies, and between the Court and the Holy Place is a veil hanging, and between the Holy Place and the Holy of Holies another veil is hanging. There is the nation gathered outside. They know perfectly well that they cannot enter into that Holy of Holies. The Levites appointed certain priests to enter the court, perhaps certain worshipers bringing offerings could enter, but they could not enter the Holy Place. Only one could go, and that man only once a year is permitted into the Holy of Holies. Who is he? The priest.

Now if we could visualize it with the simplicity of children, we would ask ourselves, What does this ritual suggest? Or to change the form of the sentence, what are the suggestions of the facts that this created ritual was intended to show?

First of all, the exclusion of man from God. That is the meaning of the Court itself, and the veil hanging between the Court and the Holy Place, and the meaning of that innermost veil hanging between the Holy of Holies and the Holy Place. You know you cannot go in, you are excluded. And the symbolism moreover, if you could be free from fanatical inhibitions and take it simply, emphasizes the fact that there is a nation with the presence of God at its midst, and shut out individually from that presence. That is not all that is suggested by the ritual. It not only excludes, it admits. There is a way by which the whole nation can draw near, and it is the way of sacrifice, and the way of a mediator and a priest. And when Aaron put on his dress and went into the Holy Place once a year, he bore with him all the nation. They could not go in, they were not allowed to go, but they did it representatively in this man who went in as a priest. You know his garments, the glory and beauty of that priestly robe, the twelve flashing stones, and upon the stones the names of the twelve tribes. Ah yes, that was for the Holy Place! And the priest goes in, a lonely man, bearing in his heart the nation. It is Gods appointment and the whole ritual said, "Sin has excluded you from communion but there is a way for man to rise, an offering and a sacrifice." And you may go there, represented by your priest

And the last thing you get in Exodus—what is it? All the way through, particularly perhaps toward the end, God persisting, God governing, God guiding. All the priesthood, and all the symbols forevermore speak of that fact, the Lord in the midst of His people—a nation which is not a monarchy, not a democracy, those two evil things that have blasted all human history. I say it patiently. Democracy is as hopeless as monarchy. I am so tired of hearing people talk about democracy, the rule of the people. We are so eager, but in God's name let Christian men and women remember that this is not the true order of life. I repeat, here it is symbolized. What then? A theocracy, a people perfectly God-governed and God-guided. Oh yes, we have seen them breaking down in this book, murmuring against God; twice over distinctly we have seen them murmuring. But there is another thing that we have seen, on the other hand: the fulfillment of the meaning of His great name Jawa, Jehovah. He gave them what they needed, bread and water, and the healing branch to go into the bitter waters. What a wonderful picture that is! And something else came out of it. Human failure is seen, and nothing here is made perfect. The mediation is not complete. The priest is not himself. I am talking of Aaron, a dreadful failure. I have sometimes been rude enough to say about Aaron—I hope I may be forgiven—all he was really good for was to wear robes, and any man can do that! There is no signal greatness when a man gets his robes on. He fell. Moses fell. Human failures. Divine persistence! And by rite and ceremony and ritual and law coming into human history, with a revelation of something that God was doing, something toward which He was moving: and that something was the answer to the dire need created by man's rebellion, the finding of a way by which man can be brought back to Him, and he can enter into fellowship with Him through sacrifice and through priesthood.

All that is suggested in Exodus.

3. LEVITICUS

We come next to Leviticus. How many people have read the book? I have been told by some that they have never read this book, and I think it is probably one of the books that is not read. It is not interesting until you really read it, but if you read it intelligently it is far from being uninteresting.

The Book of Leviticus has been very aptly called "The Handbook of the Priests," that is to say of Aaron and the priestly order of the Levites. But it is more than that. It is supremely that, as you will see in a moment, but at this point I want to turn aside to say something about priests. Quite simply, someone said to me, and said accurately, that there is in the minds of Protestants a feeling of antipathy to the very word "priests," and we are still afraid of it. I can understand it in a way, and yet I do not altogether understand it because it is a Biblical word and finds its place all through the Old Testament, and its place in the New. Of course the protest is against a false conception of priesthood that blasted the church. I join with all such people in protest. But we are not entering into that subject in that way here and I want to say three things about priests.

First of all, if you take the Hebrew word which is rendered "priest," it means simply, literally, a mediator. A priest is a mediator, one standing between God and man. I am taking the simple meaning first. When you come to the New Testament, the word translated "priest" does not mean that at all. It means consecrated, holy. The priest is therefore the holy one, the consecrated one. There is no disharmony between these two thoughts. In the Old Testament the Hebrew word helps us to understand the nature of the priestly office. It is that of mediating. The New Testament word reveals the character of those who are to fill the office. They are holy.

Now I want to go behind the Hebrew word to the Greek word of the New Testament, and see what is meant by a priest. If you go the world over into every form of religion you will find a priest—false priests, I know; priests in the midst of false systems, but there they are. And here is the simple definition of the priest, wherever you find it, whether in false or true religions, whether in the Hebrew economy or the Christian Dispensation; whether in Christendom or the darkness of idolatry, find a priest and you find one who claims access to God denied to others. Of course I stop there again to say this is the whole point of our Protestant protest. When a man comes to me today and says, "I have a right of access to God denied to you," I am always inclined, perhaps, to be a little rude to him. I am reminded of Diogenes, and how Alexander, who had conquered the known world, went to see the Greek philosopher Diogenes who was living in his tub. Diogenes was inside, and he said, "Who are you?" "I am Alexander," was the reply, "can I do anything for you?" "Yes," replied Diogenes. "What can I do?" asked Alexander. "Stand Out of my sunlight." A very good story! And if a man comes to me and tells me by his own right he has access to God denied to me, I say, "My friend, get out of my sunlight, will you, please. It was shining on me till you came." We believe that all believers are priests, and thus they have right of access to God "by whom we have access into His grace wherein we stand." That is the meaning of priesthood.

The priests of an order were not the first divine intention for the nation of Israel. That is to say, over and over again you will find God committing Himself in unfailing patience to the weakness and inability of humanity to rise to great heights. When He made this nation as we saw in Exodus, what He said to them, in effect was, "I will bring you unto myself and will make you to be a kingdom of priests." There was no order of priests there to stand between them and Himself; they were all to be priests. That was the first order. When they failed through weakness to be what they were called to be, you will see the sudden change that came to them in the darkness and lightning and thunder and flaming fire of the law, because they could not rise to that level of the order of the priest. He knew it. Of course in the counsels of God—it is always difficult to speak of that in terms of our human lives—He knew the need for priestly intervention.

What was the condition of the ordering of Aaron and Levi and the priests? You remember what it was. The first order for the priests was that they must be those who should mediate. It was a family arrangement. Every family was to be in itself a circle, and the word was this, "Every first-born that openeth the womb shall be a priest unto me." The first-born son was to be a priest, and it continued through the ordering of priests. I cannot go from that without saying that we must not forget that Jesus, after the flesh, according to that first Divine Intention was a priest. He was the first-born Son of Mary, and according to the original Divine Intention He was a priest He was never a priest after the order of Aaron nor the order of Levi, but according to the Divine Intention He was a priest, being the first-born.

The priest then is the one who has the right of access to God, and he has that right of access, not as a privilege bestowed but as a responsibility, because a priest is always in the presence of God representing others. That is the very essence of priesthood. If you are a believer you are a priest, and if you are a priest you have the right of access to God, not merely for the privilege of blessing your own poor little puny soul, but as an intercessor on behalf of others, bearing on your heart the burden of others always. The priest is doing that. Without being academic one can say quite simply that the Book of Leviticus is a Handbook of the Priest.

We saw in Exodus that God put at the center of the nation the original suggestion of the camp with its outer court, and its Holy of Holies, and in the Holy of Holies the Ark and the Propitiatory or cover of the Ark, and the everlasting wings of the cherubim and the Shekinah light. That was at the heart of the nation, and it was a ritual. Now, when the camp was completed and all arrangements for the Tribes were made, we saw them first in the Outer Circle, then coming next within the Court of that Holy Place, and then the Holy of Holies. Here in this book, we have the regulations concerning worship and the attitude of the people toward that worship and consequent upon it. Leviticus is closely linked with Exodus. Read the first verse of Leviticus. Listen! "And the Lord called unto Moses, and spake unto him out of the tent of meeting, saying," and then the rest follows on. You can give this Book of Leviticus into the hands of an intelligent person who has never read it before, and that person will ask four things, "What is it all about? Who is the Lord? Who is Moses? What is the Tent of Meeting?" We start Leviticus with that statement because those things are revealed to us in the book which has gone before. If you have read Exodus you do not ask who is Jehovah, nor who is Moses, nor what is the Tent of Meeting. It is a reference to that central place of symbolic ritual, symbolic of the great truths of the national life, and here is a book written of that order and that worship and that approach of God. Taken in its entirety, taking the whole book, there is constituted a remarkable illustration of the true evidence of priesthood and the blessings resulting from the exercise of that function. Of course I am not dealing with it in detail, but we have already seen this: First, the approach; secondly, the access; thirdly, the apprehension. God round that center, and that central fact of the Tabernacle pitched there with the very inner shrine of the Holy of Holies which is the dwelling place of God.

In the first movement there is an account of how men are to approach; in the second movement a clear enunciation of the conditions upon which, having approached, they may really have access; in the last, certain signs that show the value and meaning, the apprehension of the facts of access after the approach; Approach, Access, Apprehension.

Approach—of course that means approach to God. When the writer of the Letter to the Hebrews, with this Book of Leviticus in his mind, speaks with reference to the High Priest, he says, "Let us draw near unto God." Leviticus and Hebrews are always to be kept together in your Bible study. I say frankly, to anyone who thinks he is studying Hebrews, if he does not study Leviticus also he does not know Hebrews, for one must know the Book of Leviticus to understand Hebrews. Hebrews shows a fulfilling of everything suggested in Leviticus, in that Old Testament system of worship with its practical observance: "Let us draw near unto God." That is what is meant by Approach. There was the camp with the encamped Tribes. They are a nation and God at the center, a kingdom, only it was a kingdom that was a theocracy. How are these people to get to God, in what sense, in what way, by what measure may they approach Him? All that is shown. That is the Ritual of the Offerings, the accounts of which we have: the Burnt Offering, the Meal Offering, the Peace Offering, the Sin Offering, and the Trespass Offering—five of them, all significant.

Notice in the first place that all these offerings were brought by the people. Remember, too, that they brought them to the priests and the priests were the mediators, receiving them from the people and carrying them into the Presence of God. Always, as I say, significant.

All I want to say about the offerings is this: the Burnt Offering was the symbol of complete dedication. The Meal Offering, all parts of it, if you examine it, the result of man's hands, his tilling the ground and so forth, is an anomaly very typical of service. The Peace Offering was the central offering and was typical of communion; people coming with offerings of dedication and of service were admitted into the place of the Peace Offering, and could have communion with God. They are named in this order and with these instructions, but in another order presently. The Sin Offering was of course the offering of blood, of death, of sacrifice, the way of

approach; and beyond it, closely linked up, was the Trespass Offering. That was for definite acts of wrongdoing. The Sin Offering was concerned with any sin and the failure of humanity as a sinning people. The Trespass Offering was concerned with the acts growing out of that condition of sin. Now if we come to Approach, God says this is the ritual: these are the things that symbolize the method of our approach: dedication, service, peace, the preparation for communion, a sacrifice that deals with the sin of our nature, and offering that shows our need for personal forgiveness for individual sins. Here in this book you have the Handbook of the Priests and their rites, and solemnly they were consecrated to their office. Every act in the ritual is full of tremendous suggestiveness. If these men are to be fit to receive the offerings of the people, to approach and carry them to God, they must be consecrated men, and all the symbols of their consecration are here, a solemn ceremony of consecration.

You see here that they have two things. First of all, an offering for themselves; they too need these offerings, all of them, and their first offering was on their own behalf. Then after they had offered on their own behalf, they offered the offerings which the people had brought. This is Christ's ritual.

There is the terrible story of Nadab and Abihu, who offered false fire on the altar. I do not think that I am violating a confidence when I recall a very interesting letter I received from a minister, engaged in writing a book called *On Eagle's Wings*. It is the story of Moses and contains a reference to Nadab and Abihu, with two suggestions: first, that it was not an accident but that it was the Fire of God; and the other suggestion as to what happened—and I think this is certainly worth thinking of—was that Nadab and Abihu were drunk. I think this is patent from the story. They went into the Holy Place drunk, and in all probability whilst manipulating the Holy Oil, it broke over them and became touched with fire, and consequently they were burned. And that is how God does burn. Fire from the Lord! So it was, but it was fire very likely arising from their own sin and neglect. And that sharp little incident in the midst shows the necessity of never burning a false fire before the Lord, never going into His Presence except under the abiding stress and strain of the consecration to which all such priests must submit themselves. That was the Way of Approach.

Access to God—that does not mean merely to come to Him at that time of access but at all times. Put that in a sentence. First of all, they are revealed as a God-governed people and that is the reason why they have access to God. You may say, "We know that, everyone knows it." If you really know it, take time and read to the conclusion of Leviticus, where it is shown what it means to be God-governed. There are the great Laws of Health, and remember the time when these were enunciated; remember too the land to which they applied and the people who were to be under them. I submit without any fear of contradiction that it is the most remarkable revelation of hygiene that the world has ever seen, and that no further discoveries which are revelations have contradicted the underlying principles of health revealed here. It has to do with our food and our clothing. These may be the apparent trivial things. A God-governed people were told the material of which they were to make their garments. They were not allowed to make garments of cotton and wool mixed. Go into this carefully to see why. It was purely a health law. There were certain things they were to eat, certain things they should not eat; everything remained under divine supervision, even concerning what a man wears and eats, or a woman wears or a woman eats. A God-governed people. This is a remarkable revelation given here of how access may be made to Him. They are not only a God-governed people, they are intended to be a God-manifested people. Through them God is to be revealed, consequently their laws are strong, separating them from the practices of surrounding nations in things that are contrary to Holiness of life; they must be entirely separate. Listen! "Ye shall be holy: for I the Lord your God am holy" (19:2). Then read down that chapter and see how that fact is emphasized. "I am Jehovah, your God, be holy." "I am Jehovah, your God, I am holy." Go on reading and see, "I am Jehovah, I am Jehovah," fourteen times in one chapter. "Be ye holy for I am holy." That is to say, God is manifested through the people that He has created a nation, a people for His government, and because of that they are to be distanced from all evil actions. And there are drastic applications to the priests, more so than even to the people. These are the ways of access. See how these laws reveal the fact that these people were a people God was guiding to the right of access, and because God was to be manifested to them, they were called upon to holiness of life.

Then we come to the final section, and what is there? Feasts, and two great signs of relationship, and then interestingly enough a closing brief section on the subject of vows. They are all in the Handbook of the Priests. What do I mean by special days of feasts? I am going to name them and notice the establishing of the feasts to be observed at particular seasons constituted in their calendar. All the calendar was conditioned by feasts, and every feast was full of suggestion. The Feast of Pentecost, fifty days of harvest in its fullness, and so forth. The arresting thing is—and it is well worth working out—that a calendar of the year put down applies to the feasts, and see that all the year, winter and spring, and summer and autumn, is conditioned by feasts of the Lord. The calendar constitutes a sign of relationship. Every one of them is suggestive of the benefits accruing to those who are under His government, and whose apprehension of the glory of access of approach has been what it ought to be, all symbolized by the passing feasts.

And then beyond the order come two signs, the Sign of the Seventh, and the Sign of the Fiftieth year. The seventh year was to be a year of rest for the land, a complete rest. We may say, we have adopted it. I know we have in practice. Have we in philosophy? I am always nervous in the presence of specialists, but the only specialists I care anything about now are the farmers. Talk to a farmer and ask him, "Don't you think your land would be even more productive if every seventh year you allowed it to lie fallow?" I think you will find he will agree. God meant men to understand by that sign of relationship that the very land was there in possession by His gift, and that He cared for the land.

And then came that other marvelous sign, every fiftieth year was to be a year of jubilee. All questions of possessions were to be reconsidered, and there were to be certain re-arrangements and dispensations. Those who had by some means passed into slavery were to be allowed their freedom.

Finally, that little section on vows. It is very simple, but well worth considering. The command about vows is this: first of all, no man is asked to take a vow. Secondly, any man can take a vow if he likes, but he is perfectly free. It is not forbidden, it is not a command. Thirdly, if he takes a vow he must fulfill his vow. Very simple but well worth while pondering, even in application to our own life and times.

So there in the shortest, briefest outline we have this marvelous Book of Leviticus. Note the background: Sin excluding from God; God holy and demanding holiness. That word "holy" is found in this book more than anywhere else in our Bible. It occurs in Leviticus more than 150 times. "Holy, holy, holy" is stamped all the way through; and man, not holy, excluded.

But that is not all. That is the background. What is the foreground? God providing a way of mediation through which those excluded may return to Him. And then when all the minor things are left out, away off we can discern the central things, the Day of Atonement, that central sacrifice for sin. What did it teach? Try to go back away from all our present-day theology—I do not mean our modern theologians but our own theology, our biases—and try to escape for a moment. What do we see? As those lambs were taken to the sacrifice I see that there must be substitution, someone to take my place. And the lamb is chosen. And I see that there must be imputation, the imputing to that lamb, that sacrifice, the responsibility for my sin. And then I see this—and this is the central word—without shedding of blood there is no remission. The blood was of no avail at all; its shedding was the thing.

So with deep and profound reverence, if I am told that the blood of Jesus means the life of Jesus, I say "No." The blood of Jesus that ever speaks better things than that of Abel, the blood of Jesus representing priesthood in its completion, was the blood He shed, the blood that was poured out, death in order to live.

And the last thing I want to say about Leviticus is this. In the activity of God, the one great truth is the love of God all the way through, providing a way by which those excluded may come back to Him. It is Love that is the very essence of law, whether it be the moral law of the Sinai or the law of worship from the Tent of Meeting.

4. NUMBERS

Taken from the simple standpoint of history, the Book of Numbers is a most fascinating book. Looked at in its entirety it is a remarkable revelation of failure. But I did not say the failure of God. There is no failure in God. Here is the failure of humanity in the presence of the great movement of God, which was preparing the way for the supply of mans supreme necessity, which is the priest. Pre-eminently it is a book of failure, and the weakness is in man.

In Numbers history continues. Take up a Bible and look at two verses. Go first of all to Exodus 40:17 and then to Numbers 1:1—read them close together, and notice why we should so read them.

"And it came to pass in the first month in the second year, on the first day of the month, that the tabernacle was reared up." "And the Lord spake unto Moses in the wilderness of Sinai, in the tent of meeting, on the first day of the second month, in the second year."

Notice the tenses. In Exodus, the Tabernacle was reared up on the first day of the first month of the second year. Then turn to Numbers and read, "On the first day of the second month in the second year after they were come out of the land of Egypt." Those two readings link the history of Numbers with the history of Exodus. In between we have had the book of Laws in Leviticus. Here is the historic sequence. And it is going on, as is seen, between the horn: when the Tabernacle was reared, and the fortieth chapter of Exodus when it was completed—as the Lord commanded Moses seven times over—and the glory of the Lord filled the Tabernacle, so that Moses was not able to enter in. Only a month later, the history continues from that point in the Book of Numbers.

Surveying the whole book for a moment, it covers a period of forty years, commencing directly after the Tabernacle was completed and the glory of the Lord filled it. Then everything was ready for a forward movement, to adopt that very modern phrase. But you will find that the book ends exactly where it began, with forty years between. Go over the geographical place names. It begins at Kadesh-barnea and it ends at Kadesh-barnea; in between the beginning at Kadesh-barnea and the ending at Kadesh-barnea lay forty years which had run their course. And the whole story is the story of human failure and divine government and patience.

The first ten chapters of Numbers are full of interest because in these chapters is constituted the nation. It goes back, and we are bound to go back, to Exodus, and the emergence of the nation is seen, the whole movement beginning in the twelfth chapter of Genesis when Jehovah spoke unto Abram. And from that finding of a man came a family, and the family multiplied until there was a people, and the people went down to Egypt and passed into; slavery and remained there for 500 years. The last words of Genesis are "a coffin in Egypt," and the bones of Joseph were in that coffin. After that period of discipline in Egypt they were segregated from contamination by surrounding nations, till the hour came when they should be no longer merely a people but a nation, and in Exodus we have the account of how God brought them to Himself in the wilderness of Sinai.

Again, in this tenth chapter is the account of the camp and the arrangements made. It could be described as a picture of the nation divinely created, divinely governed, with the national life circling about the central fact of the divine presence as it is shown in the Holy of Holies. It is very interesting to look at the camp of the people which is now a nation. They had pitched their tents in the outer circle with the Tabernacle in the middle. Then came the Levites' tent on three sides. The ground in front was reserved for Moses and the priests. Glance for a moment at those twelve tribes encamped. The provision was made that they should be standard-bearing tribes. There is no means of telling how or why these particular tribes were selected as standard-bearing tribes, but it was so by the arrangement of God. One of them was on the east—that was Judah—with a standard floating there; on the south was Reuben with her standard; away in the west was Ephraim; and on the north was Dan. The Bible does not reveal the nature of these standards, but my own conviction—without giving any dogmatic assertion—is that it is absolutely without any question that we can know exactly what was on these standards from Bible literature.

On the standard of Judah there was a lion of gold on a field of scarlet. Turn round to the south from the east, and look at the standard of Reuben. A man was represented on a field of gold. Look away to the west to Ephraim, and that standard had a black ox on a field of gold. Pass to the north, and we see the standard of Dan, an eagle of gold on a field of blue. There seems no question at all, but that this accounts for these standards. Notice that they are a lion, an ox, a man, an eagle. We know the symbolism of these things. In our medieval theology we have got them mixed, and in St. Paul's and other places they are wrong, absolutely wrong. The lion was always the type of kingship, the ox of service and sacrifice, the man was the type of the highest thing in creation, and the eagle was always the type of Deity.

I read my Gospels presently, and I find Matthew and see the standard of Judah with a lion on a field of scarlet. I read Mark and I see the ox on a field of gold, the standard of Ephraim. I read Luke, and see the standard of Reuben, the man on a field of gold. And I read John, and see the standard of Dan, an eagle of gold on a field of blue. We can go on into the Book of Revelation, and find the four living ones before the throne with the same symbolic figures. These banners are very remarkable. First seen in the Book of Numbers floating across the wilderness where the camp was they are all suggestive of their part in the whole nation. Note in the first ten chapters the arrangements for worship, that centrally it remained a great act of continuous worship, and see how all gifts brought were voluntary and all equal. No wealthy man was to bring more than a poor man, and no poor man less than a wealthy man. All these things were central to the national life. The rest of these ten chapters show the arrangements for the movement of the camp. The Levites were to lead down the sacred enclosure appointed to their certain offices in certain parts of it, and with the Ark as they moved forward. The nation was to go according to the way the fiery pillar moved south. It is a romantic description.

In the eleventh chapter comes the great breakdown in national life. It begins here and runs all through the book, and if it is followed through it reveals certain things that are self-evident as the reason for breakdown. We find that the reason for the breakdown was the ignorance of the people of God. They are His people. He had brought them to Himself, given them a law, the moral law from Sinai, the ritualistic law from the Tabernacle itself. Remember the descriptions in Exodus and Leviticus, that everything was arranged for. Yet, in spite of it, they were ignorant of God. Consequently, because they were ignorant of God, came the hour of doubt. That is the story. Doubt triumphant! And all the discipline of the forty years in the wilderness followed that triumph of doubt. And the last thing we touch upon is the very significant story of the ending of the priest Aaron and his death.

Now, with that whole background in mind, glance at the content of the Book of Numbers, seeing how, from the eleventh chapter, that in the first ten verses the nation organized, arranged for a forward movement. The hour had come when they were to advance, and leave uninhabited Sinai, and march into possession of the land which God had intended for them, that it was His will they should enter into and possess. So far as God is concerned, everything is done, everything is ready for the march into possession of the land. And now what has happened? There is a murmuring among the people. We are not told very much about it except that it was there, and that God knew it was there, and it was so dangerous a thing that He visited it with sharp, decisive punishment.

I want to listen to the murmuring. We cannot hear anything that was said. At first there is no open rebellion. How does it begin? These people are conscious of the irksomeness of authority, the irksomeness of restriction. Is it a surprising thing to say that they were suffering from the fact that they had escaped from the freedom of slavery? The freedom of slavery? Yes, if that could be called freedom. Take it in all the highest sense of human possibility. They were perfectly free to live their own way, perfectly free to eat—but they were under law, they were conditioned, they were slaves, they were serfs, they were compelled. Now listen! They had no responsibility. Responsibility was carried by their taskmasters. They were told what they had to do. And there is a tremendous sense of freedom in that kind of life. Think of it. I confess to you that there are hours, often of great weakness, hours in life today when I wish for somebody to tell me exactly what to do, so that I do not have to think. It is a weak moment, a wicked moment, a terrible moment for personality when we want to be saved from thinking. They had escaped from thinking, but they had found that liberty did not mean license. They were under authority. The law of God had been promulgated and they had found its restriction irksome. Why? Because they were still ignorant of God, they still had not discovered that every line of His law was a revelation of His love. Have we discovered it? Do we yet believe it? It is a challenging question. But they did not know it. All these things irked them. Back there in Egypt— it seems almost vulgar to mention it, and I would not if the Bible did not—they said, "'We are thinking of the leeks, the garlic and the onions." And they had thought of it until their

belly had become their God. Now they had always food to eat, manna to eat, but they were murmuring. It was a murmuring caused by the sense of the irksomeness of restriction, and it was due to their ignorance of God, ignorance of the wisdom of every law enunciated and every commandment laid upon them.

And then, of course, it is a revelation of their discontent with their circumstances. They were looking back to Egypt, suggesting that it might be good to go back there, forgetting its cruelties and the incubus that had rested upon them and crushed them. Yes, because there were leeks and garlic and onions there they wanted to go back. They were ignorant of God not only as to His wisdom but as to His power. They did not realize that He who had brought them out was able to meet and supply every necessity of their lives. He was able to supply them with what they really needed. Of course, that which is beyond necessity God never covenanted to supply to anybody, not more than they needed. "My God shall supply all thy need."

Thomas Cooke once said, "It is not 'God shall supply your notion.' My notion is a house worth £ 2,000 a year. My need is a cottage, and I get the cottage, not the notion."

That is a very philosophic remark. God provided everything they needed. They did not know God. And yet there was this splendid ritual. There were priests of God ordained to come near, but that did not reveal God to the hearts of these people. So the great crisis came, but that also did not reveal God to their hearts. We know the story, but let us remind ourselves of it. They were on the march. Forty days would have carried them there, but from the beginning of the journey unto the last, forty years elapsed. What happened?

They sent spies to spy out the land. Look at the account of it. We are told distinctly that they were commanded of God to send spies. There is no question of the accuracy of that statement. But as they go on their journey from the first drift of it, it is very clear that they decided to send spies of their own choice. And God commanded. He always does that. It is His method constantly. "All right, go and do it if you want to." In this very Book of Numbers is the story of the quail. "He gave them their desire and sent leanness into their souls." God has often done that and is still doing it. It may be if you clamor long enough at heaven's gate, you will get something you are asking for, and it will hurt you. Better to take Gods first "No" than lead yourself into a place of discipline by being granted what you want.

That was their view. First they sent spies. And that shows that about the land there was questioning and suspicion. There they were. God was there. He had brought them out of Egypt. He had supplied their need, and they were on the march to go over this Jordan, and they were not sure. And so they sent spies.

Here we get that historic and wonderful story that cannot be dwelt upon at any length. There were two reports, and I rigidly adopt the modern phrasing and say there was a majority report and a minority report. I do not like to be dogmatic, but I have known in the case of this country some great Commission appointed to consider some great subject, and we were given two reports, the majority report and the minority report. It still follows. Here it was. The spies came back with their majority report and their minority report. And notice this: there was complete unanimity on the part of the majority and the minority on one subject—the desirability of the land that lay over Jordan. They said the land was good land, flowing with every good thing. They all agreed. But then they divided. Look at Numbers 13:27 and break in on the majority report: "We came unto the land whither thou sentest us, and surely it floweth with milk and honey; and this is the fruit of it." They bore back great bunches of grapes. Listen! "Howbeit…" Suppose I change that word and make it "But…" "But the people that dwell in the land are strong, and the cities are fenced and very great: and moreover we saw the children of Anak there. Amalek dwelleth there in the land of the south: and the Hittite, and the Jebusite, and the Amorite, dwell in the mountains: and the Caananite dwelleth by the sea, and along by the side of Jordan." That is the majority report.

And there is a minority report from Caleb and Joshua in verse 30: "Caleb stilled the people before Moses, and said, Let us go up at once, and possess it; for we are well able to overcome it." And then the majority talked again in verses 31-33: "We are not able to go up against these people; for they are stronger than we. And they brought up an evil report of the land which they had searched unto the children of Israel, saying, The land, through which we have gone to search it, is a land that eateth up the inhabitants thereof; and all the people that we saw in it are men of great stature. And there we saw the Nephelim, the sons of Anak, which come of the Nephelim: and we were in our own sight as grasshoppers…" Poor little things! I would like to quote something that I heard Dr. John A. Hutton say: "If you feel yourself like a grasshopper that is what you always look like to the other fellow; and moreover that is what you are like." Wait a minute. We have not finished. Caleb had simply said, "Let us go." What ground had Caleb for saying that? If you look into the next chapter you read in verse 8, "If the Lord delight in us, then he will bring us into this land, and give it us; a land which floweth with milk and honey." And then the majority got busy; and the people stoned them with stones, both the majority and the minority. And almost directly after, this people suddenly made up their minds that they had made a mistake, and they had better go. So they tried another system of advance, not under divine guidance but under their own, and they were defeated with grave disaster. What they were not prepared to attempt because God was with them, they tried in their own strength at their own fair bidding, and were overwhelmingly and disastrously defeated. And they had forty years in the wilderness as the result. The majority report and the minority report! I would not care to be dogmatic, but speaking of my own lifetime and observation of national affairs, I have found that almost invariably the minority report is true and the majority report is not. We are so fond of majorities, and yet God is always working through dynamic minorities.

And it is interesting to say baldly at once that of these people, these spies, not one of them entered the land except Caleb and Joshua, and the generation died out in those forty years.

So back to Kadesh-barnea, and there is a remarkable account, that cannot now be fully dealt with, of the death of Aaron. Before he died, his robes, representing the divine order, were transferred to his son. And while the people lamented the death of Aaron, they certainly were reminded by that act that the priest is greater than the man, and that though the man had failed, and because of his failure he was excluded from that land, none the less the idea of priesthood goes forward.

Look over the whole story at leisure. How can we account for the failure? First of all, by the fact that they had commenced with a mixed multitude, and secondly, by the fact that as the result of that and other things, their motives were mixed. It first commenced in Exodus: when they came out of Egypt there came with them not only the chosen people but a mixed multitude, and they were tolerated and allowed to go. And through all the years this tolerated, mixed multitude reacted upon the purity of purpose of the people. They had a mixed motive—the desire to please God and to be obedient, but the motive supremely seen of self-interest.

As I read this book my heart is almost overwhelmed as I watch God providing for these people, patient with them, persistent in spite of their failure. It was a complete failure. Moses and Aaron both failed and were excluded from the land. Only Caleb and Joshua entered. And as I see God gently persistent and patient, and forevermore moving a stage forward for the accomplishment of His purpose, I know that God cannot be defeated. He cannot be defeated by His enemies, as witness the waters sweeping over the Egyptian hosts. But there is a subtler danger: it is in the infidelity of His own people. But He cannot be defeated there. At last His purpose will be fulfilled.

5. DEUTERONOMY

We come now to the Book of Deuteronomy, and I want particularly to point out the boundaries of the book as shown by the opening paragraph and the closing paragraph.

Chapter 1, verse 1: "These be the words which Moses spake unto all Israel beyond Jordan in the wilderness, in the Arabah over against Suph, between Paran, and Tophel, and Laban, and Hazeroth, and Di-zahab. It is eleven days journey from Horeb by the way of mount Seir unto Kadesh-barnea. And it came to pass in the fortieth year, in the eleventh month, on the first day of the month, that Moses spake unto the children of Israel, according unto all that the Lord had given him in commandment unto them." Thus the book opens. How does it close in Chapter 34? Moses was the first speaker. But remember that Chapter 34 gives the story of his death, and nobody supposes that he wrote that himself. It is certainly the work of Joshua. Notice how it ends. Chapter 34, verse 10: "And there hath not arisen a prophet since in Israel like unto Moses, whom the Lord knew face to face in all the signs and the wonders, which the Lord sent him to do in the land of Egypt, to Pharaoh, and to all his servants, and to all his land and in all the mighty hand, and in all the great terror, which Moses wrought in the sight of all Israel"

So ends the story of the Pentateuch. And in this Book of Deuteronomy we have a background in history. Perhaps all the history in it would be covered in a few days, ten or eleven at most. I take Deuteronomy at this face value on the values revealed in this opening statement. I know perhaps all there is to know concerning: this book which was expressed during the last generation, assuring us that the book was written by Ezra. I have no argument for that sort of thing. I am just leaving it alone as being absurd. We are told in the beginning that we have in this book the words of Moses speaking unto all Israel in the wilderness. Notice how particularly the introduction tells us exactly where it happened. Now if you study the book you will find it contains what is the most authentic thing all the way through it—little historic details showing you the consecutiveness of the addresses, and yet the whole of them were delivered here in this particular region.

Look at the region in the wilderness in the Arabah, the great desert and the dark defiles between the mountains where they were gathered together, and consequently what we have here in Deuteronomy is a record of the final discourses of Moses. He is about to leave these people—Moses, the lad who by the forethought of his mother and father had been preserved from death—remember Hebrews tells you that. He has all the discipline of forty years in the court of Pharaoh, being brought up in all the learning of the Egyptians. Watch with what zeal he makes that very remarkable statement. From the mere standpoint of learning and erudition and knowledge it reveals what a remarkable man he was. Forty years, and then forty years as the result of his own action, and the overwhelming providence of it all; and he passes from all the splendors of the Egyptian court to the greater splendors of the wilderness and the mountains of God. I hope young people reading the story don't feel a bit sorry for him when he got into the wilderness. You ought to be glad for him. Those were great years and then the meaning of it all is revealed: the burning bush, the Voice divine, the holy call, the great commission. And we know what resulted.

Don't forget, forty years more in the wilderness, no longer alone with the sheep but with men and women who are more difficult to deal with than sheep, just a mob when they came out of Egypt, undisciplined except for the cruelties of slavery. Forty years he had been with them. And he is going to leave them, and he knows he is going to leave them, and this marvelous record that has been preserved for us is his farewell discourse. This book is historic in the sense that we are told the story of the disruption, and where it happened. But the thing that matters most is that we are reading the last words of this great man to these people. The farewell discourses of Moses number six, and these six discourses naturally fall into three groups of two discourses each, and are distinct.

In the first discourse (1:6—4:40) Moses spoke to them of the way along which they had come; they were looking back. In the second of these two discourses (5:1—27:10) we have a resume of laws. The laws had been given in detail from Mount Sinai and morally stated from the Tabernacle as the laws of ritual, and here we find in the second discourse a resume of those laws.

Pass to the second group, and find there first of all a great address warning the people against perils that threatened them through forgetting (27:11—28:68). In the final discourses of Moses, he is warning them against these perils, and in the second address of the second group (29:1—30:20) he is representing the effect of the words, and the immutability of the king who gives them. These are the second two in the second group.

Come to the last group and here we have a discourse ending in a song—it has often been called the "swan song" of Moses—it is a great song (31-32). And the last of all is blessing, benediction, pronounced upon these people (33:2—29). These are the three groups.

Generally summarizing: in the first two discourses the outlook is retrospective, looking back on the actual history of the people and the laws given. The next two deal with perils and warnings against them, precepts and the government of God; and we may call them introspective. Moses is looking within, at the Tabernacle and its moral and spiritual values. And then when we come to the last two, the song and the blessing, we may say they are prospective; Moses is looking on. First of all there are two in which he looks back; then two in which he looks within at the actual facts of the case before him; and then two in which in song and blessing he is lifting his eyes and looking far on.

If we have that conception, I think we shall really be helped to go back; to read these addresses one by one. I am dealing with them here by way of general analysis.

The first two discourses are contained in Chapter 1 and run on to Chapter 27:10. That is a general statement, and remember it as you read the closing words of these two discourses. Please remember that the first was a retrospect of their history, and the closing words of that retrospect are found in Chapter 4:39,40: "Know therefore this day, and lay it to thy heart, that the Lord he is God in heaven above and upon the earth beneath: there is none else. And thou shalt keep his statutes, and his commandments, which I command thee this day, that it may go well with thee, and with thy children after thee, and that thou mayest prolong thy days in the land, which the Lord thy God giveth thee for ever." Remember these are the final words and discourses in which Moses is surveying their history. It is rather dreadful to have to leave them. I would love to go over every portion. See how inexhaustible the Bible is! We can go back again and again and again, after we get through these marvelous discourses.

Remember some of the things you find in them. Moses tells these people how he led them and cared for them, how he had gone before them—and how I love this statement—they had been following a pillar of cloud for forty years, cloud by day and fire by night; and when the cloud moved they moved and they followed it and encamped where it led them. That is where we get the idea we have in one of our hymns:

Nightly pitch my moving tent,

A day's march nearer home.

And Moses tells them that the Lord went before them choosing out the place where they should pitch their tent. What a vision! And then forty years, those strange forty years, apparently with no plan at all, wandering, simply necessary movement, cloud and light leading them here and there, back, zigzag, zigzag, zigzag on about the desert that they might have crossed in eleven days. Don't you imagine some of the people wondered? And Moses tells them, among other things, that wherever they pitch their tent, God had gone before them and prepared the place in which to pitch it. And so he surveyed all their past history, and told them moreover that God had been their reward, not only going before them but following after them, and caring for them and guiding them. Moses tells them that in retrospect about their own activities, but the supreme thing is that he has been telling them of the guidance of God, showing them—and that is why we must read those closing words—that the wilderness discipline was in order to prepare them for settlement in the land. They might have gone into that land being full of their own ability, and the fact that they did not do so was because they were not ready for the land, and so came the wilderness wandering. God led them that they might learn the truth about themselves by that long discipline. That summarizes the general atmosphere, and it all closes with this statement "that thou mayest prolong thy days upon the land." That is the purpose of the wilderness, the preparation for the settlement in the land.

Now turn for a moment and take the last words of Moses in the second of these discourses, in Chapter 26, verses 18 and 19. It is the final word after the resume of the laws. And the resume of the laws is remarkable in one single thing, ending not with the mere citing of the law of Sinai or of the Levitical order; but it is changed, or rather slated in a new way. There is a new note running through it. But the laws are there. Why? The laws and the discipline of the wilderness are to prepare them for the land, and they are to take the laws with them when they enter into the land, that their characteristic may be supremely that they are a holy people, a people that bear something of the divine likeness and who are of the very character of God. We cannot state these things without saying that God always had a larger view—a poor thing to say about God, but how shall I put it? It was not merely for their own sakes, but for the surrounding peoples in the wilderness. And the summary of the laws here was not merely the law of Sinai and ritualistically—using the word in its proper sense—concerning the Tabernacle, but it is repeated here, condensed here with a different note of no lowering of the requirements, no alteration of the principle and the purpose of the law, whether of the moral significance of Sinai, whether of the ritualistic significance from the Temple, or whether, as in the wonderful resume here, the purpose was that this people should enter into the land as a holy place. And that is the last thing that Moses had to say to them in the retrospective section.

Tinning again to the second discourses, we find the introspective method of Moses. Let us glance once more here at the final words in Chapter 28, verse 68. This is not a very ordinary thing. Please don't forget that these words at the end of the first discourse in the second group contain warning to the people in view of the perils that Moses sees, and that were existing among them. And the last words are these—"And the Lord shall bring thee into Egypt again with ships, by the way whereof I said unto thee, Thou shalt see it no more again: and there ye shall sell yourselves unto your enemies for bondmen and bondwomen, and no man shall buy you." It is an amazing statement and yet a revelation such as is inevitable. God delivered them from Egypt, bringing them blessed freedom so that Egypt was behind them finally, and so it was in His purpose. But they had fallen, and were falling and were in danger of continuing failure. Moses knew it, and knew them, and is telling them what will happen at the end of this terrible discourse, and warning them not to persist in their disobedience and disloyally. Back to Egypt, back to bondage, back to slavery, and no man to redeem them—in the whole of the discourse he is warning them, and it is most terrible and yet so true and necessary.

And then we come to the second discourse of the second group, dealing with covenants. Notice how Moses begins in Chapter 29, verse 1: "These are the words of the covenant which the Lord commanded Moses to make with the children of Israel in the land of Moab, besides the covenant which he made with them at Horeb."

In Chapter 30, verse 20 we read: "To love the Lord thy God, to obey his voice, and to cleave unto him; for he is thy life, and the length of thy days; that thou mayest dwell in the land which the Lord sware unto thy fathers, to Abraham, to Isaac, and to Jacob, to give them." The covenant abides, and God abides, and that is the meaning of the citation of the covenant. It is further important to remember that the covenants of God are conditional. I know some people say they are not. But they *are* all conditional, and if through disobedience there is breaking of the covenant, there must be reaping of the harvest. God is faithful and He is true, but if I am unfaithful I am untrue and consequently while emphasizing one thing, in this discourse throughout he says (verses 11 and 12), "This commandment which I command thee this day, it is not too hard for thee, neither is it far off. It is not in heaven, that thou shouldest say, Who shall go up for us to heaven, and bring it unto us, and make us to hear it, that we may do it." Yes, "that thou mayest do it." The covenant of God is there but there is human responsibility, and it is all summarized with the command "to love the Lord thy God and to obey his voice."

So we reach the last of these groups of discourses, and we take the same method, because everything leads up to the concluding word of Chapter 32, verse 43. How wonderful, this great song of Moses! How does it end?

Rejoice, O ye nations, with his people:
For he will avenge the blood of his servants,
And will render vengeance to his adversaries,
And will make expiation for his land, and for his
people.

There is all that has gone before, all that has been said about their failure as they journeyed, their disobedience to the law and the warnings uttered and the restatement of the covenant and the fearfulness of God; and then this great song, and what a song it is! What a mixture of pean and dirge all the way through, showing us the greatness of God and the appalling failure of His people. And at the end God is still there. And the last note of the song is the declaration that He will make expiation.

And once more, to take the final discourse; it is a blessing. Read Chapter 33, verse 29 and there it is:

Happy art thou, O Israel:
Who is like unto thee, a people saved by the Lord,
The shield of thy help,
And the sword of thy excellency!
And thine enemies shall submit themselves unto thee;
And thou shalt tread upon their high places.

A people—that is the last note—saved by the Lord.

In conclusion I would like to emphasize this: This section ends, revealing to us the need for the priest, and the failure and the catastrophe and the disruption resulting from the break between God and man, the rebellion; and the necessity for some mediation if man is ever to be restored. Two matters are clearly revealed in all the five books: man's need and God's activity towards the need. But there is no finality here. God is marching on, but He has not arrived at His goal so far as human history is concerned. Man is going forward. Light is shining for him, gleams of light follow upon his way, but he is forever perpetuating his rebellion again and again. That is the history.

But there is a new note in Deuteronomy, and it is supremely a note which can be characterized by one word: *Love.* Here it breathes through everything.

If I want to consider this merely on the level of the human—and of course the human element counts—I should say that by this time Moses had come to a profound understanding of God and of His law. There is an unequivocal stem severity in the law as given by Moses on the Mount and in the Tabernacle, and yet you cannot read this through without reading all the way you go, that there is a new note.

Turn back for a moment to Chapter 4, verses 36 and 37 and find this: "Out of heaven he made thee to hear his voice, that he might instruct thee: and upon earth he made thee to see his great fire; and thou heardest his words out of the midst of the fire. And because he loved thy fathers, therefore he chose their seed after them, and brought thee out with his presence, with his great power, out of Egypt."

And one more verse in Chapter 10, verse 12: "And now, Israel, what doth the Lord thy God require of thee... Notice this verse, and I take it as an illustration rather than a final statement. Two things are declared, that God's laws are an expression of His love. God loved their fathers, therefore He brought them out, and He brought them out for Himself. And the second thing to notice is, "What doth the Lord thy God require of thee?" Here is the other side—man's love to God as the motive of obedience. There is no motive that will make any man obedient to the stem severity of the law of God except by his love, and it is love which is the answer to love. That meant the discovery that every stem commandment is the expression of unfailing love. And it gives to life and law, all through, its tremendous truth. The quotation from Browning is almost banal and yet right:

I report as a man of God's work;
All is law and all's love.

And back of the law is love, His love, love as the motive at the end; and the only motive which will make any man obedient to the severity of the uttermost law of God is love for God. "This is the whole of the law and the prophets," said Jesus, "Thou shalt love the Lord thy God with all thine heart and soul." And that meant that the second is a corollary and becomes a sequence, is like unto it, grows out of it: "Thou shalt love thy neighbour as thyself." And there under the severity of the statement of these two commandments hang all the laws and the prophets. And in Deuteronomy is found that note of tenderness and beauty running all through.

The wonderful thing, and the last thing to notice, was the command of God to write the song and teach it to the people. We notice a song will often live longer in the heart than any code of laws that was ever uttered, and the thunders of Sinai and the Tabernacle. And after that repetition of the laws and the retrospect of the history of the people, "Moses," said God, "write a song, and teach it to the people." How often we find it so, that long after hard commandments and hard, hard ethic is forgotten by a wanderer in a far country, there will begin to him the lilt of a song he heard his mother sing when he was at home. The song is more powerful than the law, and the last thing Moses had to do at the end was to write a song and teach it to the people.

6. The Fulfillment of the Pentateuch

We have noticed a connection with all the books in the Pentateuch the continuity of the story they told. With almost monotonous repetition that has been insisted upon. Taken as a whole, they do represent a great and increasing revelation of need. As to the supply of the need revealed, we have a reflection rather than a presence, a shadow more than a substance. Every separate message, Genesis, Exodus, all of them emphasized a sense of human need, and human need as created by man's rebellion against God. And yet the whole of that literature creates a confidence in God; all the way through we see Him unfailing, leading on patiently towards some glorious consummation.

Now, at once, let it be said that the fulfillment is found in Christ. Of course, this is a commonplace thing to say, because it is a natural thing to say. If we have seen the need for the priest, in Christ we have found the Priest. And I should be inclined to say, speaking very generally of course, and yet with some knowledge of the literature, that the interpretation of the way in which Christ fulfills the priestly office is found especially in the Letter to the Hebrews. I think there is some warrant for saying that we cannot read Hebrews intelligently if we are ignorant of Leviticus, and Leviticus, of course, is central to the documents to which we are here referring.

But what I want to do, very briefly, is to pass over those five books of the Pentateuch in which we heard supremely humanity's sigh for the priest, glancing at the movements of each, and then referring to Hebrews. And let it be remembered that in referring to Hebrews now, I am thinking of the one great supreme Person revealed in that wonderful literature. "God, having of old time spoken unto the fathers in the prophets by divers portions and in divers manners, hath at the end of these days spoken unto us in his Son."

Remember how it opens. Remember further, that whatever its details, whatever its technicalities of interpretation, the supreme value of Hebrews is the setting forth of the Son, as it shows that the Son is the speech of God through the Son, the final speech, always revealing Him in His sinlessness and His authority: and supremely the revelation is of the Son as the Priest.

Taking each of these books, summarizing each of them in a sentence or two, and then referring to the Letter to the Hebrews:

In Genesis we saw the life, the life of God and the life of man, and the interrelation between God and man, and further that the principle of the interrelationship was faith. When faith broke down, rapture came. Man was distanced from God by his own act. But for the moment, take the whole Book of Genesis as the supreme revealing of the nature of man, and of man resulting from his revolt and his rebellion. I open Hebrews and I find the Person of the Christ, and I find He is thus described. In Chapter 1, verse 3, He is spoken of as the very image of the divine substance. The original Adam was in the image and likeness of God, and here He is described as the very image of God, of the divine substance. I find another little phrase (and I am only taking phrases) in Chapter 2, He was "made like unto his brethren." So, whereas in Genesis we have seen man first in all his primeval glory as the divine creation, and then saw him fall; in Hebrews he is presented the man, God's man, in the very image of God, according to the substance of God and yet like His brethren. And as in Genesis faith was seen to be the principle of relationship between God and man, in Hebrews faith is constantly in the mind of the writer—and he is writing because of the peril of the early Christians falling into apostasy from faith—until he comes to the culminating movement beginning in the tenth chapter, and on into the twelfth, and he gives that list of men who lived and wrought by faith. Remember how it commences. Quoting from the end of Chapter 11, and the beginning of 12: "These all, having had witness borne to them through their faith, received not the promise, God having provided some better thing concerning us, that apart from us they should not be made perfect. Therefore… seeing we are compassed about with so great a cloud of witnesses" (to us, not those who are watching us, but those who are talking to us by the example of their life and work and service) "so great a cloud of witnesses… let us run with patience the race that is set before us, looking unto Jesus the final leader and the vindicator of faith…" That is all I want, that one statement. "The author and leader, the final leader" That is the One who takes precedence, who comes first, notwithstanding all the great leaders in Chapter 11, who emerges at the head and leads the great procession of faith, the author and final leader, the vindicator of faith. Don't put the word "our" in. I am not quarreling if you tell me He gives you faith. That is true, but that is not what this writer is saying. He says "faith." In Genesis faith breaks down and fall is the result, and misery follows all down the ages. But here is One (I have not yet reached His priestly office) who protects faith, who vindicates faith and shows the value of faith; faith in God and faith in man and faith in history.

I pass to Exodus, and in Exodus I have faith in God as the basis of obedience to divine government. The divine government rests on righteousness, and the exercise of judgment and the human attitude toward it, and that is shown to be first worship and then obedience; not worship without obedience, which is of no value.

I turn to Hebrews and I find this brief quotation again. What do I read? Christ as a Son over His own house, and the thought of the writer is that the Son learned obedience by the things He suffered. It does not at all mean He learned to be obedient, but He entered into the experience of what obedience to the will of God really means through the process of suffering.

Now take the central book, Leviticus, and here the whole subject is worship. There is the human need, sin excluding man from God. Man is excluded because of sin, and yet there is a divine provision made here, so that man through representatives can enter, not the Court only of the Holy Place but the Holy of Holies, only once a year in the ritual. But the fact remains. And when he has gone in, he comes out again and he retires into the midst of the national life. The glory remains, the place of the divine abode is there, but no man will cross that threshold again for a whole year. But when he went in, he went first of all to make an offering for his own sin.

Now in this Book of Hebrews, at its centrality, taking the very figure of speech, Jesus is seen making propitiation for the sins of His people, through His own blood obtaining eternal redemption, and entering into the Holy of Holies once for all, never again to retire from the attitude of the activity of the Priesthood; and moreover He rent the veil and left the way open for us to go in in His name and in His merit. The Priest is found, not of a nation but of all humanity, the one Priest who stands between humanity in all its relation to God; and we see Him there in Hebrews, for whom we have waited in Genesis, Leviticus, Exodus, Numbers, Deuteronomy. We saw the claims of the law, we saw the divine movement, but we never found Him. Then we come into Hebrews in the New Testament and we find Him.

We look at Numbers, and there we see the necessity of the obedience to the law of worship, and in Leviticus obedience as the necessity of those who have any right to go to God in worship. And, of course, the story is terrible. The paralysis of doubt and yet the patience of Jehovah; all the wanderings in the wilderness were evidence of His patience. When dealing with Numbers I drew attention to some of the statements, so simple, so sublime. Dealing with the abstract, and not attempting to follow the references belonging to them, but adhering to the experiences of the Book of Numbers, we saw how when the people moved, they moved at the divine signal. God ever went before them, choosing them out the place in which to pitch their tent.

We know that when these people pitched their tent, they pitched it where God had chosen. And that is the one story of the Book of Numbers. But they are a restless crowd all through, and for a moment one must go to the book that lies beyond the Pentateuch, and see them coming into the land, still restless, never finding rest. And when I come to Hebrews, I find it said of this Christ that He is the great Priest for He hath entered into His rest. That is what no priest had done before. He hath entered into His rest, and yet having entered into His rest He is touched with the feeling of our infirmity. And the Priest is there seen, not in the wilderness of wandering, not in the land of the tribulation and restlessness; but He Himself, having found His way into the place of rest, is carrying with Him in His heart all His sympathy for those who are still wandering, it may be in the wilderness, or having entered the land, not yet come into full and final possession.

Then again, to summarize Deuteronomy, I will stand by what I said, that Deuteronomy is characterized by a new note. I do not mean to say the note is utterly absent from the particular movement of the earlier books. When Moses came to deliver his great farewell discourses and addresses which are found in this book, there is certainly a new touch in the atmosphere of the revelation of God, which is not contrary to the terms of the law, but it is interpreting the law in terms of love. We cannot read Deuteronomy carefully without feeling that. God's love to man is shown as the motive for His government; and man's love to God is to be the motive of his obedience.

And then I come to Hebrews again, not for any full argument but for words that show the close identification of our Lord with ourselves and I read this: "Whom the Lord loveth he chasteneth"; and when we shall be in subjection to the Father of spirits we are in the realm of the fulfillment of love's purpose in Christ, and consequently we have entered into the new realm of love altogether in which no longer the law, hard and stem, is over us, but the tender light and compassion of God. The law was our tutor, our schoolmaster, our custodian—as it would much better be rendered—to bring us to Christ. The law held us in its severity, and there are tones of love in all the farewell discourses of Moses, but all the love and the glory of it is shining when we come into the presence of the Priest

Now I turn to Hebrews itself in conclusion, and there are two passages I want to look at close to the end of Chapter 12 at verse 18, and reading on to verse 24, especially noticing

that last verse. Notice the contrast. "For ye are not come… but…" There is that graphic description of the whole of the old economy. "…but ye are come unto mount Zion, and unto the city of the living God, the heavenly Jerusalem, and to innumerable hosts of angels, to the general assembly and church of the firstborn who are enrolled in heaven, and to God the Judge of all, and to the spirits of just men made perfect… Now listen! "…and to Jesus the mediator of a new covenant…" The One for whom all humanity has been sighing, and is still sighing, even though God has made provision. You and I can come to Him, "the mediator of a new covenant, and to the blood of sprinkling that speaketh better than that of Abel."

I want to go for a moment to the First Letter of Timothy 2:3: "This is good and acceptable in the sight of God our Saviour; who would have all men to be saved, and come to the knowledge of the truth. For there is one God, one mediator also between God and men, himself man, Christ Jesus, who gave himself a ransom for all…" These are but two extracts, but all that humanity needs on account of its revolt from God has been found on behalf of humanity by God in the person of His Son. And we are no longer excluded from God unless we persist in rebellion against God. It is possible to refuse the work of the Mediator, and it is possible even for us to boast in our right of access to God and forget all about Him. But we have no access to God though we may take His name and sing hymns about Him, save through the only way of approach through the one Mediator. The great thing is this: the Priest for whom we have heard the constant and wailing sigh in the Pentateuch is now found, and He has entered into the Holy of Holies to represent all that put their trust in Him.

PART II

THE HISTORIC BOOKS: THE CRY FOR THE KING

7. JOSHUA

Breaking the Old Testament up into its parts, we took first the division we commonly call the Pentateuch, which means the five books, called in Hebrew the Torah oar the Law of Moses. We have gone over that again, and we have found as we took that history, and followed it and listened to it, that in these first five books we heard and were conscious of humanity's need of a priest, a mediator, because of the rupture between man and God. If man were ever to find his way to God, there must be some means of reconciliation, some mediatorship, some priest—The Sigh for the Priest!

THE HISTORIC BOOKS

"They have rejected me"–I Samuel 8:7

THE HISTORIC BOOKS: THE CRY FOR THE KING	THE NEED		
	Joshua God the only King I. Moses Dead II. Possession Conquest Settlement III. Death of Joshua	**Judges, Ruth** Departure from God I. Religious Failure II. Political Failure III. Divine Deliverances	**I Samuel** A King–Like the Nations I. The Last of the Judges II. The King Asked for Saul III. The King Given David
	THE ILLUSTRATION		
	II Samuel, I Chronicles The Ideal King I. Qualifications II Samuel 5:1-3 II. Reign Judah Israel III. Failure		
	THE FAILURE		
	I Kings, II Chronicles A King–Like the Nations I. Solomon Glory Shame II. Disruption Rehoboam Jeroboam III. Israel and Judah Ahab and Asa	**II Kings, II Chronicles** Disaster Without God I. Israel to Captivity II. Hezekiah (Isaiah) III. Judah to Captivity	**Ezra, Nehemiah, Esther** God-The Only King I. Zerubbabel (Temple) II. Ezra (Reformation) III. Nehemiah (Walls)

We begin now the second of these divisions, the Historic books, which take their course through the Old Testament from Joshua to Nehemiah, through all that period of history. The first chapter of this particular history is in the Book of Joshua, and the last is in Nehemiah. And as at first we followed humanity's sigh for a priest, so I now suggest again by way of introduction, that as we follow the story we shall be conscious of humanity's quest for a king. The priest to meet the need of humanity is not found in the Pentateuch; gleams of light, promises, suggestions, but the priest is not there—until we find Him in our New Testament. So here, as we follow through this series, we hear everywhere the cry for a king, but the king is not there. There are kings there, but the King, completely fulfilling humanity's need, is not found. The need is revealed. When we want to find it supplied, we go over to the New Testament.

The Book of Joshua is a most fascinating book. There are details to which I have not space to refer here. That is not my purpose. We are studying it as a whole, taking for granted familiarity with its general outlines and its general movements.

Now the very first line, the very first sentence here is a link: "Now it came to pass after the death of Moses the servant of the Lord, that the Lord spake unto Joshua the son of Nun, Moses' minister, saying..." And so the historic event is continued in Joshua, really from Deuteronomy 34 In the last chapter is the account of the death of Moses, and we take the story up there. So the lines of history are continuous.

Spend a moment here to note this. The Book of Joshua in the Hebrew Bible is in that part of it which is known as the Prophets. Now we, in our Bible, talk of the Pentateuch, and the Prophets and the Historic books, and that is perfectly correct; but sometimes it is useful to remind ourselves of how the Hebrew Bible is divided. There is the Torah, that Law that was Moses, or the Pentateuch as it is called today. Then follow the Prophets, and third the sacred writings. The remarkable thing is—and we should pause here—that in the Hebrew Bible there were two divisions in the Prophets; in the first division referred to as the Early Prophets, not a single book that we call distinctly "prophetic" is found. We speak of the prophetic books, and they include Isaiah, Jeremiah, Ezekiel, Daniel and so on. But in the Hebrew Bible there is a section including what was called the Earlier Prophets, and that section consists of Joshua and Judges, I and II Samuel, and I and II Kings. The collateral writings in Chronicles are not found there. But we have the Book of Joshua in the section of the Hebrew Bible called the Earlier Prophets. Rather arresting! It reveals a fact that we want to bear in mind, that those old Hebrews recognized the true value of history. They knew that history really was written not to satisfy curiosity about the past, but rather to teach lessons from the past to the present generation. And so this Book of Joshua is among the Prophets, not then itself a prophetic utterance. It is a record of historic facts, but it is a record of historic facts in order that men may learn from these historic facts the lessons they have to teach.

Pass to the next books, I and II Samuel and I and II Kings. Here we have a line of history running through all the chronicles. We get the history in the Chronicles from the priestly standpoint, which has another application. But here the prophetic voice is speaking through history to the very immediate circumstances; and I go further to say, the prophetic voices of Joshua, Judges, Samuel and Kings are speaking forever of past history, in order to present necessity and present application. Bear that in mind as we approach this study of Joshua.

The period of history in Joshua covers about twenty-seven years only, and notice that it is a period concerning the nation's entry of the land. We have seen the nation created, and watched it coming to national consciousness in the wilderness; we have seen it disciplined in the wilderness through the forty years, and we see it now entering into the land. And so this book presents the nation entering the land of God's appointing and God's choosing, We must keep in mind that we are looking at it all the time in its national character, and its national character is that it is a theocracy. I use that word consistently for lack of a better. I do not know a better. We know the meaning of monarchical, the king, a person. And we know democracy, which is supposed to be a government of the people by the people. Theocracy eliminates the democratic idea of government *by* the people, but it does not eliminate the idea of the government *of* the people. And it eliminates the idea of monarchical government. That is the story coming to us here in this book, the first book of the earlier prophets, speaking, speaking,

speaking by history to humanity. The nation is seen existing in the land, entering it as a theocracy; in other words, having a King and the King is God, and there is no other king. Now this is true through the Book of Joshua. It is true also through Judges, but it is peculiarly true here. We notice the boundaries of the book. It is bounded by death. It opens with a reference to the death of Moses, and it closes with the record of the death of Joshua and Eleazar; and there is another dead thing there when the book closes. Joshua died, Eleazar the priest died, and there is the coffin there with the bones in it—the bones of Joseph are carried up. Genesis ended with "a coffin in Egypt," and Joseph's bones in it, and now these, having been preserved through all the wanderings, are carried into the land. And it is death to begin with and to end with. One of the most significant things in this book is the death of Moses—only referred to, but we must pause with it or we shall miss the whole movement that brought them into the possession of the land, first of all by conquest and then by settlement, and the death of Joshua. I should like to plead for an imagining of the occasion created by the death of Moses. For forty years he had been their statesman, soldier, poet, philosopher, lawgiver: in all their experiences, sometimes of rebellion, and sometimes of disobedience and sometimes of obedience, the nation had always been able to look to Moses. Moses had been there throughout those forty years, and now he is gone.

What a wonderful death it was! A great Hebrew writer says that Moses died of the kisses of the lips of God. It was a discipline. None of the extreme severity of the divine law shows forth more than when Moses was excluded from the land of promise; he who had led them out of Egypt through all those forty years of the wilderness was not allowed to enter the Land of Promise. It is among the most amazing statements in the Bible. Why was he excluded? No one can read that without being made to stop and think and examine themselves. He was excluded because he spoke unadvisedly with his lips. How did he speak unadvisedly with his lips? He showed a wrong spirit in a right cause. But he violated the eternal principles—another consideration, which is not our province here and now to deal with, but it is worth thinking about. He spoke unadvisedly with his lips, angry when he ought not to have been angry, provoked in a right cause when he should not have had that spirit of provocation, and so hindered the deepest truth about his God. So he was excluded.

Here is the beautiful story, the story of his passing. Called up to be alone upon the mountaintop, and dying with God. (In my own judgment, and I am not at all careful about anyone else's judgment, one of the greatest poems ever written in the English language was written by Mrs. Alexander on the burial of Moses.)

Now mark the method of Moses's removal from the nation, and the visible sign of authority. The King was still there. God had not left them. But the ambassador had been recalled to the higher courts, and he had passed out of sight. His work was done, whether as soldier, as statesman, as poet, as philosopher, and he had gone. I am not concerned for the moment with the condition of the nation, even yet so imperfect after all the wanderings in the wilderness. All the way through, the administration of Moses has been seen, and now their visible sign of authority has gone and they are left. That is how the book opens. It demands that we should pause with it. What next? Something very remarkable! "It came to pass after the death of Moses the servant of the Lord…" I imagine patient people saying, "Why stop there?" I stop in the hope that the next sentence will impress you as it impressed me. What did God say then to Joshua? Moses is dead, God speaks. What does He say? Listen! "Moses my servant is dead; now therefore arise." ("Oh! Moses is dead, what are we going to do? We had better sit down.") "Moses my servant is dead; therefore arise." The word is spoken to a man, and through the man to this nation. Notice again in that startling sentence that the first part was reference to the past. "Moses my servant"—what a wonderful phrase! He is "my servant." Everything he has done has been necessary. There could have been no forward movement into the land, or beyond the land to the fulfillment of the divine purpose, but for "Moses my servant." That phrase is the ratification of the past. And the next is the indication of the future. Don't stand still. Don't imagine there is nothing more to do. Don't let the progress end here. Arise! God has provided the means.

And what a wonderful story is the story of Joshua. I do not think we must stop to deal with it at length, but just think of him for a moment briefly. Born in slavery—in a life of slavery for forty years. He knew the bitterness, he knew the cruelties, he knew the oppression, he knew the agonies of it; even when he was born, his father and mother knew well, and they gave him a name that was very significant. When the new baby was born they called him "Hoshea." They are still slaves, but they are hoping. The baby is born, they are looking and hoping. I do not mean to say that they think this boy is going to be the instrument, but it was the passion of their hearts for deliverance. And so they called the baby Hoshea. Forty years! And then he came out, and almost at once, evidently, he became the right-hand man of Moses.

There came a day when Moses saw that young man was to succeed him, and do the work he could not do; with the thought of that he prepared him. Moses is rising there. And he changed his name, and that in the most remarkable manner. He took that name which Joshua was given by his father and mother, and after the Hebrew fashion he rendered that name of Hoshea by mixing it with the name of the Lord, Yahweh (or as we have it, Jehovah), and he took the letters from Hoshea and the letter from Yahweh and he built a name into it and called it "Joshua," which means "Salvation of the Lord."

I cannot resist running ahead! Centuries later there came the King for whom humanity was crying out, and the voice of the angel said, "Thou shalt call his name Jehoshua, Jesus, for he shall save his people from their sins." We are looking at this remarkable Joshua. So he was named, and now he comes into the Land of Promise, leading the people. First of all, a prevailing entry into the land. All the way through is seen that activity; see these people responsible for war and definite action, and yet all the while they are not halted, but are reminded that without God they can do nothing. And they come into the land and toward the river and here evidently are persons trying to stop them. I am not interested in all those people who want to explain this away. The waters of the river are there and they are piled in heaps behind them and they cross dryshod. So the nation came into the land.

And then came seven years of war. I am no soldier and do not profess to be. I have no understanding of strategy, but we should read this with an atlas and, remembering the times, notice how Joshua manipulated his armies, and how they marched and marched, and see the movement and plan of it. These have been called by some writers the most remarkable pages of human strategy in all history. I am concerned more here for a moment with the fact that so many people read these stories of the people going into Canaan, and say that some of them reflect—forgive me, I am putting it perhaps more bluntly than they do—upon God; that this is not the God of the New Testament. At any rate it is the God of the Apocalypse, the last book of the New Testament. But these emancipated people were extremely practical. They had seen the sins, the pollution, the corruption, the iniquity and beastliness of the peoples in the land, of which things they were not to be guilty. And the Lord said (Leviticus 18: 24-25), "Defile not ye yourselves in any of these things: for in all these nations are defiled which I cast out from before you; and the land is defiled: therefore I do visit the iniquity thereof upon it." And again in verse 27: "For all these abominations have the men of the land done, that were before you, and the land is defiled."

That is the meaning of the wars. As Dr. Moorehead of America said, "This is terrible surgery," but it is a surgery which is cutting out the cancer and clearing all the earth, so that a place which had become utterly profane might be clear. Do not let us make the mistake of thinking that these wars were punitive. God says His people are to be separated from abomination, a people of holiness, showing it to other nations. One of the things that halts us in life is this failure of principle, individually and nationally, and the sin of the individual becomes the sin of the community, and the sin of the one man hidden away involves a whole nation in catastrophe. The wrongdoing of Achan means the defeat of the nation at Ai. Then, there is another movement forward after that is atoned for, and the sinning man is put to death and put out of the way.

And so these strange manifestations! Not only the crossing of the Jordan, but Jericho; I wonder if you can imagine anything more utterly foolish than the idea of capturing a great walled city by having men tramp round it blowing rams' horns! Can you imagine anything more futile? Can you imagine that the walls will ever tremble because of the tread of the armies? We know better. But the people must learn obedience and they must do what they are told. Before this a visitor had been to Joshua, captain of the host. The Lord came to him, and gave him to understand he was to convey his order from a higher authority, that is he must be thinking not of the order so much as of the faith of the men who walk round the city walls of Jericho seven times, blowing rams' horns. So the nation was obedient, and did the foolish and apparently incredibly foolish thing. And God shook the earth, and the city walls fell and the city was captured.

Then followed seven years of war till Joshua was about ninety. Stop a moment and look: "And it came to pass the Lord said unto Joshua Thou art old and well stricken in years." God knew that he was getting to be an old fellow. Listen! He said to him, "Thou art old and well stricken in years, and there remaineth yet very much land to be possessed." Why, then his work is not over! That is always the way. And then there follows the setting out of the land, and its arrangements, and the settlement of the tribes, some on one side of the Jordan, some on the other. Dean Stanley said that without any argument we may call these chapters in Joshua the Doomsday Book of the Hebrew nation. It was a wonderful work. So at last they have entered into the land, and possessed it, and the people are settled and Joshua passes. In conclusion, there are two farewell addresses that he delivered to them, one in Chapters 23 and 24, as far as verse 15.I wonder if others feel as I do, that in these farewell addresses of Joshua there was a severer, even more forbidding note than in any of the farewell addresses of Moses. I understand he was a soldier, and a different man. But when we get these marvelous farewell addresses and come to summarize them, we have in the first address his dwelling upon the power and the faithfulness of God; in the second address he surveyed their history. And as I come to the close of this second address, I see he recognizes their weakness. It was there, it had always been there. And he uttered to them those miraculous words which have been made the basis of so many sermons—all of them good sermons, but not all of them good exegesis. "Choose you this day whom ye will serve." And if you take that from its context you can imagine all the things you like, and much that you imagine is right, but it is not all in the text. "Choose you this day whom ye will serve; whether the gods which your fathers served that were beyond the River, or the gods of the Amorites, in whose land ye dwell: but as for me and my house, we will serve the Lord."

In those words of Joshua there is a touch of irony. If we want to serve God we must go His way, but choose. And if we are going to have the gods of the people round us with their beastliness, choose them. "As for me and my house, we will serve the Lord." What a great ending. What a great message at the end of a great life. And then he died. The people were left with Eleazar, and then Eleazar the priest died, and they were left without the successor of Moses, and without the successor of Aaron.

8. JUDGES, RUTH

We have looked at the Book of Joshua, opening with the death of Moses (referred to as accounting for all that is to follow) and closing with the death of Joshua, who had completed his work in the national life. But the supreme thing in the Book of Joshua is that the nation is still a theocracy; no king, no president to represent the nation, no human center of authority. Moses had been that delegated by God; and in a sense, and for a certain specified purpose, Joshua was that.

Coming to Judges, with the Book of Ruth which is collateral writing for the stream of history runs through both of them, what is seen as we read this book? The nation is still seen as a theocracy. It still has no king except God. The book opens with accounts of the last days of Joshua, and the things immediately following, and the stream of history in the book begins and ends with Chapter 16. Then Chapters 17, 18 and the rest of the book constitute an appendix in which the writer gives us certain events that took place in the period covered in the history.

I turn for a moment to the boundaries. I want to notice that the recorder, whosoever he may have been (we have no means of knowing) was very careful in four references to make a statement of the boundaries. The first is found in Chapter 17:6: "In those days there was no king in Israel: every man did that which was right in his own eyes." Glance at the next chapter, verse 1, "In those days there was no king in Israel." Glance at Chapter 19:1, "And it came to pass in those days, when there was no king in Israel." And then come to the very end of the book, and the last sentence of the last chapter is this: "In those days there was no king in Israel: every man did that which was right in his own eyes." The recorder is careful to draw attention to this fact, that it was a period when the nation was without a king. There are those who think that this statement by the recorder dated the writing of the book. I am not entering into an argument concerning it. It was evident that the writer was living in days when there was a king, and he is looking back to days the record of which is found in his writing, and emphasizing the fact that there was no king. And he is saying that to show the reason of the appalling story of failure. It seems to suggest that if they had had a king it would have been all right. If this dates the writing, it does not at all affect the values of the book itself; I am bold enough to say that statement which I find first in all its fullness in Chapter 6, verse 17, and which I find in the same fullness in the last verse of the last chapter: "In those days there was no king in Israel": whether or not he was thinking from the standpoint of human kingship, shows that it was certainly an acknowledged fact that as a matter of practical value there was no king during that period. But it does not mean to say that God was no longer King and by them recognized. They were under God, and under the authority of God, and therefore he says, "Every man did that which was right in his own eyes." Call it, from the standpoint of the people, an era of democracy. Do not quarrel with me, or say that democracy does not mean that every man does that which is right in his own eyes. I am not so sure, but we will leave it at that without any argument upon the point. The fact was entered in the statement and four times repeated; the writer is drawing attention to the fact that it was in the days before the king, and not only that: he is illuminating the story by declaring that it was a period when the central authority was not recognized. There was no king and every man was running his own way and doing what seemed right in his own eyes. That statement, insisted upon by the recorder in these four instances, shows that there was no king recognized, but it does not mean that there was no king. He may have been thinking of the monarchy, but we say without any hesitation that if there is no king in this sense the King was still there: the King Himself, and there was no King other than God. The period covered by the Book of Joshua was about twenty-seven years. The period covered by the Book of Judges is roughly about 450 years, so we have a long space covered in its history.

Now notice in connection with the Book of Judges, in the second chapter (and I am back to it because it has a bearing on everything that follows) at verse 10, the writer is looking back and then looking around as he says: "And also all that generation were gathered unto their fathers: and there arose another generation after them, which knew not the Lord, nor yet the work which he had wrought for Israel." And he says definitely that this is the farewell address; and in Chapter 2:6: "The children of Israel went every man unto his inheritance to possess the land." Mark that very carefully. Joshua had now died, he had given his farewell addresses and passed; and after the solemn convention and the hearing of the addresses, every man went away to his own inheritance to possess the land. Mark the supreme interest of the people. Chapter 2:7: "And the people served the Lord all the days of Joshua, and all the days of the elders that outlived Joshua, who had seen all the great work of the Lord that he had wrought for Israel. And Joshua the son of Nun, the servant of the Lord, died; being a hundred and ten years old. And they buried him in the border of his inheritance in Timnath-heres, in the hill-country of Ephraim, on the north of the mountain of Gaash. And also all the generation were gathered unto their fathers: and there arose another generation after them, which knew not the Lord, nor yet the work which he had wrought for Israel. And the children of Israel did that which was evil in the sight of the Lord."

Now that links all the story that follows with the death of Joshua. It shows the people after his death, and after they had heard his farewell discourses, hastily dispersing, every man looking to his own inheritance that he might possess the land. Then we come to the record of the Judges. A word may be said about these men whose story is given in this book, from the first Othniel to the last Samson. Samuel judged Israel over forty years, but this book covers the period I have referred to from Othniel to Samson. And it is well to remember that these Judges had a certain amount of authority, I think an abated authority. The word "Judges" reveals that. I think in our secular history, if I may so call it, we get nearer to the idea of what Judges really were if we think of the Roman dictators. But it should be remembered that the Roman dictators in the olden days bore no comparison to the men we are calling dictators today. A Roman dictator was always a man that was raised up by some time of crisis in Roman history, and who led and guided until the crisis was over and some kind of deliverance was wrought or defeat was suffered. He was flung up by the occasion. So these men were just Judges. They were men appearing at a crisis in the history of the people, and for the time being they were leaders, and after that they passed back into the crowd. Notice that carefully. This is the story of the earlier period of Judges. Let me repeat in this connection: when you get to Samuel, he did not retire but kept on for forty years. So the people are seen approaching the idea of kingship. Samuel was no king. He did not desire a king. He was against kingship strongly, as we shall see in a subsequent series. But the people were feeling the effect of one personality, visible and seen, and that was Samuel. In the earlier period of the Judges the men were simply raised up.

This whole section gives the story of the Judges from Othniel to Samson, and shows it in seven movements. Each movement can be described by the same three words: Declension, Discipline, Deliverance.

First came the declension; then the disciplining of the people to the rule or reign of God; finally God's deliverance. In every case God raised up a man. Did you notice that when I spoke of the Roman dictators I said a man was flung up by circumstances? So here the man was flung up, and if you follow through you will find how remarkably they were fitted for the peculiar hour in which God raised them up. Every one of them had qualifications which met the necessity of that immediate moment. God is seen governing a people still disloyal, disobedient in an appalling way. And they are passing into a period of discipline seven times over. If you read that story carefully, you will see how terrible the discipline was, and that this people so wondrous in its origin, this nation so marvelous in its beginning had to pass through in suffering. It was because of discipline. But the moment God has evidence of the result of the discipline (and there was another manifestation of repentance and return to God—though as I read the story I often feel how cowardly the return was, nevertheless directly there was some evidence of that), He raises at once some man as *the man* to become the sign of deliverance.

Now the boundaries show you two dark pictures in the period. The picture of Ruth is incorporated by way of collateral history, and just for a moment look only at its very beginning. Notice how it begins: "And it came to pass in the days when the judges judged." The Book of Ruth was in this period, whether earlier or later we have no means of knowing. There are no names that link it up with any other names of the period. But the Book of Ruth I should describe as an idyll of the period showing at one side events illustrated in the boundaries. From Chapter 17 of Judges we see the dark side with all the illustrations, but the Book of Ruth shows another side during that period. That is a somewhat labored introduction, but it gives you the general idea of the book.

Now what do we see as we follow this remarkable book with its appalling story? Two things, I think, distinctly. First, the deterioration of a nation. The nation is deteriorating, going down and down, lower and lower. And secondly, we see the administration of God. They are never abandoned, never left. God is always governing, governing by discipline when there is disobedience, governing by deliverance if there is anything in the nature of repentance. That is roughly the story. Bear that in mind.

The deterioration of the nation, and the administration of God: look at these two things a little more closely. We see the deterioration of the nation, and that is manifest first in religious failure, secondly in political failure resulting from religious failure. And then we have the story of the divine activity, and the divine deliverance is wrought. Of course, if you shut God out of this history I do not think you would ever trouble to read it, but you cannot, of course, without mutilating the records.

As we go through the book, it is the story of the most appalling failure all the way through, but we cannot put God out. I find these two things closely authenticated in this order. First of all, religious failure. Where did the failure begin? I turn to the Book of Judges 2:11-13, "And the children of Israel did that which was evil in the sight of the Lord, and served the Baalim; and they forsook the Lord, the God of their fathers, who brought them out of the land of Egypt, and followed other gods, of the gods of the peoples that were round about them, and bowed themselves down unto them: and they provoked the Lord to anger. And they forsook the Lord, and served Baal and the Ashtaroth."

In that paragraph the recorder repeats the statement, not always in the same words but over and over again throughout all the history. There is where the statement first occurs, and it is a revelation of the secret of their failures. They forsook the Lord their God. There is continued history with that statement repeated over and over again. They served Baal and the Ashtaroth, they turned from God to worship false gods, the gods they found in the land, and they bowed themselves down. Of course, we can understand it in a certain way. The worship of Baal and the worship of Ashtaroth and the worship of any other god than our God is a comparatively easy matter. It does not make any demands upon the moral conscience of humanity. It runs on to freedom and to license. That was peculiarly true of the worship of Baal and Ashtaroth, but it is the most appalling story: the worship of the moon god who declared man as absolutely free to indulge in any experience he might like, without let or hindrance. These people, of course, felt the necessity for some god and they accommodated themselves to the gods they found in the land. They turned to the ways of supposed religion which lacked sovereignty and holiness. And that is the continued history that runs through these 400 years. Over and over again it is the same thing, and that wrought all the trouble. The trouble that came to these people from surrounding nations was very severe and very terrible, but it never would have come if they had not turned their back upon God.

This religious failure wrought again political failure, and social misery and breakdown. We are studying literature, and I am going to repeat something I often say. It is terribly tempting to stop and apply it to our own national life. I am not saying that this is all true of our national life, but I am saying this: that all our political futilities and breakdowns are the fruit of our religious infidelity. It is true everywhere. This literature is the one living literature, and this is the story we have been reading. Religious failure, turning from God, and the result of that was political failure. Overcome by the people they had turned to, their cleverness was of no avail against their enemies. Over and over again they were brought into conditions in that land, which was the Land of Promise, as terrible and sometimes more so than any of the conditions which had existed for their fathers in Egypt. Read the story of Gideon. Look at the people. No more traveling the highways, they had to go down the byways. They were in hiding, an unarmed people, completely broken down, at the mercy of their enemies. They gave up their God and their religion, and the result was the inevitable issue of failure. Policy, strategic diplomacy—they are of no use at all. They cannot deliver any nation that turns its back upon God. And this is illustrated throughout.

While in the presence of these conditions, glance briefly again at this story of divine deliverance, Chapter 2:16-18: "And the Lord raised up judges, who saved them out of the hand of those that spoiled them... then the Lord was with the judge." There is the statement. The King unseen, immortal, eternal, was reigning; and in that period of their deepest and direst necessity, resulting from discipline inflicted on account of their disobedience and their bowing down to other false gods, God raised up a judge. In every case it was a divine action, and the neglected King is seen still ruling in that way, ruling all the way through.

Now mark the process. These people turned their backs upon God and then they accommodated themselves to the gods that they found in the land, gods under whose influence the whole country has passed into the realm of appalling corruption. You have seen in the previous studies that God is using this nation as His instrument to lead these other nations to holy things, and yet they are seen turning to these very gods, bowing before them, becoming mastered by them. As I asked you to notice in the opening sentence, their first concern after the death of Joshua was to go to their possessions; every man went to his own inheritance, to seek out his own land. He showed his self-centered interest that adopted the gods of the people before them, and bowed down before them. But the King is still reigning and will reign. He raised up judges, according to the writer of the Letter to the Hebrews, speaking in another connection, "in the fullness of time."

What does it all lead to? What is the meaning of this Book of Judges? For the answer I go back to the Book of Ruth. This book begins by saying that "it came to pass" in that period when the judges judged; and then I look at the end and I read in verse 17 a certain reference here: "And the women her neighbors gave it a name, saying, There is a son born to Naomi; and they called his name Obed." Then go on to the same thing again in verse 22: "And Obed begat Jesse, and Jesse begat David." And it is still going on. But you must go into the New Testament, and you will find from that union of Boaz and Ruth after the flesh came Jesus the King. Vantage ground for God; in spite of all the failure, He is moving on. Now the last thing I want to say here is this: in

this Book of Judges, things of loyalty, things of beauty are seen shining against the dark background. Go over it again and pick them out. I content myself with a reference to three stories, full of beauty, full of glory, showing that in spite of the national failure God has an elect remnant of those souls whom He can trust, those men and women through whom He can move forward in the great purpose of His heart. He always has had, in spite of the failure, and it is dark enough in this nation as we look at it. And against that dark background, there are three that I should name that stand out most remarkably: the story of Deborah, the story of Gideon, the story of Ruth. The light is very beautiful in every case.

I have been reading the story of Deborah over and over again and I do not know anything more beautiful, and in some senses more wonderful, from the standpoint of literature than this marvelous story, and the song that was born in the darkness and desolation of national failure. Very interesting, isn't it, how often this is done? Over and over again out of the misery there has struck some gleam of the glory. And you will find it all in Deborah's song. This is the Song of Deborah and Barak. There is the introduction, and then it runs on:

For that the leaders took the lead in Israel,
For that the people suffered themselves willingly.
Bless ye the Lord.

You notice that Deborah was the poetic inspiration, Barak was the practical organizer. What a marvelous union it was! Deborah was the inspiration, and her song illustrates all through life the things that Barak would have done. But I am prepared to say that without Barak, Deborah's song would have been ineffective. The link between the poetic and the practical man is always necessary.

There is an illustration in the New Testament. Peter, the practical man, and John, the dreamer. Notice what close friends they became after Pentecost. Then in verse 9:

My heart is toward the governors of Israel,
That offered themselves willingly among the people:
Bless ye the Lord.

Deborah was the inspiration, the cause, and Barak had done the work, and seen to the practical side of things, and they celebrated the victory in this. "For these things bless the Lord." Recognize God. And then she passes into the finest satire. It is evident that when the tribes came to meet their enemies, the tribe of Reuben did not come. Now listen!

By the watercourses of Reuben,
There were great resolves of heart.

Oh it's fine! And he has a good many companions today. I repeat, it is poetry. I will rob Deborah for a moment of her poetic imagery and put it like this. "Those people of Reuben held conventions and passed resolutions and did nothing!" That's what was the matter with them. It is the finest satire. What were they doing? Staying by the watercourses, where the streams are gently running and listening to the piping of the flags. It is a glorious song. In it she indulged the half-humorous satire of her soul so fired that presently she breaks out,

Curse ye Meroz, said the angel of the Lord,
Curse ye bitterly the inhabitants thereof.
Why so angry?
Because they came not to the help of the Lord,
To the help of the Lord against the mighty.

What radiant light it throws! It is a radiant picture, as well as an inspiration of a movement that brought ultimate deliverance, complete deliverance for the time being by the aid of Barak; and inspired by her great song, celebrating the first action of God and then the action of the troops that came, and pouring satire upon the people that debated and did nothing.

The matchless story of Gideon reveals the fact that the God who governs depends upon a certain type of soul to do His work, and when He gets that type of soul to do His work, He can enable them to do it by inspiration without difficulty. Gideon was raised up, and Gideon called an army, and there responded 32,000 people. You know the story, and you say "A lot of people." But they are a very small percentage of the population. And God said—I am sure I shall be forgiven if I alter the wording—"Sift that crowd and find the men I want. And send back everybody who has got trembling of soul or who is fainthearted with fear. Let them go home."

The vindication of the command of God is seen in what followed. Directly Gideon made the announcement, there was one of the most remarkable military movements of history. Right about face—quick march 22,000 going home as fast as they can. Let them go. God does not want them. He cannot use them. And again that reference, using the same phrasing: "They are too many, sift them, sift them." And then came a curious test. You know the story. "Send home all those men who take unnecessary time for unnecessary things." And there was another military movement—7,000 going back. And then that word of God: "By the 300 men that lapped will I save you." These are the men that God wants. I do not want to suggest that all those who went home—29,000 all told—were all ultimately cast off. Not at all. They probably all came back presently. What for? To shout? My fellow Christians, I do not think I want to stand amid the shouting crowd if I bear no scars from the battle.

And then there is Ruth and the choice, a wonderful picture. Two souls, one of the covenant, and one a Moabite woman, and the idyllic story. Both of them true to God. And Boaz, loyal in the midst of all the defections, and every line that limns him shines. Ruth had a dreadful choice of conviction, and the words that fell from her lips have gone round the world and down the centuries as the ultimate symbol of everything that is beautiful in life: "Entreat me not to leave thee; thy people shall be my people." But don't stop there: "And thy God my God." And so history marches.

We do not know, and we do not need to know, and we do not want to know, the meaning of our life if we are utterly true to God. Who could know, gleaning in that gleaning field what that union of two righteous souls in the quiet stately march of history would bring! And yet, out of that, after the flesh, came Jesus.

9. I SAMUEL

Samuel, the book to which we come now, may be described as a period of transition in the history of the people. It is a period lasting about a hundred years, beginning with the birth of Samuel and ending with the death of Saul. Through the whole of this period the nation is still a theocracy, it is still a nation whose only King is God throughout the whole, but it is a period of transition from the period of the Judges to the period of the Monarchy. God is still the only King, but the national consciousness and recognition of that fact of the Kingship of God have lost all practical value.

Now as we survey the book through, there are three points to notice. First of all, it is the story of the last of the Judges, and then the king *asked* for, Saul; and then the king *given,* David. You will say, "Was not Saul given?" Yes, we get to that directly; but Saul was the king they wanted, and God gave them the king they asked for. David was not the king they asked for. He was wholly the king God-given. We get these accounts in this book, and these two things pre-eminently.

Take this book, beginning with the matchlessly beautiful story of the birth of Samuel. Glance at it, and thinking of it as a whole, you at once detect a difference between Joshua, and the judgeship of those who preceded him. The Judges were after the pattern of Homan dictators, who were always men raised up to meet a crisis, and when their work was done they retired.

With Samuel it was different. He maintained his judgeship for forty years. He did it by circuit, and though he was not king he certainly filled the place of a king as a visualized sign of authority. He was not king, never crowned, but it is a very interesting thing that when Peter was preaching and reviewing the history of the people in Acts 3:24 he made this reference: "All the prophets from Samuel." Now that incidentally, in a passing word, reveals the fact that there was now a new note and that it was a prophetic note, authoritative, that came into the life of the nation with Samuel. God had His prophets, His messengers, before Moses was a prophet, and none has arisen like him, say the Scriptures. But here was the beginning of something fresh. Samuel was a Judge but he was also a prophet; and all the prophets from Samuel and the order of prophets as the messengers of God arose after Samuel. That is the great succession through the centuries of names with which we are familiar.

But the prophet here emerges as the statesman, and that is what Samuel was. Notice this. God never spoke to His nation through their kings, never—the kingly office was never recognized by the divine revelation of the will of God in that way. Oh yes, He spoke to kings but through the prophets; and Samuel began that order, began the exercise of that work, and the prophets "from Samuel," said Peter, spoke in the illuminated power of the Holy Spirit. So here is the difference. A man continued to judge, and he had to do it living at Ramah and traveling round the circuit; and whilst he was going round and round exercising his judgeship, all the way he was the messenger of God, he was the prophet. The period covered reveals the appalling corruption of the priesthood. The nation was feeling as supremely troubled as was the prophet. We saw that in considering Judges. The political declension followed on the religious declension, and the social declension was the outcome of that. So here the priesthood is seen in an almost unbelievable state of corruption. Presently this corruption was manifested, when the priests said they would carry the Ark of God into battle with a superstitious idea that it would save them. It did not save them. They met with most disastrous defeat. And so the most sacred thing in the nation, the Ark of God, was not guarantee against discipline and punishment when the people were disobedient. That is the early period of the book.

In the midst of that period, the boy Samuel was born. It is a very beautiful story, which I am not going to relate, because it is well known. The story of Hannah! Take pains, when you read her grand Song after the boy was born, to see what a wonderful song it was, what a complete revelation of the fact that in the heart of a woman was a complete understanding of God and His government and His methods of guiding. And to the woman, in answer to her prayer, the boy was born. And then he was secluded because his mother devoted him at once to the service of God, and he lived a secluded life in the Temple courts shut away from the corruption of his times for a period of at least twenty years. In early boyhood there came to him that supernatural call from God. He recognized it and was obedient to it. And the lad, at that youthful age, delivered the message that was so terrible a message, to Eli. Again you have him in quietness and seclusion, at that moment of crisis to which I have already referred, when they dared to carry the Ark of God into battle superstitiously hoping that its presence would bring them victory, and instead of that the Ark of God was captured by the foe. The Philistines found that the Ark of God was no protection for the people of God against their foes, and they found out that it was one thing for the people that owned the Ark as the sign of their religion to be dazzled by its power when they were disobedient, but another thing for them, the Philistines, to think they could play the fool with the Ark of God. That is very interesting. There is the story of Ashdod. They took the Ark from place to place, and wherever the Ark came, judgment fell upon the Philistines. So we get right to the center of the book. At that point, Samuel bursts upon the life in the position of leader to the nation. That is all the first movement of the book. We see Samuel, but we have no details of what he did beyond the paragraph that he moved to Ramah, and became Judge of foe people. But it is a new beginning: leader of foe people, prophet of God, king's messenger to foe nation all foe way through. Very wonderful it was when he began his work and the finger of God had strongly intervened to give victory to His own people for then Samuel at once raised an altar. That is where we get foe name that we so often use: Eben-ezer—Hitherto hath the Lord helped us. Hitherto! And when Samuel used the word, that is its equivalent; he was looking back over all the history of the earlier judges: the Lord hath helped us. He saw the

divine fulfillment, the divine government, and that is what this altar means.

Then came the crisis, apparently from the corruption of the priesthood, the corruption of Joel and Abijah, the sons of Eli, which became ultimately intolerable even to the people themselves. The nation gathered to Samuel, and they said to him, "Eli is an old man and his sons are unworthy. We must have a change." Notice carefully when the crisis came: a corrupt priesthood, Eli incapable of directing his sons in paths of righteousness however true he may have been in his own soul to the God of his fathers, and these sons corrupting all the priesthood and the Ark proceeding into battle and travestied, and the people are in rebellion. They want to escape from the dominion of a corrupt priesthood. Is not that fine? Ah! but notice what happened. That was the occasion, and then there emerged into the clear of plain speech that which undoubtedly had been incipient and growing through a long period. They came and cited the case of these corrupt priests and they came to Samuel, still recognizing him as the leader. And you know their words, "Make us a king to judge us like the nations." We are so familiar with it, and yet go back and look at it and think of it carefully.

That was a direct contravention of the divine purpose. God had made that nation to be created, to be redeemed from captivity, and had provided for it, and followed it, and lost it, and led it in patient care through forty years in the wilderness. And He had brought them out and ruled them in patience for 450 years; and there was repeated declension, and judges were raised up to deliver them whenever there was a sign of repentance to God. He had done all this, and had created the nation to be unlike the nations, and to be unlike the nations in the interest of the nations. We must feel all that involved. God wanted a nation, to live among the nations of the world, that did not forget that it was His purpose to make of them a great nation, saying to one man, "In thy seed shall all the created nations of the earth be blessed." This nation should have no king other than Himself.

Now listen again to the people. They did not make any reference to the Kingship of God. They were tired of a corrupt priesthood. They were appealing to the leader who had been with them for forty years, asking him to make them a king like the nations. I repeat, the request was a direct contravention of the divine purpose. What was the divine purpose? What was the divine estimate of their request? In Chapter 16 it is very clearly revealed. In those days—and really it is a beautiful and pathetic thing to see him in some senses—when Samuel was mourning over Saul's declension and failure, you hear God saying to Samuel, "Why are you mourning for Saul?" "And the Lord said unto Samuel, How long wilt thou mourn for Saul, seeing I have rejected him from being king over Israel?" (16:1) Listen to these actual words: "They have not rejected thee, but they have rejected me, that I should not be king over them" (I Samuel 8:7).

These people would not have said this. They would not have said, 'We are rejecting God, we want a king, we are tired of God." They would not have put it that way, but all their life is the assurance of the truth of it.

To neglect God is to reject; to treat with indifference is to refuse; to fail to recognize is to revolt against Him when you are dealing with the fact of the Kingship of God. And the Lord summarized the whole thing when He said to Samuel, "They have not rejected thee, but they have rejected me, that I should not be king over them."

And Samuel was strangely moved, and He addressed the people in one of the great passages in all literature, and told this people what monarchy would mean, and why a king was different, and what would be the issue on the level of social relationship and national affairs. He delivered the address, but they still clamored for the king.

And now God was reigning and God said, "Give them what they ask. They have rejected me, practically, definitely they have rejected me. They are not seeking to know me or to obey my laws. They have rejected me, they have dethroned me for all practical purposes. Give them what they ask." And that is how Saul came to the throne.

Look at him. Many people are great lovers of Browning. So am I. I admit the poem "Saul" is a wonderful poem, but I submit it is absolutely false in interpretation of the man; that a bigger failure is not on record in all the Bible than that man Saul. There occurs this description in Chapter 9, "A young man and goodly: and there was not among the children of Israel a goodlier person than he: from his shoulders and upward he was higher than any of the people." A striking figure, a striking personality; indeed, looking at Saul from that standpoint, one is justified in saying he was a superb young man physically. Don't forget he was a man chosen by God, and he was chosen by God to meet the request of the people—a king like the nations. And here is the king like the nations. God chose him in that way. I don't know any more wonderful historic or collective commentary on this than something written by a psalmist long after this when he said of these very children of Israel, in other circumstances (and in saying it revealed a tremendous principle), "God gave them their request and sent leanness into their souls." It is not always good to clamor in the presence of God for something we think we would like to have; He may give it to us, that by the discipline resulting from our own choice, we may learn the folly and the wickedness of the thing chosen. That is the principle on which Saul was appointed.

If you want his biography briefly, run on to Chapter 26 and find among other things he said this: "I have played the fool"; and if you want the story of Saul that is it. "I have played the fool." What warrant have I for saying that? He said it in the moment when all the facts of his life and his activity and his impossibility and his irresponsibility and his failure were sweeping upon him. He was speaking of his attitude to David, but it told the whole story of his life.

Think of his opportunities: first of all a great personality, a commanding personality physically. I doubt whether there is any evidence of any greatness mentally in Saul. I cannot find it anywhere, but he had a commanding personality. His very presence made people look at him in a very definite way.

That is the smallest thing, it is true. "God gave him another heart"—that is, a new start. "And the spirit of God came mightily upon him" (I Samuel 10:10). What a tremendous opportunity! "And there gathered around him a band of men whose hearts God had touched." That is how he faced his opportunity.

This was the situation: himself a commanding personality; God visiting him and giving him a new heart to start the new opportunity; the spirit coming mightily upon him; and gathering round him a band of men whose hearts God had touched. And Samuel was there with him. Go through the story and see how it is the story of a man cursed with mock modesty, by impatience and self-dependence, by disobedience to the light of heaven, by irascibility of temperament until he became a madman, by hatred of David; unreasonable, until the last thing you see he is going to listen to the witch of Endor as she mutters. Saul! Do you quarrel with anything I said? Mock modesty, where do you get that? There at the very beginning after he is anointed by Samuel, when he was called to take his place, he was hiding behind the stuff. I have heard people say this was a wonderful exhibition of modesty. There is modesty that becomes blasphemy. If God calls you to the front, and you are hiding behind the stuff, you are sinning against God just as much as when you make to the front and God wants you in the rear. Evidence of weakness? It runs all through, until you get the tragic end of a man who, on the field of battle, died by his own hand. Saul! That is the king they asked for. They got the thing they asked for. All the while God is acting, granting them their requests, giving them exactly what they asked for, and then leaving them forty years to work out in their experience the stupidity and the bitterness of the experience that resulted from the fact that He was rejected from being King over them.

Now we go ahead to Chapter 16:1: "And the Lord said unto Samuel, How long wilt thou mourn for Saul, seeing I have rejected him from being king over Israel? fill thine horn with oil, and go: I will send thee to Jesse the Bethlehemite; for I have provided me a king among his sons." Take those two little sentences out: "I have rejected Saul"; "I have provided *me* a king." Now there is a new God breaking in upon the ghastly failure of the king asked for and provided, and rebuking Samuel who mourned naturally the death, saying, "It is enough for you, Samuel, prophet, my messenger, that I have rejected him, but if I have rejected him from being king, I have provided *me* a king." And Samuel, obedient to the divine voice, went where he was sent. And when he got there, the leaders of the city came to him and asked if he had come peaceably, and he said he had. And then he came to Jesse and his sons to whom he was sent, and Eliab appeared before him and he looked at him and he said, "Surely the Lord's anointed is before him." That is Samuel, thinking of the magnificent presence as a qualification for kingship. Even Samuel had not learned the lesson. "But the Lord said unto Samuel, Look not on his countenance, or on the height of his stature; because I have rejected him: for the Lord seeth not as man seeth; for man looketh on the outward appearance, but the Lord looketh on the heart" (16:7). There is the truth revealed. He gave them the king they wanted, one upon whose countenance they could look and whose stature towered above all the rest of the people. They had him for forty years. Now, God said, I have chosen *Me* a king, and upon the principle—not of outward appearance, countenance and height and stature—but upon his heart. That was the principle. And David was anointed, and we see him as king. Oh yes, he is king from that moment, but he does not come into his kingdom, he is not known, his kingship is not acknowledged.

And then by the exigence of the madness and the melancholy of Saul, this youth who is skilful upon the harp goes up in the Court to learn courtly ways, and by the playing of his instrument to exorcise occasionally the tumultuous evil spirit from Saul.

But the crisis comes and the revolt of the nation, when the enemies have got their great giant Goliath. The nation is helpless, Saul is helpless—the great man whose stature is higher than any of his own people, but who was not so big as Goliath. If we are only taking stature into account, he is perfectly fooled by the sight of Goliath. Then comes the stripling who is not as high as Saul, and is not as great in stature as Goliath. But the stripling sees things from the standpoint of the divine government by which he was appointed, and he has something in his sling. And in the name of the Lord Almighty he goes forth. And the victory is with Israel.

That matchless story of the friendship of David and Jonathan follows. It is very, very beautiful. And without reflecting on David, I never can read the story without liking Jonathan a little better than David. He is a little more self-sacrificing. A great soul was David, but their friendship was singularly beautiful.

And now Saul's hatred is increasing, and becoming deeper and he is determined to murder David. So the story goes on, and David is driven out of the land which is going to be his kingdom. He knows what the will of God is, and yet he is waiting the divine time. And he goes on alone—to use an expression in one of the Psalms—"he was hunted like a partridge upon the mountains." Twice the life of Saul was in his hand, but the man who had heard God speak was leaving the issues with God.

And then we have the whole story of Saul: "I have played the fool." And there came a moment of depression in the life of David, when he said, "Saul will surely slay me."

I close with that which brings it into line with our own conscience. There is the story of Adullam. What a story that is! Recall the description of the people gathered there, those that were in debt and danger and discontented, and in that cave, by contact with David, they became transmuted into the mighty men that were David's special guard and helpers in the days to come. That is where the story ends in Samuel.

David is not yet crowned the king, nor will he be for a good many years. Look over the whole scene. What do we see? The administration and overruling of the one King, God Almighty. Ah yes, I read the story and I learn from it that

God can be rejected, but He cannot be dethroned. They have rejected Him from being King, but they never dethroned Him, and He is still ruling; ruling by adaption of divine strength through human failure to high purpose. God is moving forward. And James Russell Lowell's words almost inevitably spring to me when I read these records: "Standeth God within the shadow, keeping watch above His own" And if we do not know what Lowell exactly meant by "His own," I think I can give it the wider meaning: Keeping watch over His own purposes and plans, guiding them forward toward consummation.

10. II Samuel, I Chronicles

We have beached the Second Book of Samuel, and I am going to refer also to the First Book of Chronicles. It gives file same history that we have in II Samuel and is what I should call a collateral writing. That is to say, in Samuel you have the book written by the historian, and in Chronicles you have the writing from the personal standpoint.

Now II Samuel may be described as the book of David. It is a very wonderful book. In period it covers about forty years. Looking back we see that God gave the people what they asked, a king like the nations. Amending that statement slightly, I should say God gave them a king after their own hearts. They had Saul for forty years. Now we are looking at David who—I am quoting—is a man after God's own heart. That is the remarkable contrast. Saul, a king like the nations, according to the desire of the people, after their own heart; and now a king raised up, a man after God's own heart. I shall refer to that again in connection with a very much challenged statement. For the moment, this is the description of this man after God's own heart. God has chosen him. He chose Saul and He gave him because the people clamored for a king like the nations. He said—I speak very reverently—If you want a king like the nations, ye shall have it; and He gave it. And it has been a ghastly failure.

And now God says, I have rejected him from being king, and have provided Myself a king, that is David. And whatever we may think about David—and no one is blind to his failure—in the matter of the Kingship of God, he ever recognized it. That was supremely characteristic of David and of his reign. I dare not stay to illustrate but I shall touch upon it again later on. Follow it, watch it; whether in victory or defeat or sin or repentance, there is not a single sentence or act in which he either ignores or forgets the Kingship of God. That is the great theme of David's reign.

Now there are three things we want to look at in David. First, the kingly qualifications, and then the reign (not in detail but glancing over the whole of it), and then the failure.

What were the qualifications? To go back to the previous book, to I Samuel 16:1: "And the Lord said unto Samuel, How long wilt thou mourn for Saul, seeing I have rejected him from being king over Israel? fill thine horn with oil, and go: I will send thee to Jesse the Bethlehemite; for I have provided me a king among his sons." That is the first qualification. God had chosen him. You remember that even

Samuel was falling into the mistake of the people, and when he saw the great big bulky fellow named Eliab, he said, "This is the man that is named" And God said, "No." God does not look upon the outward appearance. He looks upon the heart. And God looked upon the heart of this stripling, this David, and that is his first qualification. And there is no more to be said. If God has looked upon him, he is qualified.

Yet there are human elements in the subject of his qualification. We are not following the sequence for the moment; I quote this for a special reason. In II Samuel 5:1 we read: "Then came all the tribes of Israel to David unto Hebron, and spake, saying." Now this is it: "Behold, we are thy bone and thy flesh. In times past, when Saul was king over us, it was thou that leddest [us] out and broughtest in Israel; and the Lord said to thee, Thou shalt be shepherd of [feed] my people Israel, and thou shalt be prince over Israel." That was the language of the tribes when they came to crown him king, and that language reveals the qualifications of David on the human side.

First, he was all this: "of our bone and our flesh." Secondly, he was sent out the actual leader, even in Saul's time. The people had said, "Thou leddest us out." And then he was appointed leader, and finally the people recognized a divine action. These are the qualifications.

First of all we have the preparation of David for the work of the kingship as it is revealed in I Samuel. One cannot really separate these books. In the Hebrew Bible the books are not divided into First and Second Samuel as we have them. So there is a sense in which we must have in mind that when reading about David in I Samuel, we see the truth concerning him that we get in II Samuel.

That was the preparation he had to pass through for the kingly office. It was Homer who said a remarkable thing about kingship: "All kings are shepherds of the people." One may be inclined to amend that and say all kings ought to be so. But Homer was speaking ideally, and he was perfectly right. I do not hesitate to say God's idea of a king is always perfectly set forth in the idea of the shepherd. There was this lad, growing up in the fields, familiar with the work of watching over the flocks, and so being prepared for watching over the people of God and being their shepherd—and as we read, feeding them, just as a shepherd feeds his flock. This is the line of his natural preparation.

And then there was the period in which he was in the Court of Saul, a terrible period for him in many ways, but a remarkable one. Looking at it along the human level, you can see how David passed on to the Court as chief Court musician, and so became familiar with all the ways of the Court; all the incidentals of the kingship he learned in the Court; the essential meaning of the kingship as the shepherd in the fields. Then there followed the exile, when he became an outlaw, when, to use his own language, he was "hunted like a partridge upon the mountains," the terrible days of Saul's anger burning against him, and the blood lust rampant as he wanted to kill David. What was happening? The very fiber of the man was being toughened for everything that lay ahead. It was a wonderful preparation if you look at it in that simple way. First of all in the fields, then the Court, and then the exile; and every experience contributing to the make-up of the kingly character and the kingly ability.

Now we come to the story of the reign, and it is interesting to observe that although the disruption of the kingdom did not take place till the death of Solomon, it was incidentally connected very definitely with the rupture between Judah and the other princes. The remarkable thing is that when David was first crowned he was only crowned by Judah, and he was seven years king of Judah before he became king of all Israel. And that was a very terrible period. Anointed by Judah, crowned by Judah, his enemies were at work—definitely and terribly at work. Abner, that remarkable personality, was attempting to consolidate the kingdom round the house of Saul under Ishbosheth. And there are the seven years when David, anointed king, only reigned over part of the nation, over Judah, reigning all the while with the consciousness of the divine kingship: and on the other hand Abner, attempting to follow in the wake of the king who was like the nations, Saul, who had so disastrously failed, putting Ishbosheth, a mere figurehead, upon the throne in the attempt to establish a kingdom. However, when the long weary years had come to an end with the murder of Abner and Ishbosheth, the period came when David was king of all Israel, reigning roughly about thirty-three years, I can only briefly refer to the movement.

First of all, David was crowned king of the whole nation. The defeat of Abner and his death and that of Ishbosheth was the means of bringing the people together to a recognition of the fact of the real king. When they recognized him as king appointed by God, I am not prepared to say; but the real king, the real leader, was David himself. So at last they came together and they crowned him. The first recorded act in the reign of David over the whole nation was the remarkable capture of Jebus.

This story has been often misread. Jebus (which became Jerusalem) had been the stronghold of the enemies of Israel; the first great thing in the reign of David was its capture. This is followed by the wonderful revelation of the fact that David recognized the centrality of the divine government, and consequently the centrality of the religion of Jehovah to the national life. It is seen in the steps he took to bring the Ark again to the center of the national life.

So impressed was he with the centrality of religion to the life of the nation, and the absolute necessity for the recognition of the sovereignty of God, that there was born within him a passion to build the Temple. That story is fascinating. He tells his desire to Nathan, and Nathan thinks it is a fine idea, a good thing to have that passion. So possibly it was. And then what a revelation we have. God interfered, and He told Nathan, "No, I do not desire a Temple." God had provided the Tabernacle. He did not desire the Temple; He never did. The Temple was never in the divine purpose. Oh yes, He blessed it and filled it with His glory subsequently, but He did what He did, adapting Himself to human weakness in order to continue His progress and His purpose. And he said "No" to David. What a splendid revelation you get of Nathan and David. Nathan, contrary to his own conviction, carried the message to David and told the king he must not do it because God was against it. It takes a really great man to be willing to contradict his own opinion, even if he knows Gods opinion is against it. Nathan did; he went straight to the king. Now look at the greatness of David; the moment he got the message from God, he recognized the divine sovereignty and abandoned entirely his purpose of building the Temple. He obeyed, and the story moves on. But it is well to ponder it. For though David gave up his purpose of building, he did not give up his passion for a Temple, and as we read the story of his conflict and his consolidation of the nation, we find that all through he was gathering treasure. That does not emerge in the story, but it is seen presently. Treasure! For what? For the building of the Temple. For if he was not to build, he could prepare for the building of the Temple, he could get wealth together for his son or someone who should succeed him. The passion for the central place of worship burned in the heart of David.

There breaks into the story one of the idylls of the Old Testament, the story of David and Mephibosheth. The day came when David remembered his old years of stress and strain and suffering, and remembered the years of Saul's cruelty—but that was not all; he remembered Jonathan, the friend who was the son of the king, who believed in David's anointing of God and who was willing to stand aside for his succession to the throne that his friend might occupy it. He remembered all Jonathan had been to him, all he had done for him now that he had gained the kingdom entirely. And he says, "Is there yet any that is left of the house of Saul, that I may show him kindness for Jonathan's sake?" He was told about this cripple, crippled in a very sad and dreadful way. The boy Mephibosheth was lame in both feet, and that which caused the crippling was that fact that his nurse fled with him in the awful day of Jezreel when Saul and Jonathan were killed. David was told about him, that there was yet this one left, and he demanded that he should be brought to him, and there is our idyll. He restored to him all the lands that belonged to Saul—that does not mean the kingdom, but all those lands which were the property of Saul, and he put him to sit at his own table. That is a wonderful picture of grace and greatness. Think me fanciful perhaps, but I am tempted to be fanciful and say a great sermon could be preached about Mephibosheth sitting at the table of David with his lameness hidden beneath the royal banquet table. I do not want to dwell upon it, but I think of that whenever I sit with my feet beneath the table of the Lord. It is an idyll full of beauty.

The story ends with the victories over Ammon and Syria and that brings us to David's failure. And how did this failure begin? Go back to Chapter 11:1 and read this: "It came to pass, at the return of the year, at the time when kings go out to battle"—that is the springtime when a campaign that has been halted because of winter stress is to be resumed. We can read it, "When the battle should be resumed, that David sent Joab, and his servants with him, and all Israel; and they destroyed the children of Ammon, and besieged Rabbah. But David tarried at Jerusalem." That is how it all begins. He ought to have been at the head of his people in the hour of their battle. He did not go. He sent Joab. We cannot send anyone else to stand in the place where we ought to be, without disastrous results. He sent Joab while he tarried in Jerusalem, the place of idleness and of temptation. So there is the story of his fall. It can be told in about three little sentences. He saw. He desired. He took. If he had been where he ought to have been, at the head of the army, he would not have seen. That is the story of the beginning. It is an appalling story, his sin with Bathsheba. I decline to speak about his sin *against* Bathsheba. He sinned *with* her. That does not minimize the sin. You remember Thomson of Berkeley Square in the poem:

> The sins that ye do two by two,
> Ye shall answer for one by one.

Perfectly true, but that does not affect the story. He had sinned grievously against Uriah, and even there we have to get back to the East to understand it, and remember that whatever wrong he had wrought with Bathsheba, and whatever wrong he had wrought against Uriah, he was between an outer and an inner nemesis. Think quickly, horribly of David. He has committed the sin. He has stayed at home. He saw, he desired, he took, and he has committed the sin. What about Uriah? David has to choose between an appalling death for Bathsheba, or a high heroic death for Uriah, and he chose the high heroic death for Uriah. He put him in the high place of the field and he fell. I am not justifying that. I am looking at the fact, and it was a fearful thing. What then? Now we come to the point where we see something that is very remarkable. He was visited by Nathan, who came to him with a parable which aroused the ire of David against the person mentioned in the parable, and when Nathan had aroused him, looking at him and perhaps pointing the accusing finger, he said, "Thou art the man." And David saw at once his sin in the light of the divine. What did he do? Now then, all those people who say, "David! You talk about him being the man after God's own heart. What about the Bathsheba affair? Can you say that a man who can take another man's wife and get her husband murdered is a man after God's own heart?" That is the way they talk. Yes, he is a man after God's own heart—not in his sin, but in his attitude after the sin, in his repentance, in his immediate admission of the wrong to the prophet, and his confession that he had sinned.

I want to quote briefly from "Lines of Defence of the Biblical Revelation." It was written by Professor Mongolious when he was Professor of Semitic languages at Oxford. In it he refers to this incident of David: "When David is rebuked for the crime, be yields the point without argument. He is told that he has done wrong, and he receives the prophet in the prophet's name. Now that has never been done before or since. Mary Queen of Scots would have declared that she was above the law. James I would have thrown over Bathsheba. James II would have hired witnesses to swear away her character. Charles II would have publicly abrogated the commandment. Queen Elizabeth would have suspended Nathan."

I do not know a finer paragraph than that: David, the king in that period, and with these conditions, in comparison with these later days of supposed increased illumination, stands out radiantly as of fine temperament. And to know what I really mean, turn to Psalm 52 and see what he really felt. The king's heart is poured out before God in that most marvelous penitential Psalm. How he suffered. There was the awful story of Absalom, whom he had loved so tenderly: Absalom rose in rebellion against him and drove him into exile, from his throne—and how he suffered when Absalom was killed. Is there anything more poignantly pathetic and tragic in literature than his wail and lament, "O my son Absalom, my son, my son Absalom! would I had died for thee, Absalom." He was his son, and he had inherited those very forces that had blighted David's own life. Yes, "Would I had died for thee, my son, my son." And all his life was overshadowed to the end. He was restored, he was forgiven, but if I may put it this way, and I do not know a better—God could forgive him, but he never forgave himself. And he is not the only soul that has passed through that experience.

The final revelation of this man is given in the last part, in which are two Psalms. What wonderful Psalms they are! The first celebrates the sovereignty of Jehovah. He speaks of the awful supremacy of God, his conviction of the righteousness of God, his confidence of the mercy of God and conformity to the desires of God.

And then comes our last Psalm, and the last Psalm confesses sin and failure again, in another way, and God's faithfulness. It is a Psalm of the most exquisite beauty. He celebrates the purpose of God, and the power of God, and the principle upon which God works and the persistence of God, and he shows His relationship to those things. And so the book ends.

The Second Book of Samuel has traced for us what we may safely call the heroic period in the history of the nation, and it ends with that revealing account of the effect of David, and the sum total of his character upon the man who was nearest to him. David's mighty men: they were such a promiscuous crowd when they first went to the Cave of Adullam, and what mighty men they became. And as we read the story and then watch the men, there is a revelation of what David was in the deepest facts of his character. The Heroic King! The Second Book of Samuel is the epic of David.

11. I Kings, II Chronicles

We stated at the beginning of this book that if we take the whole of the Old Testament into view, its ultimate value lies in the fact that it is the divine revelation of human need. Then if you turn to the New, its ultimate value is in the fact that it is the divine revelation of the divine supply. Humanity is seen in the first in its need. God is seen in the second in His answer, in His great supply.

In our first study I suggested that if we take the Pentateuch as a whole and become imbued with its spirit—or to use a figure of speech, bend over it and listen—we hear humanity's sigh for the priest, the necessity for someone to mediate between man and God. But the priest is not found there.

Then in the historic books—the books roughly from Joshua to Nehemiah—once again if we are attentive to the whole movement and catch the spirit, we hear this time not so much the sigh for the priest, though that is still there, but the cry for the king.

We are in the midst of that section. Joshua, Judges and I Samuel reveal the need, and the movement toward the monarchy. In II Samuel there is a revelation of what humanity needs in an illustration. The illustration may be set and centered in David, and yet the story of David is the story of failure, failure in the matter of his kingship, emerging most clearly in the book we study next. The whole fact of the failure of the monarchy is revealed in I Kings, II Kings, Ezra and Nehemiah.

I am going to indulge myself once more in saying what I have often said: I have seen so many textbooks on the Old Testament, perfectly valuable in many ways, intended to help the young in the study of the history of the Old Testament, and so often I have come across this almost startling heading: "The Rise of the Hebrew People to Monarchy." What do you think of that? Do you think it was a rise? If I were writing a textbook, when I came to that section I should write as a heading, "The Fall of the Hebrew People to Monarchy." For the whole thing began when they said, "Make us a king like the nations." Gods account of them was that they had rejected Him from being King; I fail to see how you can call that a rise. However, we are in that period now, as we study the First Book of Kings. We should read along with it the Second Book of Chronicles, which is collateral writing. I am not dealing with that, because the same historic movement is discovered in each of these books. Chronicles, of course, covers both First and Second Kings. But here we are simply taking the straight historical account of the writer in the First Book of Kings.

Now think of the boundaries of the book: the death of David and the death of Ahab. It is the story of the monarchy. We do not reach the end of it in this book, but speaking of the book as a whole and reading it, what can we see? This nation—do not forget the nation is a theocracy under the divine purpose and counsel, that God brought this nation and created it to be not *like* the nations, but *unlike* them, in order to be the means of blessing to them—is the one outstanding illustration of the theocracy; not monarchy, not democracy, but theocracy.

It is the nation, according to the divine purpose, having no king other than Jehovah Himself. As this book is read, what is seen? We watch the process of deterioration. It did not begin in this book. It had already begun, but here the nation is passing from affluence and influence to poverty and paralysis. A period of a little more than 150 years is covered, and in that period the nation fades from splendor to squalor. These are not soft sounding words, but they do tell the story, and it required an ingenuity of which I am utterly incapable to read anything heroic there in the progress of the union. In their national life they had had one King, and that King has never resigned from His throne, as I shall show again presently. But as far as the people are concerned, though they have never dethroned Him, they have come to ignore Him. And that is the story of the book. It may be broken up into three parts: Solomon, of course, stands out in the first division; then, the story of the disruption, the breaking of the nation into two parts; and at the close, the story of those two nations, Israel and Judah; and a sad story it is!

We begin with Solomon. Solomon has fascinated our thinking very remarkably here. Of course, we get other things concerning him in Chronicles, but I am focusing attention on the Book of Kings. Notice, first of all, that he was crowned king before his father died, and the crowning of Solomon was due to a rebellion against David under Adonijah, and then thereafter the death of David. I want to dismiss it in brief words. If there is anything that reveals his failure in his kingship, these last stories do. They cannot be read without seeing how he has failed as a king. I am not now speaking of a man, I am talking of the king; and when a man comes to old age and is concerned in his thinking with the troubles that exist in the kingdom over which he has been king, and is giving instructions as to how they are to be dealt with after his death, and that certain men should be put to death, it is evident at once that the kingdom has been a failure under David. I know much has been said about David and his charge of Solomon concerning how he was to deal with those men who were troublers of the nation, but I am not forgetting he knew his men. He was a man of keen understanding, and he knew the men, and he knew the trouble they were likely to make. From the standpoint of pure policy, he was right in the instructions he gave to Solomon as to how they were to be treated. I am not arguing it, I leave it at that. All I want to emphasize is the kingdom here in a condition of failure, national failure; a kingdom that has in it the last elements of discord so bitter as to rouse the spirit of a dying king, who for forty years has been reigning over it and inspiring it, to give instructions as to how to deal with the men who are the origin of those troubles. It is a kingdom that has failed.

Then Solomon emerges, and there are two stories of him which are revealing: First of all, revealing Solomon in all his glory, and then Solomon as tired and distressed and shamed. I shall summarize my own conviction by saying that I do not know a more disastrous failure in all the pages of the Old Testament than that of Solomon. People say, "Yes, he failed, but he was restored." I believe that to be right.

We have only to study his writings and see the experience through which he passed. If we study Ecclesiastes there is Solomon, the pessimist of pessimists. We have had a great many volumes characterized by blank pessimism in this country during recent years, most especially since the 1914-18 War. It is all in Ecclesiastes, exactly the same experience, resulting from exactly the same attitude to life. It is the cry of pessimism and failure. His Proverbs reveal another side to him, and when we reach the Song of Solomon, which to me always has its mystical value, I think we have the writing of a man who has been brought back into a place of fellowship with God. A leader may go wrong, tragically wrong, and the result may be that his nation, his people that have owned him, go wrong. That man, I daresay, may be restored, but he cannot bring back with him the people that have been wronged. That harm has been done. That is the story of Solomon.

Look at him for a moment as he is revealed here in all his glory. First of all, he entered on a great inheritance. That was a great thing; and he reaped, as he entered into the possession, all the national benefits that had accrued to the nation, all the political benefits and the territorial benefits. Simply looking at it on the material side, he entered a great inheritance. I can only use the phrases and pass on.

Solomon stands out as a man of vast intellectual equipment, mentally a great man. And not only a man of natural mental equipment, but of great culture. It is evident all through, even in the midst of the pessimism of Ecclesiastes. It bursts through again and again in the almost unmatched wisdom of the Proverbs that came from him, and it sings poetry in the Song of Solomon. He was a remarkable man as to natural equipment.

And I go further. At the great crisis of his life he made the right choice. I want you to glance at the story in the third chapter. God said, "Ask what I shall give thee." Now listen. "O Lord my God, thou hast made thy servant king instead of David my father: and I am but a little child; I know not how to go out or come in. And thy servant is in the midst of thy people which thou hast chosen, a great people, that cannot be numbered nor counted for multitude. Give thy servant therefore an understanding heart to judge thy people, that I may discern between good and evil; for who is able to judge this thy great people?" Can you find anything finer than that? And read further: "And the speech pleased the Lord, that Solomon had asked this thing. And God said unto him, Because thou hast asked this thing, and hast not asked for thyself long life neither hast asked riches for thyself, nor hast asked the life of thine enemies but hast asked for thyself understanding to discern justice; behold, I have done according to thy word."

We cannot read that without being halted at the remarkable choice he made that God approved right there, when he was entering into his inheritance and his king-ship. He made the true choice. It is almost appalling to read it, and then think of all that happened. God always knows what is in a man, and I want to say this almost with bated breath but with very sincere conviction: God, in dealing with a man, always puts him in circumstances that will bring out what is in him. Follow on in Chapter 3: "I have also given thee that which thou hast not asked, both riches and honor, so that there shall not be any among the kings like unto thee, all thy days."

And that constituted the testing of the man. God gave him riches, and honor, and yet it was right there he broke down; in the possession of riches and honor he failed. Yes, God always leads a man to the circumstances that will show what really is within him. The most startling and classic illustration of it in all the Bible is the story of Judas. Remember that he was a thief, and he had the bag. Christ knew what was in him, and He gave him the bag, and the guarding of it gave him the chance of developing what was really in him. There, in the presence of his weakness, he could take refuge in the strength of His Master.

And so it was with Solomon. He made a great choice, and then he found himself possessed of noble riches, and there follows that period in the life of Solomon and the kingdom over which he reigned, which was the kingdom of material magnificence. Never in the history of Israel did they reach such a height either before or after. It bore in upon him, and at once the nation was surrounded with every evidence of lavish expenditure and magnificence. He ground them under his heel. I never read this story without thinking of a more modern story in history, the story of Lorenzo de Medici in Florence. It is just another story of splendid equipment, and magnificent display, lulling the people for the time being into security and into a certain attitude of obedience toward him, until Savonarola arose. And when Savonarola arose, things were altered; and he said to Lorenzo de Medici, when Lorenzo ordered him away from Florence, "It is not I that shall go, but thou that shall go." There we have it. Material magnificence reaching such a height as never before.

But at the very time of his choice there is the hint of shame, in the beginning of this third chapter; even before he made his choice his shame was exposed. It is there; "And Solomon made affinity with Pharaoh king of Egypt.

…And Solomon loved the Lord, walking in the statutes of David his father: *only* he sacrificed and burnt incense in the high places." There was an exhibition of weakness in the affinity with the king of Egypt, and the bringing of his daughter into the city of God, and the toleration of certain forms of worship which were not the worship of the holy place.

The whole story is revealed in that wonderful building of the Temple, Chapter 6:38, "And in the eleventh year …was the house finished throughout all the parts thereof, and according to all the fashion of it. So was he seven years in building it" Chapter 7:1 "And Solomon was building his own house thirteen years, and he finished all his house." Does that strike us in reading it? He is building the Temple, the wonderful Temple, and took seven years to do it. And he was thirteen years building his own house. And as we read we see that the house he built for himself, for his own self-centered life, exceeded in splendor and glory even the wonderful Temple that he had built for God.

Go on a step further to Chapter 11: "Now king Solomon loved many foreign women... of the nations concerning which the Lord said unto the children of Israel, Ye shall not go among them, neither shall they come among you: for surely they will turn away your heart after their gods: Solomon clave unto these in love." Run down to the ninth verse: "And the Lord was angry with Solomon, because his heart was turned away from the Lord, the God of Israel, who had appeared unto him twice… Wherefore the Lord said unto Solomon, Forasmuch as this is done of thee, and thou hast not kept my covenant and my statutes, which I have commanded thee, I will surely rend the kingdom from thee, and will give it to thy servant." Now notice that the man is seen in his weakness, and he is seen bringing there unto his kingdom these women, and with them their laws and their rites and their ceremonies and their forms of religion, tolerating them while he himself still ostensibly observed the worship of Jehovah.

And then comes the account of the nemesis twice over which is very striking in that chapter. "And the Lord raised up an adversary unto Solomon, Hadad the Edomite." "And God raised up another adversary, Rexon…" And the adversaries were there outside and they inflicted conflict upon Jeroboam, until afraid for his life, he fled to the city of Shishak, king of Egypt, until Solomon was dead. The glory and the shame of Solomon was definitely self-evident.

What is the picture you have here? The picture of spiritual strength superseded by material magnificence—and the real condition of the kingdom is revealed in Chapter 12. I quote it resolutely out of its context, and this is the whole story. At verse 4 is an account of the rebellion. But in that verse the people are saying to Rehoboam, "Thy father made our yoke grievous: now therefore make thou the grievous service of thy father, and his heavy yoke which he put upon us, lighter, and we will serve thee." It is the revolt of the people against the government of Solomon, in which he had placed burdens of taxation upon them for the maintenance of the material magnificence. We see spiritual power superseded by material magnificence, in many ways which were entirely human, by the greatest king in the history of the people.

Then came the disruption. Rehoboam tried hereditary autocracy. Yes, I cannot help laughing a little again. It is so utterly foolish and yet listen to this. In that very Chapter 12, at verse 14, Rehoboam is saying this: "My father made your yoke heavy, but I will add to your yoke: my father chastised you with whips, but I will chastise you with scorpions." Hereditary autocracy! The fool, the fool, you cannot do it! It has never been done, and never can be done. But see what it meant. Rehoboam represented the doctrine with which they were familiar, that of the phrase which came into use after long, long centuries of the divine rights of kings. That is what Rehoboam was to represent.

On the other hand, Jeroboam had become king, through the reaction of a popular movement. When Jeroboam made this reply, what did the people say? "Then we have no part in David. To your tents, O Israel." It was the language of rebellion against power, and Jeroboam became the leader until the people made him also king, and when they did it was by divine arrangement. Certainly it was God giving the man, so that He might fulfill His purpose. But the kingdom was rent in twain. True, David reigned seven years over Judah before Israel came in. But now the rift is deeper, and from that moment there will be no place between those two kingdoms rent in two. And so we have the history of the rise of Israel and Judah, and the history of those two kings, two of them Abijam and Asa: and then the kings of Israel from Nadab to Ahab. Do you know anything more tragic than the story of the kings of Israel? One succeeded another, each man after the murder of his predecessor; and there is the ghastly commentary on the kingship which forgets God, and the spiritual death issuing in moral poverty. In II Kings we have an appalling picture of human failure.

This is not a lonely story. It is the story of other vast kingdoms and empires, and it is the story of the futility of monarchy.

Rehoboam forces on the degradation of national life, and it is the clamoring to be heard under the guidance of the man placed upon the throne. And yet look again. As we have read that story we have seen—I am sure we have—the throne of God, and the government of God, the overruling majesty of the Most High. It is manifested in two ways: by listening to the prophetic voice, and by reading the account of the actual divine interferences. "The Lord reigneth…" The Lord was reigning all the way through. He sent them those prophets, Abijah and Shemiah, Elijah and Micaiah—God speaking through His prophets, and insisting upon His sovereignty. Then, His direct appearances! God appeared to Solomon twice over, and raised up adversaries to him; this followed by that wonderful story of Carmel and the prophets of Ahab flaunting their god. We observe the human failure: the cry for the king, and the King Eternal there and unrecognized; disobedient, ignorant of God, all human kings breaking down and the falling of the nation to degeneracy.

12. II Kings, II Chronicles

We come now to II Kings, the book that records the end of the monarchy. The history of this book alternates very largely between the two nations of Israel and Judah, until first Israel and finally Judah are carried away into captivity and the kingdom ends. It is well that we remember now that this was the period of the great prophets whose writings have been preserved for us. I do not mean to say that every prophet whose prophecy was here is found in that period, though most of them who were great prophets, whose writings we have, all exercised their ministry in this period. This final, later period in which the earthly choice of the monarchy is working itself out to the end, was the particular period in which God spoke definitely to His people through His prophets.

As I have said in previous chapters—and it is well that we should remember it—God never did speak to these people through kings. He used them, permitted them, helped them, guided them, governed them when they were willing to be helped and guided and governed, but His messages did not come through kings but through prophets. And it was in this period of final failure that the great prophets arose and uttered their message.

Now to understand the landmarks the book covers: First Israel and captivity; then the shining of a wonderful light in the story of Hezekiah; and following that, Judah and captivity. I want to repeat that this is the end. When you get to the other books—Ezra, Nehemiah, and so forth—there was no king. The monarchy was over.

In the first section we have an alternative history between the two kingdoms of Israel and Judah, the account of the succession of kings misgoverning the nation. It is a terrible picture, because you find that again and again one king succeeded another upon the murder of his predecessor. Just imagine that monotheist nation, called and created by God; and the ascent to the monarchy was from that. It is an appalling story. And as you study the conditions, you will find that during this period the nation was more and more given over to idolatry and the practice of those very abominations that were strictly forbidden at the beginning of their history, and for the ending of which in human life this nation had been created.

If we go back to Leviticus 18:21, at the very beginning of the Law, and again to Chapter 20 in the early verses, we will find how strictly these things were forbidden, and yet we see this nation setting up the groves of Baalim and worshiping him. We see something far more terrible, almost unbelievable—these very people worshiping Moloch. The passages referred to in Leviticus distinctly name and forbid that particular form of worship. It was a brutal form of worship, closely allied undoubtedly to the worship of Baal, paganism, in its most brutal and corrupt and terrible form. Its particular activity was sacrifice, and the sacrifice of children. These were sacrificed through fire to Moloch, who was represented as a great animal with a human head and arms, and when the effigy was worshiped a furnace could be lit inside, and the children were put in the arms and offered to Moloch. This was distinctly forbidden as the most terrible form of corrupt paganism in existence, and these people were to have nothing to do with it, and especially nothing to do with making their children pass through fire. I find that when Micah uttered his great prophecy he named this tendency, this weakness and wickedness of the people, and when he sees the soul as bowed down in the presence of the Lord, his reply was, "Shall I give the fruit of my body for the sin of my soul?" That was what Moloch was demanding, and that is what the worshipers of Moloch were doing. It is almost unbelievable but it is true. The places of the worship of God were still standing, neglected very largely but still there, certain forms of ritual had to be observed, nevertheless the people were worshiping at the groves of Baal, and worshiping Moloch, and offering their children in sacrifice to him.

Moloch is first mentioned in Leviticus, but you will find him again and again through the prophetic utterances. He appears once in the New Testament, and then we hear nothing of him after; that one occasion was the great Apology of Stephen where, referring to the history of the people, he mentions this very fact of their worship of Moloch.

And so it went on, one king succeeding another on the murder of his predecessor; and the people, corrupt, decadent, worshiping along the worst forms of degrading worship, until there came the final catastrophe. It began when Hoshea submitted to Shalmaneser, practically became his vassal, and almost immediately afterwards the whole kingdom was subjugated to Shalmaneser, and carried away into captivity. That is the history. Look at Chapter 17:16: "They forsook all the commandments of the Lord their God," and verse 17, "And they caused their sons and their daughters to pass through the fire, and used divination and enchantments, and sold themselves to do that which was evil in the sight of the Lord, to provoke him to anger." That is a condensed form of all I have been saying. "Therefore the Lord was very angry with Israel, and removed them out of his sight: there was none left but the tribe of Judah only." Shalmaneser came on to Hoshea and absolutely overwhelmed the whole kingdom and carried the folk away into captivity.

This is the deeper truth, the truth behind the historic fact, that the Lord was angry and removed them out of His sight. So ended that one kingdom. We have seen it all through the past.

Now in the book you have the story of Hezekiah. Chapter 18:1, "Now it came to pass in the third year of Hoshea son of Elah king of Israel, that Hezekiah the son of Ahaz king of Judah began to reign." Look at verse 2: "Twenty and five years old was he when he began to reign; and he reigned twenty and nine years in Jerusalem." Run on through verses 5, 6 and 7 and see what a wonderful picture it is of Hezekiah. He stands out upon the page in the most radiant and wonderful fashion. What had been the influence of his life before he came to the throne? His mother is named. But the thing I wanted you to notice is that he was the son of Ahaz, and it is a remarkable illustration of a man reacting from all the evil he had seen. I believe that played a great part in the making of Hezekiah. He had seen the evil and his soul was against it. Then the supreme thing is his friendship with Isaiah. It comes out again and again in the man as he is grown up. He was twenty-five when he came to the throne, and had undoubtedly grown up under the influence of Isaiah. These two things are formative influences in his life: his vision of his fathers evil and his reactions from it; and that larger view of the interpretation of the throne of God which he received from the prophet Isaiah. The story of the things he did after he came to the throne is fascinating reading. He opened and cleansed the Temple. Yes, opened it. It had grown into such practical disuse that it had been practically closed. Notice in reading what condition the Temple was in. The Priests of the Levites took ten days carrying away rubbish before they could begin to cleanse it. Hezekiah had the rubbish carried away and cleansed it. Then he instituted the Passover, which I think is one of the greatest recorded things that he did. He sent invitations to attend it, not only to the priests in his own kingdom but to Samaria, and to Galilee beyond Jordan. He seems to have thought that amongst those subjugated people there might well be souls that hungered and yearned for the God of their fathers. So Hezekiah invited not merely those of his own kingdom, but he sent his invitations over the border line. It is a wonderful gleam of revelation of the man's character.

Then we are told that he destroyed the places of false worship. And a wonderful little story reveals the condition of the people and the greatness of Hezekiah. What was it? In connection with their history they had been preserving all the time the brazen serpent that had been erected in the wilderness. Remember the story of Moses and the brazen serpent? This had never been destroyed, and the people had become so superstitious that they were treating it as an object of worship. That which God gave them for their deliverance had been turned into an object of human worship. Notice what Hezekiah did! He smashed it to pieces. He called it Nehustan. What does that mean? Simply this—"a bit of brass." He gave it its right name. That which they had invested with some superstitious values for worship he ground to powder in their sight. Only a bit of brass! And I think that might be repeated in many ways in the days in which we live. How many things there are among us that once were gifts of God, and thereafter became objects of superstitious idolatry. What a good thing to smash them and give them their right names. Dismiss them! Hezekiah is seen doing that.

He was also a remarkable man in a literary way. In the Book of Proverbs there are sixteen chapters of which I think undoubtedly Hezekiah was the author. And there is no doubt that he wrote a group of the Psalms in the Psalter, and that he took some of David's Psalms and recast them to meet the necessities of the age in which he lived. He was a great and remarkable man.

Of course there is a shadow across the story—the picture of his weakness. His weakness was seen in his reception of the king of Babylon. There can be no doubt whatever it was an action of pride, a mistaken action, which appears in Isaiah's sharp rebuke. Isaiah was there by his side, and Hezekiah's strength is seen in his immediate submission to the message of Isaiah. What a wonderful story it is right here in these times of darkness, the shining of this light. I have sometimes said, though I do not know if I am warranted in doing so, that Hezekiah was the greatest king of Judah, if not the greatest of the kings—greater than David, certainly greater than Solomon—a remarkable man. And this man is seen to be nearly the last of the line.

Coming to the last section, we find that on the death of Hezekiah there was a reaction which was terribly—to use the word I do not like—interesting. But so it is, to watch the national movement. First of all, Manasseh, corrupt and corrupting, one of the weakest of men, reigning for fifty-five years, despising the nation, and leading them back into ways of pagan idolatry. He was followed by Amon who only reigned two years. And then there is another breaking of light in the story of Josiah, a wonderful story, which was the last attempt to reform in the history of the people. It is a beautiful story of the boy attempting to lead the people to reformation and restoration. And the significant thing in that story again is its revelation of the condition of the people. He finds the Book of the Law. Yes, finds it. Evidently it had become hidden, forgotten, out of use somewhere. That is the actual fact. And then the king got to work, attempting to bring the people to conformity with the revelation found in that Book of the Law. Just think of it! The central thing in their national life, as to its code of spiritual and moral living, is lost in the debris and the confusion, and the king finds it and uses it to show the real meaning of the national life. It was a great attempt on the part of Josiah to do a thing of real value. Before he embarked upon his campaign, he visited the prophetess Huldah, and she told him that he was right in his desire to go forward, that it was a good thing to do; but she told him it would be of no use, and it was of no use. There was no real reform.

And then came the end, and once more the people went into vassalage and captivity. The Northern Kingdom and the Southern Kingdom; and the days of the monarchy were over. Do not forget that the nation never again had a king, never has had a king since. Some may say, "What about King Herod?" Yes, he bore the tide, but it was granted to him by Rome, a concession to his vanity. He was a vassal of Rome. After this, the nation never had a king. Monarchy had been tried and passed away.

But during all the period, the King they rejected had been ruling and overruling and moving toward the accomplishment of His own great purpose. Yes, you can reject God, you can dethrone God, but as you read the Book you will see God there all the way through.

What did we say about the values of monarchy? Hosea summarizes the whole story in one brief sentence in which he has recorded God as speaking about this business. It is in Chapter 13:11: "I have given thee a king in mine anger, and have taken him away in my wrath." The divine overruling! The king granted in order that it may be proved by experience what was the will of God. The supreme value of it? The folly of rejecting God. "I gave thee a king in mine anger." The words cut across decades and centuries. You have seen them working out as the things have happened. "I have taken him away in my wrath." And there was no king left. The cry for the king! But the king is never there. But he is foreshadowed throughout. There came a wonderful light shining for the king.

I have said they never had a king since. Let me put that in another way. They nailed Him upon a cross, and the representatives of the people that were holding them in slavery wrote a great inscription in letters of Hebrew, and Latin and Greek: "Jesus of Nazareth, the King of the Jews."

And the only hope for the people is that they shall see Him whom they pierced, and shall mourn, and shall crown Him God's appointed and anointed King.

13. EZRA, NEHEMIAH, ESTHER

We come now to consider Ezra and Nehemiah (and a collateral writing, Esther), and I want to begin with a reminder that here we have two books in our Bibles, but not in the Hebrew Bible. There is one book in the Hebrew Bible. There has been a great deal of scholarly debate as to what it was first called, into which I am not attempting to enter. I only want to say that the story is one in the Hebrew Bible: the two books constitute one complete book.

Again, these books are peculiar in this. They are not in strict chronological sequence. It is true that they cover one period, but that one period is not due to design, a straight piece of history as we have been finding in the other books. I should be inclined to say that these two books, taken alone or as one book, are of opposite character, but I do not think that

anyone would care to be dogmatic as to who wrote "them" or who wrote "it." Someone says, "There is no doubt Ezra did." That applies to certain parts. Someone else says, "Surely Nehemiah wrote this book." That applies to certain parts. It is equally to the point to say that there is no doubt we have the writing of Ezra, and the writing of Nehemiah, but we have other parts certainly written not by Ezra or Nehemiah. Students can follow carefully, and notice the changes from the first person to the third person when referring to the Book of Ezra or Nehemiah, and so it is a composite book made up by some compiler.

It is possible, perhaps even probable, that Ezra was the final compiler, and there may be times when he refers to himself or his own work in the third person. It is not inconceivable. I just mention that the bulk of it is in Hebrew, and other parts are in Aramaic. That is another indication of the composite nature.

Moreover, as we read carefully we find that things chronologically may be repeated and references repeated, but it is a perfect revelation, not of sequence in period, but to a whole period with reference to some of the things therein. When reading Ezra—to take our name for the first part—we notice that between Chapters 6 and 7, there are sixty years unaccounted for; we are left with no trace of these sixty years at all. The whole period covered by these books may be about 100 to 110 years.

This book follows a gap of seventy years in the history of the people. Remember we saw them at the end of everything, carried into captivity; first Israel; and then that wonderful period of the reign of Hezekiah, and then at last Judah was also carried into captivity. Now, for years, the whole nation was carried away into captivity.

Notice how the Book of Ezra begins: "In the first year of Cyrus king of Persia, that the word of the Lord by the mouth of Jeremiah might be accomplished…" That is all we want Of course, we know the Book of Jeremiah, and can remember how clearly Jeremiah foretold what would happen to the nations of Israel and Judah, that they would be carried away into captivity. He clearly indicated the fact that captivity would last for seventy years. The story is taken up there, "that the word of the Lord might be fulfilled." Seventy years have now elapsed, in which Jeremiah had foretold there would be captivity and the subjection of the race. That period has elapsed, but remember this: during that period the people had been without a land, without a city, without a Temple, without a king. And the study of the book itself and its references and contemporary history show that during that period they had largely settled down in captivity, and in their captivity they had prospered materially. Away from their land, away from their city, away from their Temple, without any visible king, they were in captivity: nevertheless, materially vast multitudes of them had succeeded and prospered. I only refer to it now, but shall mention it again. When they did return, not more than between thirty and forty thousand did so. Comparatively a very small percentage of the people were willing to go back when the hour of return came: so had they settled to conditions of subjection and comparative slavery in which they had a certain amount of freedom, and of course they had prospered materially. So much for the seventy years.

Then came the divine interference, and a forward move in the divine program, and these books of Ezra and Nehemiah give us an account of that period and of that movement. One King is seen acting. God is revealed. And notice how wonderful the revelation is, and the instruments He used to carry out His purposes and to move forward in the program. Outside the covenant, outside the nation, outside the people that were His own peculiar people, He used Cyrus, Darius, and Artaxerxes, great and mighty monarchs. How far they knew He was doing so I am unable to say, but the finger of God was using them. And then, inside the nation appeared three men—Zerubbabel, Ezra and Nehemiah. God acting, God interfering, and again and again God is revealed making a way to the accomplishment of His purpose; He takes Cyrus, Darius, and Artaxerxes, those monarchs of the pagan world, and uses them within the borders of His own nation, followed by Zerubbabel, Ezra, and Nehemiah. So much for the incidence.

Our immediate consideration covers what these three men did, and there are three things to notice. Under Zerubbabel, the return and the Temple was the central and first thing; under Ezra, their return and the law given back to the people; and under Nehemiah, the city and its walls. Can we visualize—I do not know that I am using the right word at all—can we see the whole movement? Seventy years of captivity! People may say, "Why do you stop there?" That you may think. It is a great thing to stop sometimes for people to think. Seventy years! Just imagine! Perhaps two generations as we count generations now. How many would be left alive there who were alive when they were carried away? Some of them, and some of the old men made great nuisances of themselves after a while. But the vast majority carried away were gone, as were their sons and their daughters and their children. But the hour has struck; for that nation God created for His own purpose has passed through a period of discipline in slavery; and now the time has come for them to go back, and God is overruling. Cyrus, Darius, Artaxerxes—kings independent of God. What? No king was ever born and no dictator has ever lived who is independent of God. He may think he is, he may boldly declare that he is, but he is a fool, whosoever he may be. He is not independent of God. If God wants Cyrus, He will gird him. If God wants Darius to help in the forward movement, He will inspire him. If God needs Artaxerxes in the midst of this corruption, to do something that will forward the divine program, He will use him. But the chief instruments are these men Zerubbabel, Ezra and Nehemiah, the direct instruments of God. Let us just briefly look at these men and what they did.

Now we touch upon something that I at once admit may be an open question, but I personally do not think there is a question about it. In Ezra 1:7 we read that they brought the vessels of the house of the Lord and gave them to Sheshbazzar, the prince of Judah. And there is no doubt that Sheshbazzar is identified with Zembbabel. That can be followed out. It was to Sheshbazzar, as named there, that the treasures were handed over, but it was Zembbabel who became the active leader and possessor of these treasures and the carrier of them back to Jerusalem. Both these names, Sheshbazzar and Zembbabel, were Babylonian names. It is possible that they were two different men, but I do not think that it follows. We sometimes find that a man's name is altered, and pronounced like the names of the people he is amongst, as was the case of Shadrach, Meshach and Abednego. I do not think that militates against the fact that these two were one. It was Zembbabel who took the treasure back to Jerusalem, and he was evidently a man certainly of Hebrew, or Jewish people—as I prefer to say—and born in Babylon. Moreover, he was the grandson of Jehoakim and we can call to mind that it was under Jehoakim that their captivity was consummated. For some reason Jehoakim gained the favor of the king of Babylon, who gave him a position among the princes. Now it is his grandson; and there he was, representative of David's dynasty. What made this man do what he did? What inspired this man to go up to Jerusalem and lead the people up there?

Go back and look once more, and get the emphasis upon something I have already been saying. Chapter 1:1-3, "In the first year of Cyrus king of Persia, that the word of the Lord... might be accomplished, the Lord Stirred up the spirit of Cyrus king of Persia, so that he made a proclamation throughout all his kingdom, and put it also in writing, saying, Thus saith Cyrus king of Persia, All the kingdoms of the earth hath the Lord, the God of heaven, given me; and he hath charged me to build him a house in Jerusalem, which is in Judah. Whosoever there is among you of all his people, his God be with him, and let him go up to Jerusalem, which is in Judah, and build the house of the Lord, the God of Israel (he is God), which is in Jerusalem."

It is a most remarkable document. Read it at leisure, for I am not now attempting to deal with it. But notice this record says "the Lord stirred up the spirit of Cyrus." That accounts for everything. God acting. No, I am not prepared to say that Cyrus understood. Personally, I think very likely he did, even if Darius never did or Artaxerxes never did. I think there are references found in other of the prophets of his consciousness that he was in the hands of God, in spite of the fact that it was said unto him, "Although thou hast not known me I have girded thee."

I have done a great deal of reading of a most interesting and delightful nature around this story. I am amused by the way in which men try to account for what Cyrus did. It is very interesting: that it was merely a political move; that he was threatened by Egypt and wanted to get the Jews back to Palestine to be a bulwark against Egypt. Possibly! We do not know. All sorts of things are said and suggestions made as to why he did it. We have these references, and the reason is that the Lord stirred up the spirit of Cyrus. God was at the back of it, whatever else happened. And even if these men that He so girded were unconscious that they were His instruments, they carried out His sovereign will. "The Lord stirred up the spirit of Cyrus." And then they returned.

We get lists—and what wonderful lists they are too—of heads of the families. There were between thirty and forty thousand, and with their families as well, probably it would be a larger number. But the fact, I repeat, is that a vast number remained behind. They were not going to take this new venture, They were not prepared to. Away in Babylon, beaten and bowed down before the governor that the king set over them, they said, "We are getting on very well. Let us stop where we are." It is human nature. We know that at the very beginning the predecessors of these people, when they got away from Egypt—it is a somewhat vulgar story but it is a true one—these people, just away from Egypt, out of its brutish bondage, because of the difficulties in the way were sighing for the leeks and the garlics and the onions. People may well smile. I think the recorder chose the most savory things he could think of. There it was, and there the people are again. But God is not on the side of the big battalions, and God never has been dependent upon vast numbers. The mightiest work of God, as we trace it all through history— and it is going on still—is being wrought by an elect remnant. And Zerubbabel led them back. It is interesting to see what happened. The first thing they did, the very first, was to raise the altar. The altar was raised, and they gathered around it and worshiped God. And that altar having been raised, the Temple was commenced. The work went on for a little while and then it was suspended, till presently there was another edict of the king, the edict of Darius, and the work was completed. That is the period of the prophecies of Haggai and Zechariah. From these two prophets, as they are read, comes a light on that period, and we see what these people were doing. They had gone back. They were presumably occupied looking after themselves, and then they neglected the house of God. They began to build, raised the altar, began the work of the Temple; and then I think that for twelve or fourteen years it stood without a stone being added because of supposed difficulties. Remember Haggai: "Is it a time for you yourselves to dwell in your ceiled houses?" Ceiled houses! That is a very remarkable and illuminating phrase. Beautiful houses? Yes, decorated and ornate and splendid; and there was the house of God lying waste for twelve or fourteen years, nothing done. Have we ever happened to see a building started, foundations laid, with its great concrete and stone blocks ready, and then for some reason, abandoned? I saw it once in an American city in the Middle West—the building started, bricks there and foundations laid and not completed. It had been left and the work stopped, and there it was, grass tracks over it, weed infested. That was the condition of the Temple.

There follows the edict of Cyrus and this matchless story of how that edict became promulgated: and the Temple was completed. That is the story of Zerubbabel.

Going on to Ezra, he was a priest, a direct descendant of Aaron. As Zerubbabel was a direct descendant in the kingly line of David, Ezra was a direct descendant of Aaron in the priestly line. And see what he did. Once again God made him

act, and he acted as the result of a decree of Artaxerxes. Again he is moving back to final consummation, and some who went were born probably after the first returns were made. They go back, and we must take the story as it is. But the amazing fact remains that when you find them back, Ezra discovered that the people were practicing pagan rites, the very things that had brought about the downfall of the nation and driven them into captivity for seventy years. They are doing the same thing again, forming alliances by marriage with outside people, forming alliances of a political nature, indulging in heathen rites and ceremonies and practices. And when Ezra got there we have an account of a great confession. I cannot deal with it but as a summary. What a wonderful story it is of this great confession, which he poured out in the presence of God. And that ends the story of Ezra, so far. But it does not end it! We meet it again in a remarkable way. But so, I say, it ends the story of the book named by the name of Ezra.

And Nehemiah appears upon the scene. Now who was he? It is doubtful what tribe he belonged to. There are two views held, and I am not going to debate between them. Some believe he was a Levite of the tribe of Levi, and others believe he was of the tribe of Judah. But, at any rate, the man had risen to a position of great responsibility and authority in the court of the king. He was the king's cupbearer, which means far more than it may appear to mean in our English phrase. He occupied a position of great responsibility. But he knew about Jerusalem and he knew about the people there. And even though he were a much younger man, which he probably was, he was concerned about them. He enquired about them, and the news he got concerning conditions in the city of Jerusalem and among the people filled him with sorrow. He was so obsessed by this sorrow that he could not hide it, and even in the presence of the king he manifested the fact that his life was overclouded by some great sorrow. So the king sent for Nehemiah to learn about it, and Nehemiah told him of his concern about Jerusalem, and sought permission to go to the city. And Artaxerxes, in the hands of God, gave his cupbearer permission to go. Probably he was away about twelve years, but he allowed him to go. He gave him a royal commission to go up and see how his people fared, and serve them.

Is there anything more fascinating than the whole story of Nehemiah? I follow it in words only. When he first arrived at Jerusalem he told no one. He indulged in quiet inspection, and he found an alarming state of things. The gates of the city were burned with fire, and the walls—not wholly but largely—broken down and left. The Temple was there by that time, but the walls of the city were destroyed and its life had passed into a period of corruption. So Nehemiah set himself to build a wall. Is there anything, I wonder, in the story of architecture and building much more wonderful than what he did? Do you know he built the walls in fifty-two days? And he got everyone to work. "The people"—is not that a great text? I think every preacher has preached on it some time—"The people had a mind to work." And the organization! What a story it is—listen! He set every man to build opposite his own house. The men who were building were set to the wall nearest where they lived, and so they built. A full list of the builders is given. It is healthy work reading that list. Go through it and see who they were. They built in danger of opposition from outside, and they built with the trowel and with the sword at their side. Building and battling! There it is, the perpetual methods of God are there, building and battling! That is what our Lord meant when He said, "I will build my church and the gates of hell shall not prevail against it." Building and battling! And so Nehemiah built. There was difficult opposition, and difficult days, but they overcame them all. What a man he was! I sometimes think that the Book of Nehemiah, by reason of its size, is more full of possible texts for preachers than any other book.

And then the last sentence of the story. "And *so* the wall was finished." Read it. Why "So"? Go back and read how. "So." By consecrated endeavor, by persistent toil, by a great unity of purpose, by a determination to work. So the wall was finished.

And there was a great ceremony at the dedication, and they finished it all. Then Ezra appears again. He was described in the earlier part in these words: "He is a ready scribe in the law of Moses." The word "scribe" occurs often in the Old Testament, and signifies an officer of the Court of the king, largely responsible for keeping the records, the archives. But here it emerges with a new note. It means here a man familiar with the law of Moses, knowing the law of Moses: and not only that, but able to interpret the law.

Then there followed that marvelous movement, that wonderful movement, the reading of the Law. He erected a pulpit of wood, and a really great gathering was held throughout the land; a convention—to take our modem word. They heard the Law, the Law that was being ignored, the Law that was largely forgotten, the Law therefore that was not understood. And that was the next step. The walls are built. Now, now comes the Law, and it was at that moment that the Law took its supreme place in the national life. As Paul says, "The law is our schoolmaster to bring us to Christ." There never was a more unfortunate piece of misleading translation than that word "schoolmaster." It is very interesting how often traces are found in modern life and language of unconscious Biblical imitation. Pedagogy comes from a Greek word, and it is the word Paul used, but never used it as a teacher. He was never a teacher, he was a custodian who saw to it that the boy went to school each morning. But he did not teach him. The Law did not teach, but it was the custodian of these people and led them on until Christ came Himself. And this is the moment when the Law moved to the center of national life and significance. Nehemiah read the Law.

And the last picture is the picture of Nehemiah coming back again. What a time he had! He came back and he found abuses restored that he had swept out on his first visit, and that had been put an end to for the time by the very reading of the Law. And then I see Nehemiah, the great iconoclast, in his majesty sweeping out these things.

And there the history of the Old Testament ends. The people are without a long on the earthly level. So ends the historic section, and it reveals the need for a king, and still through man's rejection of God as King, it reveals man's inability to provide a king equal to the government of men.

And still once more, one King is overruling.

Esther is a collateral writing, a very interesting book in many ways. First of all, there is no doubt it refers to that period between Chapters 6 and 7 in Ezra where I said there was a gap of sixty years, and it has nothing to do with the land. It is not of the land. God is not named in the Book of Esther, but you cannot read it without seeing God and seeing Him as you see Him everywhere. He is quietly manifest. There is no doubt that in this little Book of Esther is a fragment taken directly from the Persian records. It is the story of some of the people who did not return under Zerubbabel, and who had been brought into the place of danger, and the everlasting God is caring for them. And the Feast of Purim was established, which is still observed by the Hebrew people. Mark the historicity of the things recorded here. A wonderful story, a pagan story, about those people away from the land and away from the movement under Ezra and Nehemiah, but *not* away God.

PART III

THE DIDACTIC BOOKS: THE QUEST FOR THE PROPHET

24. JOEL, JONAH, OBADIAH

We reach now the last sequence of the Old Testament. In using the word "sequence," I am taking all the rest of the books under the general heading of the Didactic books, those books that are more specifically books of teaching.

When we finish this section, we have to say once more that *the* final Prophet is not found, though this is the section dealing with the quest for the prophet.

It is important that we should begin this section by seeking first some interpretation of the general theme as indicated in the phrase "The Quest for the Prophet." In what sense is that phrase employed? Begin with the prophet. The word "prophet" is used here in its widest sense. There is a very definite word for the Prophet in the Old Testament in the Hebrew, *nabiy*. There is an equally definite word in the New Testament, and the first is almost more significant than the word found in the New Testament. The Old Testament word means, taken in its fullness, "to speak by inspiration." That thought is not found in the word that is translated "prophet" in the Greek language. But in the Old Testament, which in a very remarkable way has the relationship which is prophetic, the very word used constantly and used repeatedly from beginning to end almost without exception is a word that means "to speak by inspiration." There is exactly the same thought in the New Testament where we are told that in preaching men spake as they were borne along by the Holy Spirit, as they were moved by the Holy Spirit. And if we want a pure translation of the word in the Greek language, it means "caught up by," and accurately, "borne onward by the Spirit." Does not that characterize the very word that is used to describe the prophet through the whole Testament?

THE DIDACTIC BOOKS

"Divers portions . . . divers manners"—Hebrews 1:1

THE DIDACTIC BOOKS: THE QUEST FOR THE PROPHET	THE NEED		
	Joel, Jonah, Obadiah Activities I. The Fact The Day of the Lord II. Compassion Nineveh III. Anger Edom	*Amos, Hosea* Attitudes I. Government All the Nations Specially His Own II. Grace Sin Judgment Love	*Isaiah, Micah* Authority I. The Throne Government Grace II. The Rule False Shepherds The True King
	THE ILLUSTRATION		
	Wisdom: *Job, Proverbs, Ecclesiastes* Worship: *Psalms, Song of Solomon* I. Unveilings Of Human Need Of the Way of Wisdom Of the Way of Folly II. Expressions Of All Experiences Of Perfect Fellowship		
	THE FAILURE		
	Nahum, Habakkuk, Zephaniah Activities I. Judgment Nineveh II. Method Chaldeans III. Nature Goodness and Severity	*Jeremiah, Daniel, Ezekiel* Attitudes I. Grace Sin Judgment Love II. Government His Own All Nations All Ages	*Haggai, Zechariah, Malachi* Authority I. The Immediate Worship Visions II. The Ultimate The Coming One The Coming Day

Prophet! What does it really mean? We are always a little in danger—and I want to put it kindly—of thinking of one who foretells. The word does mean that. But what do you mean by foretelling? If you are using the word "fore" to mark a time, a period, then you can be mistaken entirely in the real thought of the word. The word literally means "speaking in front of," not ahead in the matter of time, but before those who are listening, to speak in front of: to be more literal still, to speak in the sense of making a showing forth. That is the word, and where a prophet is referred to in the New Testament, if the reference is in the Old Testament dispensation or in the New, this is the thought. It is an old theme. I have often said, but it is worth repeating, that the real meaning of prophet is not so much foreteller as forth-teller. He is a man who tells forth. The word of the prophet may have to do with the past. It constantly has to do with the present. And it certainly has to do with the future, and then it becomes foretelling often enough. Sometimes its work is forth-telling in interpretation as to the future. The prophet! Who is the prophet? What is the meaning of the prophet's office? Whether you take it in the suggestiveness of the Old, or whether you take the meaning in the New Testament as

interpreted in the New Testament, the prophet is one who speaks for God. That covers the whole ground.

Recall the passage at the beginning of the Letter to the Hebrews. "God, who at sundry times and in divers manners spake in time past unto the fathers by the prophets…" (I am quoting from the Old Version), "Hath in these last days spoken unto us [not in that way but] by his Son." I must not attempt to stop over the passage, and interpret it at any length. I want to say only two or three things about it, because it has a bearing on what we are doing now in studying this section of Old Testament literature. First of all, there is the antithesis in that Old Testament passage, how one idea has been upset now. "In times past," and "now." In times past the voice of God spoke through the prophets. Now God is still speaking, but He does it through His Son. That is a very remarkable note. The word used for the speech of God in both these cases, whether it refers to the past or to the present, to the past economy through the prophets or the present through His Son, is the same verb. God talking—talking in the most intimate way.

A friend of mine, Dr. Cunningham Pike, long ago pointed out that the Greek word is the word from which we get our English word "lullaby." I do not mean to suggest God's talking was a lullaby in our ordinary sense of the word, but in a deep profound sense of the word everything that God has said to restless, feverish, crying, agonized humanity is a great lullaby. He spoke!

Now the Old Version, referring to that old economy says "at sundry times and in divers manners." The Revised Version has changed that first adjective and it now reads "by divers portions and in divers manners." The same adjective has been used twice over.

It is tempting to carry over the similarity in the prefix between the two Greek words so translated. It is worth doing. "Sundry" said the Old Version, "divers" says the New. And yet there is a difference in the two words, and there is a reason for both. It Says, God spoke to the fathers through the prophets, first of all "in divers manners." This should be "in divers portions," as we have now rendered it. It signifies parts. There is no completeness, there can be no completeness.

Over the whole of what God said to men before the coming of His Son can be written what His Son said to men when He did come. I declare that God might have said to all those through whom He spoke and to whom He spoke, "I have many things to say unto you but ye cannot bear them now." And so they had sections and portions, and that is what we have in the New Testament.

But then the other word has another meaning, not only many sections, or many parts, but "divers" manners. I am not at all sure that I like that. If we take this Greek word and translate it—it almost sounds baffling in our language—it means "by many terms," that is, with many applications. And that second Greek word "in divers manners," as we have now rendered it, speaks of the versatility of the speech of God. I think I do no violence whatever to the real thought that is in either statement when I say we might read it thus: "God spake unto the fathers through the prophets in many sections and on many topics." But do not forget the sections—nothing complete, nothing perfect. And only a cursory glance over these wonderful, writings will reveal how marvelous are the subjects dealt with, and many sections provided; and when we finish Malachi we can say, *"Now we need the Prophet."* That was the final word, the quest for the prophet.

So to pass on. Our use of the word "quest" there reveals our own examination. We are questing for the prophet as we pass over the books. But it reveals more. It does reveal the note of humanity's need against the background of history. Is that clear? Let me struggle with it for a moment. Humanity constantly needs something that it does not know it needs. And history reveals it, and God answers that need in the divers sections and the divers or many topics. What was a quest for the prophet? As you go through and look at the beginning of the history, it does not seem as if these people were questing for a prophet very much. We are inclined to think that their quest consisted in an attempt to find ways by which they might avoid the issue, and disobey the prophets. And yet there is suffering, searching, in respect of the word that the prophets of God sent and spoke to them.

All this has been necessary as an introduction to this section. Our attempt now will be to keep in mind the background of the history as it is revealed in any dating. I want to emphasize the fact that we must approach these prophetic writings as determined by the dating of the context found in the writings, where there is such dating. I know perfectly well that there is in many of them none at all; but wherever the dating is found in the writings, we try to remember the background of history for which they are dated.

I am inclined to stop just for a moment here, and go back to the time when I was speaking of the arrangement in our Bible. At the beginning of Isaiah there are these words: "The vision of Isaiah the son of Amoz, which he saw concerning Judah and Jerusalem, in the days of Uzziah, Jotham, Ahaz, and Hezekiah, kings of Judah." That is what I mean by dating. I am not going to enter into any argument of scholarship, although Isaiah was modern enough by what is known as "modern scholarship." Any dating of the background of history is found in a knowledge of the reigns referred to, stretching from Uzziah away to Hezekiah. It is evident what that does. It cuts away the idea of two books in Isaiah because Hezekiah comes in the second part. Two sections? Yes, but not two books.

In the matter of the books of Joel, Jonah, and Obadiah, two of these, Joel and Obadiah are undated, though they are open to speculation, and there has been a great deal of that about Joel. I think I summarize accurately when I say some very eminent scholars believe he was one of the very latest of the prophets, others believe that he was one of the earliest. I am not going to give any reasons for either case, but so far as I am concerned, I think Joel was one of the very earliest prophets of that period. It is equally true to say that we have no definite dating at all in that one page we call a prophecy.

Jonah is very clearly dated, as we remember how it begins. "The word of the Lord came unto Jonah the son of Amittai…" Go back into the II Kings 14:25: "He restored the coast of Israel from the entering of Hamath unto the sea of Arabah, according to the word of the Lord God of Israel, which he spake by the hand of his servant Jonah, the son of Amittai, the prophet, which was of Gath-hepher."

I think that places Jonah definitely, for there can be no doubt that he was the son of Amittai. So let us remember Jonah, and consider the historic background of the reign of Jeroboam.

What have we in these three prophets, Joel, Jonah and Obadiah? We have the revelation of the activity of God. That summarizes all three. In Joel, the divine activity is emphasized; in Jonah, it is the compassion moving the divine activity that is revealed; and in Obadiah, it is anger moving the divine activity that is revealed.

Now take the Book of Joel, and there is nothing so emphatic in it unquestionably as that one phrase, "the day of the Lord." It occurs five times in the course of this very brief prophecy, and it stands in relation to what the prophet is saying round them all; it is the key of the whole book. It constitutes the burden that lay upon the heart of Joel. He had been bound to deliver the fact of the day of the Lord. Look at it! In what sense was he saying it? If we follow through, he applies it in three ways. First of all, to the immediate conditions in the midst of which they were living; and secondly, to something in the future, menacing, unescapable, that was coming; and thirdly, to some great ultimate. Whether he looked at the moment or the imminent or the ultimate, in every case it was the day of the Lord.

The immediate moment was a locust plague. The locust plague swept the country moving right along and sweeping its devastating ranks over all. In this country we are not very familiar with that. Travelers in the East know what it means. Once in my life I passed through 400 miles of country in Southern California that had the previous week been swept by a locust plague. I never shall forget it. There was not a leaf to be seen on a tree or a blade of grass. Everything was gone, a devastation of the most complete kind. These people passed through an experience like that. Imagine the calamity that had overtaken them. Think of the terror of it! No food, for they were almost without food for the time being; certainly there were no gifts for the Temple. And the prophet refers to these things. I think I can almost believe that humanity was then what it is now, and that there would not be wanting those who were asking, "Why did God permit it?" "Permit it," says Joel, "he caused it." It was the day of the Lord. God was acting, God was abroad, and every beating wing of the rushing locusts was under divine control. It was the day of the Lord. He was calling them to realize that God was acting in chastisement and punishment, and that it was His intention to bring them back into right relationship with Him.

But having declared that the day of the Lord was there in the locust plague, he lifted his eyes and saw before the horizon an invading army. And we would not describe an invading army under the same figure as the locusts. It was far more terrible an army, especially armed, that would invade and destroy them forever, overwhelming them. And this is what they said: "What shall we do in the crisis? What shall we do to prevent it?" "Prevent it," said Joel, "it is God, it is the day of the Lord. He is at the head of the armies. He is leading them. It is His mighty discipline."

Then occurred what is perhaps in many ways one of the most remarkable things of the Old Testament, and especially in prophetic writings; looking from the immediate and the devastation of the locust plague, and the imminent and the army invading, his eyes swept down the ages and he had to halt. He saw something which was different from anything, and he spoke of it as the poured-out Spirit of God upon all flesh. Jew though he was, and a Jewish prophet (or Hebrew as he was and as I prefer to say, with all Hebrew prejudice), he said that that spirit, would fall, not upon those of his own nation, but upon all flesh. "Your sons and your daughters shall prophesy, your old men shall dream dreams, your young men shall see visions." It was still the day of the Lord. God was still acting, and acting in a strange and wonderful way that called forth such a dramatic outburst. We know what Joel was describing. In the New Testament we find the day of the Lord. The Apostle, in the first message delivered after Pentecost, said, "This is that which was spoken of by the prophet Joel." Joel got a glimpse of the day, and then beyond that he saw something else: he saw the day of the Lord which would bring the consummation to a high level; a day of anger, a day beyond the period of grace. That day has not come. Whether it is near or not I am not prepared to say, but that it must be I am profoundly convinced.

Now the fact that is revealed in this prophecy of Joel is that the day of the Lord is always present and always coming. He emphasizes the unbroken continuity of the divine government, the day of the Lord. Today it looks very much like man's day. It is not man's day. This is the day of the Lord. And all the things we see and cannot understand and do not pretend to understand! We believe it *is* the day when God is working His purpose out This is the fact that is emphasized in Joel.

With the other two books we need not tarry long. Jonah— what a wonderful servant! I have often said in talking about Jonah that some people are so busy with a tape measure trying to find the dimensions of a whale's belly that they never see God at all. The Book of Jonah was of the time of the kingdom of Jeroboam, and with that background of history this experience of Jonah took place in a strange time in the national outlook, and a contradiction of attitude on behalf of the nation. First of all, they were daring to make political alliances with other nations, contrary to the will of God. Secondly, they were observing the utmost bitterness regarding those nations religiously, while admitting them to many offices. There were these two things: mixing with the nations politically, and excluding the nations religiously.

That was the national outlook and the story of the prophet; and the heroism of Jonah is seen in the fact that he ever wrote it. It is a revelation of his own disastrous failure, and of Gods incomparable grace in dealing with him, and ultimately of his success. In many ways it is a wonderful story. What does it tell? The reluctance of this man to do what he was told. What was he told to do? To go outside the nation, to go outside the people of the covenant, and to give the word of God to a heathen, pagan, cruel city named Nineveh. Why was he reluctant? Let me put it bluntly.

He was reluctant to go because he knew God so well. I wander if that is at all surprising. I think it is, if we are familiar with the book. He knew God so well. Read this in Chapter 4: "It displeased Jonah exceedingly, and he was angry. And he prayed unto the Lord, and said I pray thee." Jonah was a very fine man. He ran away, but he never escaped from the situation even though he tried. How often we try to run away from God! And there was a ship just conveniently there. It is wonderful when we want to run away from God how often we find a ship close at hand. And what I like about it is that he paid his fare. If he was going to be disobedient he was going to do the thing honestly. He paid his fare. But however determined we are to find our ship and pay our fare, we won't get away from God. And he talked to God. He was angry. What did he say? "O Lord, was not this my saying, when I was yet in my country? Therefore I hasted to flee unto Tarshish; for I knew that thou art a gracious God, and merciful, slow to anger, and abundant in lovingkindness, and repentest thee of the evil. Therefore now, O Lord, take, I beseech thee, my life from me."

Poor Jonah! Now we understand why he didn't want to go; because he knew God so well, and he didn't like what he knew about God. He didn't want any pity shown to Nineveh. He thought it was a great mistake. Oh yes, he knew God's nature, full of compassion, and he knew that if there was repentance God would repent, and he didn't want Him to. That is the story of Jonah. But it ends very beautifully in the same Chapter 4. Look at the end of the chapter: "Then said the Lord, Thou hast had pity on the gourd, for the which thou hast not laboured, neither madest it grow; which came up in a night, and perished in a night: And should not I spare Nineveh, that great city; wherein are more than sixscore thousand persons that cannot discern between their right hand and their left hand; and also much cattle?"

And it was because Jonah knew that, that he ran away. Then he came back, still angry, and God talked to him; and there is a strong note of heroism in Jonah seen in the fact that when the day came to write the story, he revealed his early foolishness. He revealed two great facts: first, that God gave him a second chance, the word of the Lord came a second time; and He had pity on Nineveh—the activity of God in compassion.

Then we look at Obadiah. Don't forget that in Obadiah there is but one page, which brings into the clearest revelation the age-long hostility between Jacob and Edom. That is the story. It is not over.

What is the matter with the world today? Exactly the same thing. It is the age-long hostility between Jacob and Edom. The times? What were they? It was a time of calamity for the nation of Israel, and of terrible calamity for Edom. Read it carefully. What was its attitude? First of all, aloofness. It was neutral but it watched; not entirely neutral insofar as it was rejoicing over the calamity which was falling upon Jacob—until it was no longer neutral. The aloofness of Edom! And it presents the burden of the cruelty falling upon Jacob. And God watching—the divine activity. And here in this page of the Book of Obadiah we find two things close together in verses 3 and 4: "O thou that dwellest in the clefts of the rock, whose habitation is high; that saith in his heart, Who shall bring me down to the ground? Though thou mount on high as the eagle, and though thy nest be set among the stars, I will bring thee down from thence, saith the Lord." Of course, geographically that was true. Edom was dwelling in the rocky fastnesses that we now call Pera, and dwelling there they seemed invincible, and felt that they were safe. And we know what Edom was saying: "Who shall bring me down to the ground?" Here is God's answer: "Though thou mount on high as the eagle, and though thy nest be set among the stars, I will bring thee down from thence, saith the Lord." How will He do it? "All the men of thy confederacy have brought thee on thy way, even to the border: the men that were at peace with thee have deceived thee, and prevailed against thee…" And why? "For the violence done to thy brother Jacob, shame shall cover thee." God is angry, and He is angry with Edom. And what was the reason for His anger? Pride which challenged God, and said, "Who will bring me down?" And the answer of God's anger to that attitude is always the same. *He* will bring them down.

So in these three books, thus briefly glanced at, we see the activity of God; the great fact of it—doing! He is always acting. The day of the Lord yesterday, and the day of the Lord today, and the day of the Lord tomorrow, and every tomorrow. God is never inactive, and the character of His activity is dependent upon the attitudes that men take toward Him. If they repent, His compassion moves and they are spared. If they rebel, anger falls and they are swept away.

15. AMOS, HOSEA

I am going to suggest that the prophecies of Amos and Hosea reveal another aspect of the one truth of the special attitudes of God, as we have looked at His activities as revealed in Jonah, Joel and Obadiah. Now we are to look at His attitude toward man as revealed in these two prophets. The historic background is found in Hosea with a definite date (and here we have prophets with their own dating, and where the prophet is dated, as I have said, I believe in the dating given in the prophecy). It is given in Chapter 1:1: "The word of the Lord that came unto Hosea, the son of Beeri, in the days of Uzziah, Jotham, Ahaz, and Hezekiah, kings of Judah, and in the days of Jeroboam the son of Joash, king of Israel."

Then, if we turn to the prophecy of Amos, we have the dating given in Chapter 1:1: "The words of Amos, who was among the herdsmen of Tekoa, which he saw concerning Israel in the days of Uzziah king of Judah, and in days of

Jeroboam the son of Joash king of Israel, two years before the earthquake."

From that we gather the dating of these two prophets. Therefore, when we turn to Amos, which we take first, we notice that he prophesied when Jeroboam was reigning in Israel and Uzziah reigning in Judah, and the historic background emerges by these familiar references in the Old Testament. Jeroboam was reigning in Israel when Hosea exercised his ministry, whilst Uzziah, Jotham, Ahaz, and Hezekiah were kings in Judah: so the two prophets were contemporary, at least in part of their work. Personally, I think the ministry of Amos was a brief one, comparatively toward the end of the period of the reign of Jeroboam; and that of Hosea—as I shall note again more particularly—was of long duration. In all probability we have in Amos the accounts of two or three discourses, perhaps only one long continuous one. I cannot say which, but the book is divided into certain sections. In Hosea, on the other hand, undoubtedly the notes were compiled and written by the prophet himself after a long period. By no means a full record of his prophecy is contained there, and everything was not covered.

Perhaps I should say at once that both of these prophets were specifically prophets of Israel, the northern kingdom, though Judah was not lost sight of either by Amos or Hosea. Amos was a son of Judah. He came from Tekoa, and it is very interesting to read what he said about himself in Chapter 7, in answer to the criticisms that were raised concerning his work, and the pressure that was being brought to bear upon him to give up his persistency, and clear away off to prophesy in the northern kingdom. He came from Judah to the northern kingdom, and in verse 14 he said this: "I was no prophet, neither was I a prophet's son; but I was a herdsman, and a dresser of sycomore-trees."

Another reading is: "I am no prophet, nor am I a prophet's son," and there is no question he was writing of his past. He says, "I am no prophet nor was I a prophet's son"; or, as the margin renders it, "Neither was I one of the sons of the school of the prophets"—which means in our own modern language that he was an untrained man: that is, untrained as a prophet in the usual way of training. In our modern phraseology, he had never had any theological training. It is very interesting to notice that, because there has been other such in the history of the ministry of The Holy Word of God. Here is a man who was no prophet in that sense, neither did he belong to one of the schools of the prophets, but he says: "I was a herdsman, and a dresser of sycomore-trees: and the Lord took me from following the flock, and the Lord said unto me, Go, prophesy unto my people Israel." That is a very interesting personal reference as to this man. He was no prophet in the ordinary acceptation of the term; he had no training in one of the schools of the prophets of their day, but he was a prophet, as he claims, because the Lord commanded him to "Go, and prophesy." And let it be said that when it ever happens that the Lord may say to a man directly, so that there can be no mistake in his soul, "Go and prophesy," whereas it may be an advantage in certain senses to pass through one of the schools of the prophets, if the Lord sent him directly, he should go. So did Amos the herdsman. I want to picture him: a rough and splendid character of a man, a herdsman, a dresser of sycamore trees, who went up to the northern kingdom and to the very special northern life of the Samaritan Court, and carried with him all the atmosphere of the wilderness of Tekoa. All he said was characterized by the splendid granite roughness of his early life and his early training.

Hosea also was a remarkable man, unquestionably a native of the northern kingdom. Both he and Amos were specifically prophets of Israel, though, as we observe, Judah is not lost sight of in all their prophecies; they were called the Messengers of God, speaking for God.

Going back for a moment to the background of history here, what do we find? So far as the northern kingdom is concerned, Jeroboam was king, and his reign was characterized by very remarkable material prosperity. It was equally characterized by times of spiritual and moral degeneracy. In that northern kingdom—and what was true of the north was true of the south too—they had fallen into the terrible fallacy of believing that their material prosperity was evidence of the provision and goodness of God, in spite of their moral declension and delinquency. They were boasting in their material prosperity, although they were morally corrupt and rapidly passing on to nemesis. In Hosea, Jeroboam is named as king of Israel, and there follows this long list of kings, Uzziah, Jotham, Ahaz and Hezekiah in Judah. To run a little ahead in our present study, it is evident that he was prophesying contemporaneously with Isaiah. There is practically the same list of kings, and the same world conditions. In the reign of Uzziah, the people had a great period of material prosperity, yet all the while there was declension and failure until Uzziah became utterly corrupt and a leper. There is the historical background, and against that we have these two voices. In Amos, the subject is that of the government of God. It is a revelation of the attitude of God toward human affairs in government. I do not think one can say anything else about Hosea, save that it is a revelation of the grace of God, the attitude of God in grace. So, through these contemporary prophets we have their message, which brings us face to face with these two things concerning the attitude of God: His Government and His Grace.

Now look at Amos. The outlook of Amos was a unique one amongst all the prophets of Israel. There were others who had inklings and glimmerings of the great truth, and in certain senses declared it; but the method of Amos is very remarkable, and the remarkable thing is that his earlier prophecy, from the beginning of the book through Chapter 2:3 had nothing to do with Israel in detail, nothing to do with Judah in detail. In principle, yes. In other words, the outlook of Amos was international. It is worthy of record that a title concerning God which may be found so often in these prophetic writings, "The God of Israel," never occurs in Amos. No one will imagine I am saying that Amos forgot He was God of Israel. Of course not! To tell this was the purpose of his ministry in the northern kingdom. But he takes a wide sweep. Look in a map of Palestine for the outline of those different places mentioned in Amos. Listen: Damascus, Gaza, Tyre, Edom, Ammon, Moab, Judah, Israel. There is no simpler outline in the work of map-making than that strip of land with its elbow in the middle, Palestine. Mark all those different places, and see what a remarkable method Amos had. He swept around Israel. Dr. Wilbur White once described the course of Amos as a "spiral." I do not know that that is good, but at any rate we know what it meant. He swept round and round, and kept coming closer and closer, until at last he got to Israel. He began with Damascus, which was on the extreme northeast, and delivered his message there; he swept clean round the map until he got southwest to Gaza. Next, he swept up until he got to the northeast to Tyre; and then he circled across toward the west and away down until he found himself at Edom in the south. Here is the movement. How is he going to come round to Israel? Away he goes round the north until he comes towards the west and swoops down to Ammon. He comes down again over Ammon, and goes a little inward toward Moab, and when he has delivered his message there, starts north to Judah, and passing through Judah he delivers his message. And at last he reaches Israel. We are looking now at these people before they are carried away into captivity, both the northern and the southern kingdoms, and they are seen hemmed in by nations, all of them hostile: Damascus, Gaza, Tyre, Edom, Ammon, Moab, all hostile peoples. And this herdsman from Tekoa went up to the northern capital and began to preach and prophesy and utter the Word of the Lord. He began by saying—mark it well: "The Lord will roar from Zion, and utter his voice from Jerusalem; and the pastures of the shepherds shall mourn, and the top of Carmel shall wither."

That is the introduction. And then he goes on: "Thus saith the Lord: For three transgressions of Gaza, yea, for four…" (1:6). "Thus saith the Lord: For three transgressions of Tyre, yea, for four…" (1:9). "Thus saith the Lord: For three transgressions of Edom, yea, for four…" (1:11). "Thus saith the Lord: For three transgressions of the children of Ammon, yea, for four…" (1:13). "Thus saith the Lord: For three transgressions of Moab, yea, for four…" (2:1). "Thus saith the Lord: For three transgressions of Judah, yea, for four…" (2:4). "Thus saith the Lord: For three transgressions of Israel, yea, for four…" (2:6).

The same formula opens every one of these passages. The Lord is roaring from Mount Zion, speaking to the centers of international life, Damascus, Gaza, Tyre, Edom, Ammon, Moab, and then Judah and Israel. In all these messages there is the universal fact on which the prophet was insisting—the fact of God's knowledge of the nations. These people living in Judah and Israel were living as if God had no care for any of these surrounding nations, except perhaps that of hostility, and some of the messages of Amos seem to ratify that view of Gods activity. And let me break in at once to say it is very interesting to watch, that as long as He was chastening surrounding nations everyone was complacent, but when He reached Israel and His message became more specific, more directly applied to them, they got angry. Is that not true of human nature? That is what this prophet was doing; speaking out of Gods knowledge of these nations, and the things going on in these nations, and speaking of God as governing.

God is heard denouncing the condition of their national life and declaring what the consequent issue will be. The government of God is that upon which Amos is insisting, and he is revealing the fact that responsibility is according to privilege. He has said nothing so far about Damascus. He has said lots about Judah, and especially about Israel. It will be seen that according to the privilege of the nation, such is their responsibility in the government of God. And all the way through, in the messages to the nations outside and the messages to Judah and Israel, that is his theme. Did you notice that repetition? What did he say in every case: "For three transgressions, yea, for four…" That is a Hebraism that marks the fact of God's patience. It does not mean up to one, two, three, four, and so on, but that He would be patient in spite of transgressions until the cup of iniquity was full. We have a saying which I just quote, "The third time pays for all." God went beyond that, and said up to three, four, and so on, until the cup of iniquity is filled, and then God acts, and acts in punishment. But mark the patience with Damascus, and with all of them.

And then, of course, these messages reveal the inescapable issues of the things denounced. One would like to take time there. We see the national sins denounced in this message, every one of them. It is worth while looking carefully through, and seeing what were the things for which these nations were denounced in the government of God. And yet everything moves through toward the ultimate result, for the purpose of God's government as seen—even in the first place—is ultimately that of judgment. Remember, one prophet speaks of judgment as being the strange act of God. This judgment is punishment, which is necessary in view of conditions. Nothing is more patent than that everything moves toward it; and this preacher, Amos, is looking forward to the day when the divine government will reach its own goal and says in Chapter 9:11-13: "In that day will I raise up the tabernacle of David that is fallen, and close up the breaches thereof; and I will raise up its ruins, and I will build it as in the days of old; that they may possess the remnant of Edom, and all the nations that are called by my name, saith the Lord that doeth this. Behold, the days come, saith the Lord, that the ploughman shall overtake the reaper…"

There it is. That is the ultimate in divine government. It is a fact based upon the divine knowledge, and issuing in an ultimate result which, through judgment and punishment, reaches the divine purpose.

We turn to the prophecy of Hosea, and here we have the notes of a long ministry. If we look at these reigns, and arrange them, it will be found that if Hosea was a prophet during that period, or in some of that period of those reigns, his ministry lasted for seventy years. It was a long ministry, and yet in the most marvelous way we have condensed into this comparatively brief book the burden of his prophesying, and a revelation of the inspiration of that prophesying.

Again, the messages of Hosea were learned from personal experience that seemed perchance to have nothing to do with national affairs, a purely personal tragedy in the prophets life that broke his heart and crushed him. I need only say that out of his own experience he gained the great messages; that in the midst of his tragic experience—the infidelity of Gomer, and the fact that she had deserted him and become a harlot and adulteress—out of his own breaking heart he learned something of God, and he learned it by command of God that was purely personal. We see it. God told him to go and find that woman, and love her and bring her back home. Hosea found out that that was God's attitude, and it underlies all his prophecies. According to Hosea, what is the ultimate nature of Sin? He deals with it—infidelity to love. He learned the agony of it in his own experience, but he learned that God suffers in the presence of the infidelity of His people. The great burden of Hosea is first a recognition of sin, and sin in its ultimate and worst form, infidelity to love. The supreme sin is disloyalty to the love of God, and it is all here in Hosea.

But he not only shows you the sin. He shows you judgment, and he brings out very clearly the fact that judgment is inherent in sin; that there is a sense in which we are not correct when we talk about God punishing. It is punishing because of love. I have heard men glibly say that a man carries hell in his own soul. So he does. But very often when he has said that, he has not touched the depths. Infidelity to love, rebellion against the government of God, which is the government of infinite grace—that is the truth brought out here, and it is in these elements that at last will be grown and ripen the devastating harvest of the soul. And that is what is taught in this prophecy.

And yet, having said that—and these things must be said because they are here—the great undertone running all through it, and breaking out ever and anon into some marvelous expressions, is that of the constancy of love. Most of us are familiar with Shakespeare's words,

… Love is not love
Which alters when it alteration finds.

How far we can apply that to human love I am not going to say, but it is true of God. His love is there. His love is all through.

And secondly, the great revelation of Hosea is that of the grace of God in that way. I turn for a moment to Hosea, and even though it is a little paragraph, I want to quote it. God is speaking through the prophet in Chapter 11:1-4, 8: "When Israel was a child, then I loved him, and called my son out of Egypt. The more the prophets called them, the more they went from them: they sacrificed unto the Baalim, and burned incense to graven images. Yet I taught Ephraim to walk; I took them on my arms; but they knew not that I healed them. I drew them with cords of a man, with bands of love; and I was to them as they that lift up the yoke on their jaws; and I laid food before them… How shall I give thee up, Ephraim? how shall I cast thee off, Israel? how shall I make thee as Admah? how shall I set thee as Zeboiim? my heart is turned within me, my compassions are kindled together."

I always dislike comparisons about the Bible. I am not really doing it. But do you know of any passage in the Old Testament or the New, more wonderful in its revelation of the love of God than that? That one central word, "How shall I give thee up, Ephraim?" is the revelation of God. Ephraim is referred to all through Hosea, because Ephraim had become the dominant tribe in the northern kingdom of Israel. Once God has to say to him, "Thy goodness is like a morning cloud," something that is full of promise, and alas, the hope of the day is not kept.

"Ephraim is a cake not turned," burnt on the one side, and soft and flat on the other. "Ephraim, how shall I give thee up?" And when the end of Hosea is reached, we find that wonderful passage in which he says, "I will" and "Thou shalt," until the day shall come that even Ephraim shall say, "What have I to do any more with idols? I have answered, and will regard him: I am like a green fir-tree; from me is thy fruit found."

So, from this inadequate glancing at the two prophecies, we learn from them this, at any rate, as to the attitudes of God: that the inspiration of Gods government is always His grace.

But we also learn that grace never abrogates government; and in the background and with the conditions of these people, we listen to these voices, with these two things shining with great clearness.

16. ISAIAH, MICAH

Coming now to Isaiah and Micah: To read these prophecies is to realize the majesty of them, especially perhaps of Isaiah, though Micah is equally important. Both these two prophets pre-eminently reveal and emphasize the fact of the authority of God. We have studied the activities of God, the attitudes of God, and now the one great theme of both these prophets is that of authority, and that, the authority of God.

The dating of these prophets is very clear. In Isaiah 1:1 we read: "The vision of Isaiah the son of Amoz, which he saw concerning Judah and Jerusalem, in the days of Uzziah, Jotham, Ahaz and Hezekiah, kings of Judah."

In Micah 1:1 equally clear dating is found: "The word of the Lord that came to Micah the Morashtite in the days of Jotham, Ahaz, and Hezekiah, kings of Judah, which he saw concerning Samaria and Jerusalem." These two verses give us the dates of the prophecies. Notice Isaiah covers that long period beginning in the reign of Uzziah, running on through Jotham, Ahaz and Hezekiah; in reading we see where these things begin. The first five prophecies were uttered exclusively in the days of Uzziah. Then in Chapter 6 are given the prophecies during the time of Ahaz, "In the year King Uzziah died." The references follow up to the death of Ahaz. It is interesting that Jotham is not referred to during the prophecies, though he reigned for sixteen years, most of the time as vice-regent and not as king, because of the lingering and dying illness of Uzziah. Next pass from Uzziah to Ahaz; and after the death of Ahaz comes the period when Hezekiah began.

Notice that in Micah there are the same kings, except that Uzziah is not mentioned. Micah prophesied during the reigns of Jotham, Ahaz and Hezekiah. Thus these prophets were there part of the time as contemporaries. Micah began his ministry after the death of Uzziah, and continued it in the reigns of Jotham, Ahaz and Hezekiah. Evidently he and Isaiah both prophesied in Damascus during part of the time.

The history of the background of these days is seen in the names of the kings given in the case of Isaiah and Micah. Practically, the background is exactly the same as it was in the days of Amos and Hosea, but it must be remembered they were specifically sent as prophets to the northern kingdom, whereas Micah and Isaiah were prophets to the southern part, the kingdom of Judah. But in both the earlier prophecies—and when I refer to "earlier" I mean earlier in the sense of reference—Israel is referred to: yet specifically, the first two prophecies are to Israel, and the other prophecies were to both Israel and Judah.

There is, however, one theme especially in these two prophets of Isaiah and Micah, the theme of the authority of God. Roughly dividing between them, I should say that in Isaiah the great fact insisted upon is the Throne of God. In Micah, we have the same fact in mind, the same authority. But he is dealing, not with the direct authority of God, but with the authority of God as delegated, with rulers for the people who ought to have been representing God, and were supposed to be representing God. Micah sees the necessity for the delegation of the divine authority but it remains the divine authority, and in nothing that the delegate can say or do, has he any right to say or do anything except upon the basis of divine authority. That is specifically the note of Micah. It may be remembered that Paul said the powers that be were ordained of God, and that some of the powers in existence were manifestly evil. Yet what he meant to say was that behind all the delegated authority, there was the same final supreme authority; and that is the supreme thought brought out in Micah.

Look now at the message of Isaiah. I have said that its great theme—and I am not sure that the word "theme" is correct—is the divine authority, the divine sovereignty. But the great final point and final word is seen in the attention which was drawn, in a very remarkable manner, to the fact that he ever kept in view as he delivered his message, the Throne itself. Specifically he is speaking to Judah, but in speaking to Judah he has much to say about all the surrounding nations that were encamped against Judah. Even to glance through the prophecy means at least to notice messages to Babylon, Assyria, Philistia, Moab, Damascus, and Israel, all uniting with each other for the time politically.

The same method is seen in Amos, where he went up to the northern kingdom and preached specifically to Israel. He began by giving messages to all the surrounding nations, working round and going inward, but there was the same method and the same outlook. This prophet sees these nations all round about, and he has something to say concerning all of them, until finally in the messages of Isaiah, the outlook is to the larger Israel, the larger Judah, and to the surrounding nations: but whether it be Judah or Israel or the nations I have referred to, or the whole world, everything seen is under the dominion of the one Throne.

I want to pause at the point which is in many ways the central one, certainly from the standpoint of his theme and his teaching—the vision that came to him when King Uzziah died. There are some expositors who say that that vision in itself is prophetic work. I do not believe that. I feel that in the earlier chapters Isaiah is still speaking, and speaking during the reign of Uzziah. I need not debate it; it is not important. Whether his vision came before he commenced his work at all; or, as I believe, several years after he commenced it, it was to him an unveiling, a revelation from which he never escaped and which became invincibly the increasing burden of his appeal, as it was the light on his outlook. Of course, it is significant that that vision did come—as we are told—at the death of Uzziah: "In the year that King Uzziah died." I think it is good to pause and think what that meant to this young prophet. Uzziah, who had been on the throne for half a century and a little more, is dead, and on the national level everything must have looked different. Now mark the significance: "In the year that king Uzziah died I saw the Lord sitting upon a throne, high and lifted up; and his train filled the temple" (6:1).

An empty throne! The throne that was not empty. The king is dead. The King lives for ever! The year of the Lord, and he saw the Lord lifted upon the throne. That passage is so full of fascination, but I cannot tarry with it. Suffice it to say that he looked at the vision, and the enthroned Jehovah, and all the surroundings were the surroundings of infinite majesty and glory. But listen to the chanting of the seraphim: "Holy, holy, holy, is the Lord of Hosts: the whole earth is full of his glory" (6:3). And that vision of the throne of God, and the glory of the throne of God that filled the temple, and that sound of the anthems of the seventy, produced in the prophet a sense of deep abasement. In the presence of the glory he cried out: "Woe is me! For I am undone; because I am a man of unclean lips, and I dwell in the midst of a people of unclean lips: for mine eyes have seen the King, the Lord of Hosts" (6:5).

He had preached the sovereignty of God before that, he had announced the reign of Jehovah before, but there was granted to him in some form an intensive vision of the uplifted Throne flinging the empty throne of earth into the darkness. He heard those angels, those seraphim, celebrating the holiness of God, and that too with the uttermost reverence, wings veiling feet and faces, ready to fly at the command of God. And in the presence of that light and that glory and that tremendous manifestation he was deeply and profoundly abased, and from that sense of abasement he cried out, "Woe is me!" And then something happened.

There is nothing more marvelous in all the Scriptures than this. Isaiah saw the glory of the Lord. Isaiah was made aware of the holiness of God, and the majesty of God. And the effect of it penetrated to earthly facts, and the whole earth was filled with the glory of the Lord. He saw the vision, and he cried out, "Woe is me! In the presence of that light I am unclean, and I am exercising my ministry among people unclean."

"Then flew one of the seraphim unto me, having a live coal in his hand, which he had taken with the tongs from off the altar: and he touched my mouth with it, and said, Lo, this hath touched thy lips; and thine iniquity is taken away, and thy sin forgiven. And I heard the voice of the Lord, saying, Whom shall I send, and who will go for us? Then I said, Here am I; send me" (6:6-8).

I think I should almost spoil it by saying anything. Only notice that Isaiah saw two things supremely revealed to him concerning the authority of God. First, that of the actual government: God rules. Thrones empty, Gods Throne is filled, and He is sitting in the midst of the holy glory and the glorious holiness, the governing God enthroned. The Throne is not on earth; that is to say, it has never trembled; it has never been vacant. Isaiah saw that. And then he found out this amazing fact about God, which I personally do not think he had grasped though there are evidences of it even in the earlier chapters. But I think it came to him with all the wonder of a new revelation, that that reigning God was the God of grace. How? When a lonely man, burdened with the sense of his own uncleanness and his own unworthiness, cries out in the agony of his sin and abasement, "Woe *is* me, I am undone," then God, he learned, will stop the chanting of the seraphim to answer the sobbing of a sinner. Grace and the Lord. That cleanses sin. And when that was done, and he had seen the glory and been filled with abasement, had felt the burning touch of the live coal, and was conscious that he was a cleansed man, then he heard God making the enquiry, "Who will go for me and whom shall I send?" And he answered, "Here am I, send me." There it is! That is Isaiah. That is the very center and heart, that is the revelation of the burden that lay upon his heart. God, in all His holy majesty, had sent him; and the authority of God was the infinite grace of God. That, as I have said, was the beginning of his prophetic work. In the reign of Uzziah, as is seen in the first five chapters of this book, are found things that tell of the consciousness of both these facts. In both these places the facts are there, but this vision intensified his conviction of the righteous government of God, and the infinite grace of God.

Then he went on to show how God in righteous government was proceeding by the ways of judgment, for the ultimate establishment of peace. He showed how, all through human history, the work of God would be done through the servant of the Lord, and the servant of the Lord was abased. Isaiah 53 is in mind: through travail to triumph, through suffering to the establishment of sovereignty. But it is the one God, and the one Throne, and the one authority. We hear reverberating the voices of holiness till we read the last movement of the book, and twice over distinctly that great word thunders out, "There is no peace, saith my God, for the wicked." The Prince of Peace, working toward peace by the pathway of His own travail, but no peace to the wicked. So the Throne thunders its holiness and reveals its grace in the prophecy of Isaiah.

Turn to Micah, and we see the same great principles. His messages were principally to the cities. Listen to this opening phrase again in the first six verses concerning Samaria and Jerusalem. These are the capital cities: Samaria, the capital city of Israel, and Jerusalem, the capital city of Judah; and thus the prophet is saying things concerning the great centers of life. Notice that in the first chapter he says, "Hear, ye peoples, all of yon; hearken, O earth, and all that therein is." And then turn over to Chapter 3:1 and read, "Hear, I pray you, ye heads of Jacob, and rulers of the house of Israel." And so he is dealing with those who are specially in charge with delegated authority. Most clearly it is easy to see, all the way through, the reigning Jehovah. The Throne that Isaiah saw he also saw, but he saw God seated above the earth and its earthly rulers. He is looking at and speaking to those to whom authority is delegated. He described the false authority that is being exercised, and then comes his prophetic talk on the true authority. To go carefully through it is to see the elements of falseness in rule. Micah is denouncing men in authority in Jerusalem and Samaria. What is he saying to them? How does he describe them?

We read in Chapter 3:11: "The heads thereof judge for reward, and the priests thereof teach for hire, and the prophets thereof divine for money." These men are in authority, heads or princes or judges, but each of them taking bribes. They judged for reward, not for justice. The priests taught because they were hired, and if they were not hired they were not prepared to teach. And lastly, dishonorable prophets (and he does not say "prophesy," but uses that mystic evil word "divine," the divination by mystic methods), divined for money. We can put another word in there, and put the same word in each case, self-centered rulers who cared for themselves, and stooped to taking care of themselves and took bribes from people. Read the prophecy through as I am only summarizing. He is denouncing authorities; and the authority was delegated: and the great majority of these men—princes and rulers and prophets—were all taking money. They were forgetting the position to which God had delegated them, and were forgetful of the righteousness of His Throne, and the holiness of His being, and were seeking their own ends for reward, for hire, for money. The degradation of authority!

Again we have one great passage in which he described the true authority. It is a prophetic word in Chapter 5:1-4: "Now shalt thou gather thyself in troops, O daughter of troops: he hath laid siege against us; they shall smite the judge of Israel with a rod upon the cheek. But thou, Bethlehem Ephrathah, which art little to be among the thousands of Judah, out of thee shall one come forth unto me that is to be ruler in Israel; whose goings forth are from of old, from everlasting. Therefore will he give them up, until the time that she who travaileth hath brought forth: then the residue of his brethren shall return unto the children of Israel. [It ought not to be forgotten that there is a sense in which this third verse is in parenthesis, but a very important one.] And he [the one who is to come forth from Ephrathah] shall stand, and shall feed his flock in the strength of the Lord, in the majesty of the name of the Lord his God: and they shall abide; for now shall he be great unto the ends of the earth. And this man shall be our peace."

Micah has been borne aloft He uses Peters words; and carried across the years, he sees beyond the failure of delegated authority, the coming of One to whom all authority shall be given in heaven and on earth. And in that majestic position He is rising. Notice He has come from obscurity, from a place where men were not looking for their princes or their priests or their prophets. "Thou Bethlehem, thou art little to be counted." Obscure? He was to come from there.

Is that all? No. "Their goings forth are from of old, from everlasting." He was to rule, He was to come out of obscurity, out of the little town of Judah itself, and yet He shall come out of eternity: "Your *goings* forth are from eternity." And he saw the Ruler to whom authority was to be delegated, and he tells how He shall reign in two little phrases: "He shall stand, and shall feed." And the work of the shepherd is to feed; and the work of the king is to feed. Here is delegated authority, realizing the purpose of God, of whom he says: "This man shall be our peace."

Immediately after the declaration that this Man shall be our peace, it is seen that through Him there will be ultimately the destruction of all false methods of government. Isaiah saw the Throne, and he saw Grace on the Throne. Micah sees that Throne, and he sees its authority delegated, and prostituted and blasted. But he said that is not the last thing. There is One coming to whom that authority shall be delegated, and He shall come from obscurity out of the eternities, and He will stand and none can move Him. He will feed, and there shall be perfect satisfaction. So he saw delegated authority, and its upward intention realized in One who will come. I have not yet referred to the fulfillment, but we do know how that passage is quoted in the New Testament, and that word from Micah is fulfilled in our Lord Himself.

One final word. We have examined Isaiah and Micah. Isaiah saw and proclaimed and insisted upon the central eternal fact of the Throne of God. Micah saw the exercise of delegated authority in relation to the central and eternal fact of the Throne of God. And where the recognition was lost there was disaster, and where the recognition has been in our time fulfilled, there has been glory and the movement toward ultimate peace. But in both the prophecy of Isaiah and that of Micah we see all the way the intimate relationship between the government and the grace of God.

17. JOB, PROVERBS, ECCLESIASTES

There is a story told of Carlyle, that when visiting a house on one occasion he was asked incidentally if he would take the Bible reading for prayers at the family altar. The tough old sage said yes, he would, and he took the Bible and started to read the Book of Job. He never stopped till he had finished it. Gradually the servants all retired, and then others, and by the time he had finished he was left alone with his host and hostess. "Well," he remarked, "that is very interesting." But he was some time at it! Of course, the Book of Job can be read nicely through in two hours.

I want, by way of introduction before surveying these three books, to deal with the fact of why they are called "wisdom literature." They are pre-eminently wisdom books. And what *is* meant by that? I will put it crudely at first. Wisdom is a name for philosophy. There is a sense in which we may speak of these books as the philosophic books of the Old Testament. We should be quite accurate in a certain sense, and yet it is well for us to remember that there is a difference. I want to pause for a moment to consider the difference between these books, and all other systems of philosophy. We are all familiar with the word "philosophy," but I think it is good sometimes to remind the young especially what the word means. It does not mean wisdom. It means the *method* of wisdom. Pythagoras, it is said, would not allow himself to be called a wise man, but a man who loved wisdom. Philosophy is the love of wisdom, and a philosopher is one who loves wisdom.

And there is a difference. The Hebrew Bible does not speak of the love of wisdom but of wisdom itself. All philosophies have been questing in the love of wisdom, but these Hebrew philosophers started with the declaration of wisdom as existing, as a fact, not as something to be conceded. And there is an elemental difference between every system of philosophy and the philosophic books of the Bible. I wish only to touch upon it very lightly.

All systems of philosophy—all of them—begin with a question. Let no one imagine that I am speaking slightingly of philosophy. I think it is one of the most engaging and wonderful studies in which the mind of man has ever been engaged. And I am not saying it is wrong to start these investigations with a question. Every thinker has begun the study that is now called the study of philosophy with an inquiry; that inquiry, strangely enough, that fell from the lips of Pilate when he stood confronting Jesus: "What is truth?"

Bacon begins one of his Essays by saying, " 'What is truth?' said jesting Pilate, and did not wait for an answer." With great admiration for the particular work of Bacon, I join issue entirely with him at the beginning. Pilate was not jesting. He was puzzled, perplexed by Jesus' personality and His claims and His position, and at last, looking at Him when he said He came into the world to bear witness to the truth, said Pilate, "What is truth?" That is what the philosopher has been asking all down the running centuries, and it has been a great quest.

Now the Hebrew philosophers did begin with a question and this book reveals that fact. You get some of it in the Apocrypha, in the Jewish writings, in some of the Psalms in our collection that are peculiarly philosophic, and in the Epistle of James in the New Testament. The Hebrew philosophy is seen distinctly in the mind of James. This philosophy begins with an affirmation. What was it? *God is.* They did not start with inquiry. Some people may say that is not fair. I am not discussing its fairness. I am discussing the fact.

On the basis of that affirmation he made a second, and it was this: all wisdom is in God; the truth is known to God; there are no secrets from God. Those Hebrew philosophers started with these things. And then they immediately made a deduction. It is a familiar one, and to be found in the books. What is it? The fear of the Lord is the beginning of wisdom for man. You see! God is all wisdom, all truth is in Him. If we want to know wisdom, we must start with that assumption of the fear of God. That is the basis of Hebrew philosophy from beginning to end. But they were not called philosophers. What is the term? Go through our Bible and we find the term, the "wise men." And if we watch carefully, the term is used in the Old Testament on a dozen occasions of wise men who were not philosophers. It is interesting that the first reference is found concerning Egypt, when Pharaoh brought out his magicians and wise men. And we have here all the way through this recognition of wise men.

Taking these three books, Job, Proverbs, Ecclesiastes, in review, let me first say that they are not theological. I am not saying there is no theology in them by assumption, but they are not theological in the strict sense of the word. It is very interesting to notice the absence of Jewish phraseology in these books. There is very little reference at all to the Mosaic Law or the Mosaic Ritual. The Law, as it appears in these books, is moral rather than ceremonial. It is definitely there, but that is its nature.

Further, the outlook of these philosophers in all of these books of wisdom takes in the whole range of human life. The king on his throne, the workman at his task, the Court, with all its courtiers and its habits—all are seen in relation to the fact of God. Job is pre-eminently the revelation of human need and humanity's need of the *wisdom* of God. Proverbs is the revelation of the true way of wisdom, a description of life when it is lived according to wisdom. Wisdom is therein defined. Ecclesiastes is the supreme revelation of the way of folly, what life becomes when this philosophy of life or this wisdom is forgotten.

The Book of Job is a remarkable book. No one can tell who wrote it. As to locality, there has been endless debate as to where Uz really was, or if there really was a land of Uz; we have not been able to find a distinct site. The date is uncertain. There are those who believe, as I believe my self, that this is one of the oldest writings in the Old Testament, going back to patriarchal times. The book is a dramatic poem with an historic basis. There is no doubt that this man Job really lived; his story is told in dramatic form, centering very largely around him in the days of his suffering and sorrow and loss. The book is the account of how he was visited during that time by his friends, and what they said to him and what he replied. I do not know that it is necessary to believe that Eliphaz spoke exactly in the form in which the things he said are recorded, but rather the drift of his speeches is there, and that is so in the case of every one.

What are the essential and final values of this book? Long ago I lectured on Job and published my lectures in my

Analysed Bible, calling the Book of Job "The Problem of Pain." I should not call it that now. There is a sense in which I should agree, but let me say at once that if Job gives you the problem of pain—and it does—it does not give you the solution of that problem, but the problem is presented. The first value of the book—I name it first emphatically—is that it reveals the breakdown of human wisdom at its highest level, the breakdown of human philosophy in its attempt to account for the experience of the human soul.

Consider these men, Eliphaz, Bildad, Zophar, Elihu, as you read their speeches. I like these men for certain reasons which I think are fine and remarkable. I like them first of all because they came to see Job when he was in trouble. I think they deserved to be named friends on that account. I like them in the second place a little more because they were wise enough to sit still for seven days and shut their mouths and be silent. They only made a mistake when they opened them. And yet I like them again because when they did open their mouths, they said what they had to say about Job *to* Job, and not to someone else *about* him. These things apply to our own friendships. You will find that you cannot take exception to the spirit of anything said by Eliphaz, Bildad, Zophar, or Elihu. Leaving Job out for a moment, listen to the speeches, to their philosophy. I challenge you to find anything objectionable. In Chapter 22 Eliphaz says, "Acquaint now thyself with him, and be at peace." We cannot quarrel with it Supposing we hear what Job has to say. He answered and said, "Oh that I knew where I might find him." The philosophy was all right, and Job heard it, and he did not contradict it; but he went on to say, "I go forward, but he is not there; and backward, but I cannot perceive him." A philosophy that gives a definition but cannot find any solution or key to the problem does not account for the human soul. I content myself with that one reference, because it is perhaps the central and most wonderful bit out of these speeches. They were all uttered to Job, and the picture of him is there, seen in his misery, listening.

There are three cycles in these speeches. They are all directed to one point, trying to prove to Job that all his suffering was somehow the result of his own sin. They were wrong, and yet there are men who do not bear the name of Eliphaz but who seem to hold the same philosophy still. They see somebody passing through periods of difficulty and trial and anguish and they say, "Something is wrong." For God's sake, shut your mouth, my friend. That is what these men did. They could not account for it. There it was. Their philosophy was right, so far as it went; but it did not go far enough. They could not account for the suffering of the man and they did not know enough of the signs (which may be noticed at the beginning of the book), how heaven and hell are holding controversy, debating the development of Job, and arguing between the lie of hell and the truth of heaven. They did not know that. Philosophy finds no answer to this application. So, I say, the first value of the book is the picture of the breakdown of human philosophy when it sees the breakdown of the soul in certain human experiences.

What is next? The greatness of human personality. We feel the sense of that as we look at the opening of the book, and watch this man—the greatest of the men in the East—with his family around him. Watch him from the standpoint of their religion. As these sons had their birthday celebrations, he became a priest going to God with his prayers. And then the man is revealed stripped of everything; stripped of his children, of health, stripped of wealth, of possessions, at last even of the sympathy of his wife. I cannot pass without saying a word on behalf of his wife. I have no patience with people who abuse her. You have no right to abuse her until you have sat down and watched your husband, or your best loved friend, passing through the agony he passed through; and when she says in her unutterable foolishness, "Curse God and die, and let me see you out of your misery," what strange, pathetic tenderness lay in that supplication. Listen! We see Job at last, smitten from head to foot with disease, children dead, wealth gone, possessions gone, friends gone: and he talks about them, the friends of the day of prosperity, all scattered except these three, and at last the fourth, Elihu. And yet how great Job was—great in his day, and in the things he spoke to these men: great things, splendid satire, showing the awakening of spiritual conception. I think I hear him and catch the vibrant satire in his voice when he said,

No doubt but ye are the people,
And wisdom shall die with you (12:2).

There is seen a great personality, great in his bearing, and in the words he spoke to God, a wonderful unveiling of the way of wisdom. That is what he needed. It is found in that matchless twenty-eighth chapter. He begins:

Surely there is a mine for silver,
And a place for gold which they refine.

And so it runs, until he comes to this pregnant question, "Where shall wisdom be found?" He has shown where other things shall be found.

Where shall wisdom be found?
And where is the place of understanding?

And with a dramatic touch he goes on to tell where it is *not* found. "Man knoweth not the price thereof." So he tells in forceful poetic language where one cannot find wisdom, until he says,

Behold, the fear of the Lord, that is wisdom;
And to depart from evil is understanding.

Job knew that he was on the highway to solution in the fear of the Lord.

Then follows that matchless part of the book in which God speaks to him. He breaks in upon Elihu, that remarkable man whose speeches are in some senses the most wonderful of all of them, showing that pain and suffering are educational. A storm arises, and the voice of God is heard out of the storm saying,

Who is this that darkeneth counsel
By words without knowledge?

That is how God silences the voice of philosophy. What does God do for this man to interpret his problem now? He makes His glory pass before him. We have the great theophanies, as they may be called, of these two addresses of Jehovah. And how does it end?

> And Job answered the Lord, and said,
> I know that thou canst do all things,
> And that no purpose of thine can be restrained.

Job then plays with words, playing with Elihu:

> Who is this that hideth counsel without knowledge?
> Therefore have I uttered that which I understood not,
> Things too wonderful for me, which I knew not.
> Hear, I beseech thee, and I will speak;
> I will demand of thee, and declare thou unto me.
> I had heard of thee by the hearing of the ear;
> But now mine eye seeth thee;
> Wherefore I abhor myself,
> And repent in dust and ashes.

No solution of the problem, but we have seen human philosophy at fault, we have seen the greatness of the human soul in its possibilities as perhaps it is unveiled in no one else in the Old Testament.

Let us glance now at the Book of Proverbs. In that we have the way of wisdom. Forgive a little reminiscence. When I was once lecturing and analyzing the different books, a lady said to me as I was approaching Proverbs, "You will get beaten when you get to the Book of Proverbs." I said, "What do you mean?" She said, "You cannot analyze that. It is a collection of thoughts." That is what some people think. As a matter of fact, there is no book in the Old Testament that yields itself more readily to definite, clear analysis than the Book of Proverbs. There is the introduction, then the discourses before we reach the Proverbs at all. We never reach the collection of Proverbs until we get to Chapter 10. From Chapter 1:8 to the end of Chapter 9, we are listening to addresses being delivered. Then follow two collections of Proverbs, one beginning with Chapter 10; and then at Chapter 25 we have the second collection, made under Hezekiah. Simply looking at the book, I want to notice what it says itself as to its authorship and its purpose: "The proverbs of Solomon the son of David, king of Israel." That is the man who is responsible; he is the author. And then at the heading of Chapter 25, "These also are the proverbs of Solomon, which the men of Hezekiah king of Judah copied out." Hezekiah did not write them, he collected them; and I think we can take it that the work here is the proverbs of Solomon. All we need is to read this book. This is the introduction to the book:

> To know wisdom and instruction;
> To discern the words of understanding;
> To receive instruction in wise dealing,
> In righteousness and justice and equity.
> To give subtilty to the simple,
> To the young man knowledge and discretion:
> That the wise man may hear, and increase in learning;

> And that the man of understanding may attain unto sound
> counsels:
> To understand a proverb, and a figure;
> The words of the wise, and their dark sayings.
> The fear of the Lord is the beginning of knowledge,
> But the foolish despise wisdom and instruction.

After this introduction comes the movement. As I have said, Chapter 1:8 on to the close of Chapter 9 consists of a series of discourses on wisdom; then, a series of ten addresses—if that is the right word to use—delivered by a father to a son. Run through them, and you will find ten times, "My son, hear, my son, hear my words, my son, hear me." It represents the father talking to his son in all that part of the book. Bearing this in mind, we find that the addresses have to do with the child, with the youth, and then with the man. See the order of the movement. Or to put that perhaps in another way: first of all the child is at home, and wisdom tells it how to behave towards the father and the mother. Then see the youth making friends outside the home. It is so utterly human and natural. It is always so—the children first at home; but you cannot keep your children there, and try to manage them in your home altogether. They must get out to make friends. It is right that they should for the development of personality. So we get the series of discourses to the youth about friends, and the making of the sort of friends that will be of real value to him, and warning him against those friends who will hinder him. Then we find him coming to full young manhood. And as we read, we see him in the midst of the city. Listen to the words about the streets, the broad places, the chief places of the congregation and the city. The youth is passing out into civic life in the busy streets, where the crowds are jostling one another, to the place where they gather together. And wisdom is speaking to the youth who is soon becoming a man. There are ten addresses to the son through his childhood to the development of youth until he arrives at manhood: in them we see the wisdom that is warning him against perils that threaten to ruin him, and in favor of the forces that will make him strong.

What is a proverb, by the way? The Hebrew word means a ruling or maxim, a very good definition; a maxim is considered to have in it an element of rule and government of mans life. We get the ruling maxims on wisdom in both classes of Proverbs.

The final value of the Book of Proverbs is its revelation of the application of wisdom to all sorts and conditions of people, and to the ordinary affairs of human life. It is very interesting to study the Proverbs. They are very forceful, and picturesque, all revealing of the value of this high wisdom that starts with God, believes that all wisdom is in Him, and that in fear of Him is the success of life.

By contrast look at the Book of Ecclesiastes. It opens with these words: "The words of the Preacher, the son of David, king in Jerusalem." That may leave the subject in doubt as to who the writer was, but I have not one single doubt that the son of David referred to is Solomon. Did you notice especially how he is described as "the Preacher"? I think I am right in saying that we owe that translation of the Hebrew word to Martin Luther. I think he made a terrible mistake. It does not mean a preacher in the sense in which we use the word. We should have been far nearer the mark if we had used the word "debater" instead of preacher. What is he doing? He is debating, he is arguing, and he is doing it all through. He tells of the theme in the first verse: "the words of the debater." What is his finding? He states his finding first, and then he masses his proofs. "Vanity of vanities, saith the Debater; vanity of vanities, all is vanity." That is the summing up of his outlook on life: nothing lasting, nothing solid, nothing worth while—"Vanity of vanities, all is vanity."

Then, in a very remarkable way, he proceeds to prove his assertion. He does so first of all by giving personal experience, and then giving the result of his observations of things generally in the world in which he lives. He starts from there to get his personal experience, and having said "Vanity of vanities," he says, "What profit hath man of all his labor wherein he laboreth under the sun?" And he answers: "One generation goeth, and another generation cometh; but the earth abideth for ever. The sun also ariseth, and the sun goeth down, and hasteth to its place where it ariseth. The wind goeth toward the south, and turneth about unto the north." Observe how he describes what seems to him to be the monotonous mechanical drive of the universe. He looks upon himself as living in the universe like that and then gives his reasons for that outlook. There are four in his own experience.

He tells you the things he has tried. He tried knowledge, learning, the amassing of knowledge, and he says that it was all vanity. He turned from that and tried mirth and had a good time, letting loose his passions, and he found that it was vanity. Then he had a third try and tried wealth, amassing it in vast quantities, and then he found that all he had gathered was vanity. And then he tried life, just life itself, letting it run and have its own way, and all his experience led him to the conclusion that there was nothing worth while. Yet he took a new line, looking out upon the universe and repeating more fully what he had said at the beginning, looking at it as a mechanical thing; he looked out upon the psychological conditions in the midst of which he was living, upon the general agony, and in every case he came to the conclusion that there was nothing worth while. It was empty, void, vanity—until we reach his closing address on this subject, at the very end of this book, in which he defines his case as wholly worldly. It is rather interesting on the human side. There, for instance, he says, "Whatever thy hand findeth to do, do it with thy might." And the man is asked to do it because he won't be here long, so he must do all he can while he is here. It is pessimism from beginning to end, until we come to the end of the book.

In Chapter 11:9-10 we find this remarkable outlook: "Rejoice, O young man, in thy youth, and let thy heart cheer thee in the days of thy youth, and walk in the ways of thy heart, and in the sight of thine eyes; but know thou, that for all these things God will bring thee into judgment. Therefore remove sorrow from thy heart, and put away evil from thy flesh: for youth and the prime of life are vanity." And so on through that marvelous chapter, until we reach the words, "This is the whole of man." "Whole duty," you say; "you left out a word." No, I have not. It is here, but not in the Hebrew: "This is the whole of man." Man, in his entirety, must begin with God; the whole of man, the fear of God. Suddenly, at the end of that period, why this allusion? This man saw the bright shining of deep truth. Over and over again, listening to him in his pessimistic wailings, we hear recurring almost monotonously one little phrase: "Under the sun, under the sun." This man had been living through all these experiences under the sun, concerned with nothing above the sun, on the modern level of experience in the realm of the material, until there came a moment in which he had seen the whole of life. And there was something over the sun. It is only as a man takes account of that which is over the sun as well as that which is under the sun that things under the sun are seen in their true light.

So if Proverbs reveals most remarkably—by way of maxims—how to be wise, here is shown the way of folly: the way of folly is that of forgetting God and trying to satisfy a human soul with the things which are of the dust.

The teaching of this wisdom, considering the three books and thinking of the whole, is this: that to enthrone God, and to act in harmony with that enthronement is to discover the secret of life: and the application of that is as varied as life itself. When this is understood, we see the appalling folly of any philosophy of life that begins in the dust, and stays in the dust, and grovels in the dust, and yields to the dust, and tells the abysmal lie that vanity is everything.

18. THE PSALMS, THE SONG OF SOLOMON

The Book of psalms consists of five books, although they are bound up as one in our Revised Version, indicating that they are one Psalter. There are 150 Psalms in that collection, which were largely composed for and used in the Temple worship. The word "Psalm"—I do not mean our word, although it is so in some senses; but the Hebrew word, *Maschil*—is never found in the Book of Psalms except in titles, and you will find it in fifty-seven of them. The meaning of the word is something that makes music, and the use of it is always meant to refer to a song with instrumental accompaniment.

Notice that there is a superscription: "To the Chief Musician." That is the preface to fifty-seven Psalms, and means that they were for use in public, and so it was written for the Chief Musician, who was responsible for the public worship of the sacred Psalm.

Then, of course, it is an old debatable subject as to what exactly is meant by that little word "Selah." It occurs again and again. Whatever it means, whatever the particular value of it, one thing is certain—it was a musical term. We notice it is connected with a pause, indicating a new beginning. It is a musical term, something like singers used to show where they might pause. In certain of our hymn books you will find down the margin of the page the musical terms, "f.," "ff." or "pp " You do not always observe them if you see them, but nevertheless they are there! And so Selah was a musical term.

Going through the Book of Psalms, you will see that some of them were by, or for, as the case may be, the sons of Korah. By another reference in the Old Testament, we learn that the sons of Korah were set over the service of song in the House of the Lord.

And then, of course, there is Asaph, who was David's principal musician concerned with the music and the adaptability of the music to the words. Some Psalms tell of the occasion for which they were written; for instance, the Dedication of the Temple. Suffice it to say that the Psalms are lyrical poetry. I am always a little chary of explaining things that everyone knows. Most people are familiar with this word, so I am not telling you, I am reminding you. What does lyrical mean? If I had a class of boys, I would ask them and let them tell me. It simply means written for the lyre. Notice the spelling of that word! Written to be accompanied by the lyre, and "lyrical" just means set to music. These are all Psalms set to music, and lyrical poetry is poetry expressing the individual emotions of the soul and set to music.

I spoke of the Book of Psalms as containing five books. The dating of these books is very wonderful. Taking up the Psalter, we can note the dating of the Psalms which, by the way, is not Christian but Hebrew. Each book ends with the Doxology; and if we study the Doxology and the names of God employed there, it is seen how the Doxology catches and summarizes and thunders forth the great masterly thought of that particular book. The book is preeminently the book of worship.

Now, to take the general atmosphere: the Book of the Psalms—as we have already stated, and I want to say it again in this connection—is the book in which the emotions of the human soul find expression. Whatever your mood, and I suppose you have changing moods as well as I do, if you could tell me sincerely and accurately, I can find you a Psalm that will help to express it. Are you glad? I can find you a Psalm that you can sing. Are you sad? I can find you a Psalm that will suit that occasion. Are you mad (I do not mean beside yourself, but angry)? I can find you a Psalm that will suit that occasion.

Dr. Joseph Parker once said that if any man could invent a form of words that could be used by the clergy under circumstances of great provocation, he would confer a lasting benefit upon that order. I do not want you to invent a form of that kind, for I can find something that can express anything, whether it be about the persecution of the Jews, or the brutalities of dictatorship. The Psalms range over the whole gamut of human emotions. Yes, but now hear me carefully. They were all written for us in the consciousness of and in the sense of the presence of God. I do not care who the writer was, or whether—as I think is true in the majority of cases—it was David himself, or whether Hezekiah or whether Asaph or the son of Korah, every singer has poured out the emotions of his soul in the presence of God. Herein the Book of the Psalms is differentiated from every other volume of poetry you have ever read. And you cannot find any other collection of poems of which this is true. In every one of these Psalms, from the first to the last, whatever the particular tone, whether major or minor, the singer is conscious of God. That gives peculiar character to the Book of Psalms.

What is their purview? their scope? what do they cover? The singers are looking at past history, at existing conditions, and at prophetic hopes. They are looking back, looking round, and looking on. All these things are to be found in the Book of Psalms.

Then mark their infinite variety. As to method, some of these Psalms are addressed to God directly; some are meditations of the soul in its loneliness, but always remembering God, always realizing Him; they are meditations on life and circumstances.

Then mark the variety in tone that appears in this book. I only touch upon two of the things that characterize it: honesty and emotional consciousness. That is the wonder of it all. If they are perplexed, they say so honestly, and they say so to God; and what they have to say about God, they say to God. These singers are perfectly honest about their disappointments, their disillusionments. They are perfectly honest about sin and their sense of sin. Look at some of the Psalms which we call penitential and read them through; there is no mistaking of sin, no suggesting that it is a shadow cast by turning, or the underside of good, or such neurotic humbug as is reserved for the degenerate period in which we are living. Sin is sin. "Against thee, thee only have I sinned." There is the greatest word of all found in the Book of Psalms.

Then look at the emotional consciousness of all the subjects. Some of the Psalms are dirges, some of them are glorious peans of praise; and some of them show, in the course of their writing or singing or utterance, a change from one emotion to another. Remember how the Psalmist says on one occasion at the beginning of his Psalm: "At what time I am afraid I will trust in thee." Go on, and by the time he is at the end of the Psalm, he is getting a great deal higher than that for he says at the end, "I will trust and not be afraid." And you see the change from "At what time I am afraid I will trust." That is great. I should think that that Psalm was used in a crisis, don't you? I hope from henceforth you will go on to the end of it and say, "I will trust and *not* be afraid." That is just one little passing incident, indicative of the expression of change in the singer during the course of the song.

Now one other thing. The inclusive value of the Psalms is that they are songs of worship. What is worship? The very meaning of the Hebrew word will help you there. It is persistently "bowing down," but it is always persistent in the consciousness that you are in the presence of the Superior and the Supreme. That is worship. You are not worshiping if you are standing erect and singing Psalms cheerfully. It is worship when you bow in the presence of God, not in slavish fear, but in enduring wonder and submission. That is the value of these Psalms: that you are bowing, that you are adoring God. And you can be honest with Him and cry out, "O Lord, how long?" And you reveal the agony of your heart, as these Psalms do, and yet you are worshiping all the time. And all the earth is called upon to worship.

The attitudes of worship are revealed here. What are they? Fear, and I suppose there is always a little reluctance to use the word, and yet we must go on using it because the wisdom books teach and emphasize the value of it. "The fear of the Lord is the beginning of wisdom." That does not mean something cringing and cowardly, but that awe that holds the soul in check and in poise, because of His majesty and glory. And you will find all that in the Psalms. That is the completeness of the wonderful collection of poems here, marvelous expressions of every mood of the human soul, always in the presence of God.

Then, for a brief consideration, turn over to the Song of Solomon, or Canticles. It was used by the Hebrews in their religious services on the fifth day of the Passover; that means that to the Hebrew people, at any rate, the Song of Solomon had its allegorical interpretation. They would not have used it in their worship if it had been merely and purely a human love song. It is that, but they understood that it had some deeper meaning. What is the theme? First, love; the love of man to woman. It was an Eastern love song. There is no need to deny that. What is the idea of the book? The man who says it is a love song and nothing more, and therefore has no value, is wrong. It is a song celebrating the holiest emotions and possibilities of human life—love, and love between man and woman in the foreground; but, as I believe undoubtedly was in the mind of the writer of the song (and certainly in the understanding of the Hebrew expositors, and equally certain in the interpretation of all the early Church fathers) it is a sacramental song representing the love of God for His people.

We recall how that figure was used by prophets: "I have betrothed thee unto me for ever," and so on—until in the early Church it came to be symbolical of the love of Christ for His Church, and then the love of Christ for the individual Christian. That was St. Augustines definition of the book's value. And so it has its place in the higher reaches of worship. Of course, this is the supreme passage on love. Let those who know literature generally see if they can find another. This is the crown of literature.

> Set me as a seal upon thy heart
> As a seal upon thine arm:
> For love is strong as death;
> Jealousy is cruel as the grave;
> The flashes thereof are flashes of fire,
> A very flame of the Lord.
> Many waters cannot quench love,
> Neither can floods drown it:
> If a man would give all the substance
> of his house for love,
> He would utterly be contemned.

Is there any greater passage on love, if you speak of love merely of the man and the woman? But if you lift it, then you see that it is truly great. It is an outstanding passage in the supreme value of the whole book, whether the story is of the bridal or the betrothal. You find it in the relationship between Solomon and the Shulammite, and if it is studied it gives an interpretation of love. What is the foundation of love between two? Mutual satisfaction. I did not say attraction. I said satisfaction. That is a very different matter. It is eternal, it is indissoluble. Its methods? the marvelous merging and mastery and yielding. Its exercises are so: and its experience—perfect rest, perfect joy and perfect kindness. This is the great Book of Canticles and of worship.

In conclusion, I would remind you of the great value of psalmody in worship. The Hebrew people were a singing people. The Christian Church is a singing society, and I do not agree with Christian people who, for any reason, try to silence the voice of music in their worship. They have been weakened by that silence.

You remember Paul said: "Be filled with the spirit…" true, that is the beginning "…speaking one to another in psalms and hymns and spiritual songs, singing and making melody with your heart to the Lord" (Ephesians 5:19). Let your song come from the heart. And Paul says the same thing in the Letter to the Colossians 3:16, only he begins with this: "Let the word of Christ dwell in you richly," and then he goes on to the same teaching. Be filled with the spirit, be filled with the indwelling word; then let the song be uttered. And don't miss that remarkable declaration of one of the Psalms. "Whoso," says God, "offers praise glorifieth me." Don't forget it! When a Christian assembly rises to sing, and the song is a song of adoration, we are glorifying God.

This is a wonderful collection of literature, the worship books of the Hebrew people.

19. NAHUM, HABAKKUK, ZEPHANIAH

In this study of the second group of Prophets, as we draw to the end of our examination of the Old Testament, we are next concerned with the books of Nahum, Habakkuk and Zephaniah. And once again in these three we have a revelation of the activities of God. I want to glance at each of them briefly.

First, the Prophet Nahum. I am inclined to say that at the moment I am slightly perplexed that in this particular age and in this period when the authority of the Old Testament is called in question in many quarters, I have never found any very definite attack upon the Prophet Nahum. Let it be said immediately that amongst all the prophets he is the most terrific and the most terrible. Perhaps it is a hopeful sign that this book has not been attacked.

Now if we look at this prophecy, what about its dating? No date is given to us, but it is certain as to the period in which it falls. I am referring for the moment to Chapter 3:8 where the Prophet is addressing the people; talking of the bloody city of Nineveh, he says, "Art thou better than No-amon, that was situate among the rivers, that had the waters round about her; whose rampart was the sea, and her wall was of the sea? Ethiopia and Egypt were her strength, and it was infinite;

Put and Lubim were thy helpers." Now No-amon was another name for Thebes, and evidently the Prophet was looking back to a time when Thebes, in spite of its arrogance, had been swept away, and he is asking Nineveh, "Art thou better than Thebes or No-amon?" Consequently we may know that the prophecy was uttered between the fall of Thebes and Nineveh. The prophecy is a prediction of the fall of the Assyrian power and the overthrow of Nineveh.

The Prophet himself is utterly unknown. I am inclined to think that his name is a suggestive one, for the word simply means "comfort" or "consolation." I think we might take the Hebrew word and translate it in a phrase "full of exceeding comfort." I have said it is a most terrible prophecy, but it must be remembered it was a prophecy concerning Nineveh. It was uttered to the nation of God, and to them it was a message of exceeding comfort. There may be no particular significance in that, but I am inclined to think that it was a prophetic name, gathered from the nature of the message he had to deliver.

What was the historic background between the fall of Thebes and the fall of Nineveh? So far as is known, as we have already seen in our consideration of these historic books, Israel was no more; she had gone into captivity. Judah was threatened by Assyria. The Assyrians were gathering their forces together at the height of their arrogant power: and to really know what I mean by this arrogant power, go to the Book of Isaiah and read Chapter 30. There is a picture of the arrogance of these enemies of the chosen people. That was the period in history; and to these people of Judah, surrounded and threatened by this masterful, arrogant, cruel Assyria, the Prophet came. And he delivered his message, putting the whole thing into a sentence by his declaration to them that Assyria would be completely overthrown and Nineveh utterly destroyed.

What do we find in this book? It has one subject, and that is the terrifying aspect of it, but it is very definite. That clear-cut subject is the vengeance of God. Reading it all through, it may perhaps evoke almost a little inclination to wonderment. Yet it is a clear revelation of the eternal truth concerning God. It is a picture of the activity of God in retribution and in vengeance. There is a threefold vision granted to the Prophet and declared by him to the nation. The first is a picture of Jehovah Himself. It is immediately followed by a picture of Jehovah in anger. That leads, of course, to the picture of Jehovah acting in anger. There is the theme of the book from beginning to end.

Referring to the revelation of Jehovah in anger, here is a very simple thing, but it is interesting. Take the opening section in which there is the revelation of Jehovah, and notice how it opens—"The Lord [Jehovah] is a jealous God and avengeth; the Lord avengeth and is full of wrath; the Lord taketh vengeance on his adversaries, and he reserveth wrath for his enemies. The Lord is slow to anger, and great in power, and will by no means dear the guilty: the Lord hath his way in the whirlwind and in the storm, and the clouds are the dust of his feet." Right through the whole of that first section in which the Prophet is describing Jehovah Himself,

Jehovah is angry. And we find this simple thing to which I was referring, and yet a remarkable thing: in the course of that brief opening paragraph, there are seven words which the Prophet uses to describe this particular attitude of God as accounting for His activity in the case of Nineveh.

What are the words? "Jealous"; "vengeance"; "wrath"; "anger"; "indignation"; "fierceness"; "fury." We can go through the whole of the Old Testament and find here and there many references to these aspects of the divine character and the divine activity; but every Hebrew word is pressed by the Prophet into this brief section in describing this tremendous truth about God. Every one is suggestive and has a distinct picture value. "Jealous," "vengeance": they deal with the emotions. Vengeance is volitional. "Wrath," a common word, and yet what a remarkable word. The Hebrew word for it means "crossing over"; God, taking up a new attitude on the realization of certain facts. "Anger" is a pictorial word. "Indignation" is the twin word to anger. "Fierceness" and "fury" are words that vibrate, and they are used to describe the attitude and the activities of God.

Why was God jealous, why was God a God of vengeance? Why this wrath and anger and indignation and fierceness and fury? Why? Because, to put it bluntly and simply, this city of Nineveh had repented of its repentance. This prophecy was uttered just about a hundred years after Jonah had visited Nineveh. We remember the story of Jonah going to Nineveh to proclaim the word of the Lord most unwillingly, and yet he proclaimed it. And as the result, the king and the rulers and the whole city were halted in their iniquity and a fast was proclaimed; they repented and Nineveh was spared. Within forty days Nineveh was to be destroyed—that was Jonah's message. A hundred years had passed, and Nineveh had not been destroyed.

There is a sidelight that is very important: God changes His dates. Just before Jesus left His disciples they asked Him, "Dost thou at this time restore the kingdom to Israel?" So many people today are dating and fixing things. And what was our Lords reply to the disciples' question? He told them, "It is not for you to know times and seasons [mark it carefully] which the Father hath set" (or "the Father hath fixed"). Paul, speaking to the apostles, said the same thing. Jesus used the expression, Paul used it, and it is to be found in our Old Testament: "He ehangeth the times and the seasons." So do not get out a little calendar and fall into the stupid blunder of trying to find out dates. Leave them alone. They are not our business. God changes them. Forty days, and Nineveh shall be destroyed! And it was not destroyed in forty days. God changed His date. Why? Because Nineveh changed her attitude as the result of His message, and repented.

And a hundred years have run their course, and in that process the city of Nineveh has repented of its repentance, and the picture is one of utter cruelty and diabolical oppression. The cup of her iniquity is absolutely full, and all the nations are realizing the appalling pressure of her arrogance. That is why God was angry. The cup of her iniquity is full. And you will find what that means: her sin against God, her arrogance against God, her challenge to God. In Chapter 50 of Isaiah the people were warned against thinking that God would care more for them than for any nation—that was the great sin of Israel. I think that is the trouble with many of us just now. God is always against any nation and any ruler who, in pride and arrogance, lifts himself up and challenges God. Judgment may be long delayed, but it is as inevitable as God is God. That is the sin.

And the result? Mark how these things—shall I say, hang together. First the sin of Nineveh, proud and arrogant and challenging and rebelling against the fact of God's everlasting government. And secondly, there is the result of that sin, the sin against men in cruelty and oppressive mastery. These two things always go together. Any nation or any ruler in history who has become arrogant enough to deny the government of God has become cruel and despotic and brutal, indulging in every form of cruelty that was in them. And that is why Nineveh was destroyed.

Those who have been over there may have actually visited the place where Nineveh stood. She was swept out, wiped away by God in retribution. He waits until the cup is full, and then He makes, as the Prophet says, a full and a complete end. And every word the Prophet uses to describe the anger of God is needed, every word is justified, and even in their combination they only show what the wrath of God actually is. I am so thankful to have Nahum, and to know that the God who is governing is that kind of God. But that is not all this prophecy teaches. Did you notice in it that "the Lord is slow to anger"? That is perfectly true. Did you notice that "The Lord is good, a stronghold in the day of trouble; and he knoweth them that put their trust in him. But with an over-running flood he will make a full end of the place thereof." Yes, He is slow to anger, but when the limits have been passed and the cup of iniquity is full, thank God, He is a God of vengeance.

We turn now to Habakkuk, and there is a sense in which we need not tarry long with it because it is so well-known and so wonderful a book. Glance at it briefly. What does it reveal supremely? I am asking that question carefully. It reveals the discipline of God, His method of disciplining His own.

What is the date? That is unknown, but probably before the downfall of Babylon. Who is the Prophet? He is unknown. His name only occurs in the superscription. Nothing more is known about him than that.

But we do know the historic background. We get the picture of it in the opening part of this prophecy. Remember now that the opening paragraph gives the most appalling condition of the national life. In all probability this prophecy was uttered after the death of Hezekiah in the last years of the later part of the reign of Manasseh and Amon. We must refer to the historic books to find out the character of those reigns. It is found in II Kings: 21 and 22 where there is revealed the appalling condition of affairs. I am not concerned, however, with the historic statements there found, although they are important, but with what this Prophet says about them. Listen! I want to mention certain things. Let me name them separately.

He speaks of "violence." That is the one great word. "How long shall I cry, and thou wilt not hear? I cry unto thee of violence and thou wilt not save." Violence! Iniquity, perverseness, spoiling, strife, contention! "The law is slacked, and judgment doth never go forth [judgment failing to be exercised]; for the wicked doth compass about the righteous." There is more of it, and it all shows the condition of national life when Habakkuk exercised his ministry. Now, with that condition creating a problem in the mind of this man—who may have been, who must have been evidently a man who knew God, and who lived in fellowship with God—we can almost hear his anguish.

It was the fact that he knew God that created his greatest trouble. In the opening prophecy he is telling the story of his own experience. Of course, Habakkuk is a story of experience, just as Jonah was, and he has written for his people the story of his own experience, telling them how these conditions trouble him. Indeed, it is not so much the trouble, but the fact of these conditions. And though he is troubled by them, what is troubling him is this: he has cried to God and had no answer. As we listen to the appalling state of affairs, he does not see that God is anywhere interfering or acting. "Behold ye among the nations, and regard, and wonder marvelously; for I work a work in your days, which ye will not believe though it be told you." Habakkuk said in effect—I say it reverently—"God is doing nothing. What is He doing? Why doesn't He do something?" Don't be angry with him. Some of us have said the same thing in recent years. And God's answer, in effect, is this: "It is not correct that I am negative. It is not correct that I am doing nothing. I am working, I am at work and you will wonder, and you will wonder marvelously. I shall do so strange a thing that you won't believe it though I tell it to you." What is it? What art Thou doing? if I may reverently imagine I am addressing God in place of Habakkuk. We cannot see any results. What art Thou doing?

What was God doing? He was employing another nation, raising up the Chaldeans to scourge His own people on account of their wrongdoing. He was causing its armies to move in, as they did move in, and causing them to act on His behalf for the cleansing of that nation of its sin, for its dire and disastrous and final punishment. God's method of discipline! Yet that puzzled the Prophet more than ever. He could not understand it. It was because, as I have said, he knew God so well, that he says, "Art not thou from everlasting, O Lord my God, my Holy One?" He cannot understand how God can use a nation like that to the accomplishment of His purpose.

And that led to the next answer of God, and in that answer He declared the eternal principle underlying all life, whether national or individual. When the Prophet has told God that he did not understand what seemed to him a greater problem in God's answer, he said, "I will stand upon my watch, and set me upon the tower, and will look forth to see what he will speak with me, and what I shall answer concerning my complaint. And the Lord answered me, and said, Write the vision, and make it plain upon tablets, that he may run that readeth it [not as we rendered it, that he that runs may read]. For the vision is yet for the appointed time, and it hasteth toward the end, and shall not he: though it tarry, wait for it."

See how God has called him to wait! And then this: "Behold, his soul is puffed up [that is the whole nation of the Chaldeans], it is not upright in him; but the just shall five by his faith."

The declaration of an eternal principle in a contrast. Oh, yes, the Chaldeans are coming, but this is not the end. God is using them. They are puffed up, arrogant, rebellious; but He is employing them. The puffed up are always coming to an end, but the just shall live by his faith. The method of the divine discipline is the overruling of the wrath of man, and the employment of it in His own service. So He raised up the Chaldeans, that bitter and hasty nation; but the eternal truth proved the end of Chaldea and the end of the puffed up, but the righteous shall live by their faith.

Let us glance at the last of these three prophets, Zephaniah. The date of Zephaniah is very clearly marked for us in the opening statement: "The word of the Lord which came unto Zephaniah the son of Cushi, the son of Gedaliah, the son of Amariah, the son of Hezekiah, in the days of Josiah the son of Amon, king of Judah." Hezekiah had passed, Manasseh's long reign was over, Amon's short reign was at an end, and Josiah was reigning when this prophet arose. Notice that he was in kingly descent. I suppose, to use our language, he was the great grandson of Hezekiah, of royal blood. He seems to have inherited the loyalties, not of his father or his grandfather but of Hezekiah. So this was the Prophet Zephaniah.

What was the historic background? It was a remarkable story. He states here he gave himself to a very vigorous and wonderful attempt to recall the nation. He was very popular. The book of the Law had been discovered and had been reopened by Josiah. Before he started his great service, he went to consult a woman who was a prophetess, Huldah. Huldah received him and told him this remarkable thing: that what he had in his heart to do was right and good, but that there would be no value in it. It is possible to produce a comparative reformation upon the ground of popularity with a nation, but there will be no heart-turning to God. But he went on to do his work, and a wonderful work it was; and this man Zephaniah prophesied through that period.

I repeat, as to historic background, there was considerable reform under Josiah. And here is the remarkable thing: Zephaniah makes no distinct reference to these reforms, as we read his story, although they seem to have been very varied and drastic. But they were trivial. And this prophet, with the same straight insight that characterized Hezekiah, saw that there was no value in them, no real turning to God. So he gives this prophecy in which he sets forth first the sovereignty of God. The keynote of Zephaniah is found there, "the day of the Lord." Joel made great use of that phrase, and Zephaniah uses the same words.

But he sees more than that, for he sees the day of the Lord, the government of God, the authority and activity of God; and he saw that government and that activity operating in two ways. Turn first to Chapter 1:2: "I will utterly consume things [nations] from off the face of the ground, saith the Lord." Now read 2:1,4: "Gather yourselves together, yea, gather together, O nation that hath no shame… For Gaza shall be forsaken, and Ashkelon a desolation; they shall drive out Ashdod at noonday, and Ekron shall be rooted up." Come to 3:17: "The Lord thy God is in the midst of thee, a mighty one who will save; he will rejoice over thee with joy; he will rest in his love; he will joy over thee with singing. I will gather them that sorrow for the solemn assembly, who were of thee."

You can put these texts together—the very desperation of the prophecy: "I will utterly consume all things from off the face of the ground"; and "The Lord thy God in the midst of thee… he will rejoice over thee with joy… he will joy over thee with singing." These texts stand in the most remarkable contrast.

With very profound respect I want to say this: that even so scholarly and profound and eminent an interpreter as George Adam Smith says that Zephaniah must have been the work of two prophets, because it would be impossible for any one to say two such contradictory things. With profound respect I say that I think the learned professor failed entirely in his understanding. These two things are definitely and always found in God: His sovereignty and His goodness. Nahum celebrates that side in which He will consume all things, but there is always a reason for it; it is when the cup of iniquity is full.

But it is equally true, of course, and I think there is nothing more beautiful in Bible literature than that description of God: "He will rejoice over thee with joy… he will joy over thee with singing." That is the most exquisite picture of motherhood. Look at the mother with her child. She rejoices over it with joy. She is silent in her love until silence becomes vocal and she sings to the child. That is God. And in this one little prophecy we have these two things brought together in the most pregnant way, the sovereignty of God and the goodness of God: and they are the two aspects of the one nature.

Glancing over these three prophets, what do I find? I find when I read Nahum this very remarkable fact emerging at the end. Let me state it first: that God does act, and in their profound judgment men agree with the righteousness of what He has done. Notice how Nahum ends: "Thy shepherds slumber, O king of Assyria; thy nobles are at rest; thy people are scattered upon the mountains, and there is none to gather them. There is no assuaging of thy hurt; thy wound is grievous: all that hear the report of thee clap their hands over thee; for upon whom hath not thy wickedness passed continually?" All the nations agree with the righteous action of God in the overthrow of Nineveh.

I learn too as I look at these three prophets that no nation is outside His compelling government, for He will use them.

As I have already said, He will make the wrath of man to praise Him, and the remainder He will restrain.

The sovereignty and the goodness of God are the twin aspects of the One Being of God.

20. JEREMIAH

We are getting near the end of the section contained in the Old Testament, and at present we are considering that section concerned with the Didactic writings, the quest for the prophet. We have reached the prophecy of Jeremiah. To read Jeremiah means that we must also read Lamentations, for one cannot study Jeremiah and leave out his Lamentations. In thinking of the whole message contained in the book, I wonder what effect it has had. It has had a remarkable effect upon me as I have gone through it again. I say "again" because I have been in some senses strangely influenced by this prophecy for many years.

Indeed, in my publications you will find this influence. In the *Analysed Bible* there is a chapter given to its content, and in addition, a chapter to its essential message. And when I take up the Book of Jeremiah, I do so not only with some amount of familiarity, but also with an abiding sense of having been almost always in the presence of this book, and I think that sense has been deepened as I have gone over the book again.

Jeremiah stands out to me, among all the prophets of the Old Testament, as far and away the most striking. Of course, a statement like that may lead to a man being charged with differentiating between the value of this book of the Bible and that book of the Bible. I submit I am doing nothing of the kind. I am speaking of the heroism of this man Jeremiah. There are senses in which Isaiah may be a greater book. But if you take these commonly called Major Prophets or the Minor, this man stands out as the most marvelous in his heroism.

As we approach the book let us glance at three things: first of all noticing the dating, then trying to look at the man himself, and then, of course, considering his message. I won't say "his messages," for that would be too great a subject for us here, but the great message of the book itself.

For the dating we go to the beginning of the book, and read these words in Chapter 1:1-2: "The words of Jeremiah the son of Hilkiah, of the priests that were in Anathoth in the land of Benjamin: to whom the word of the Lord came in the days of Josiah the son of Amon, king of Judah, in the thirteenth year of his reign." There is the plain dating of the prophecy. When we remember the historic movement represented by that dating we shall find that he leaves out two kings in the list. He mentions Josiah, Jehoiakim and Zedekiah, but he omits Jehoahaz and Jehoiachin. I do not know that there is any significance in that except that their reigns were trivial, insignificant and unimportant. Between Josiah and Jehoiakim, Jehoahaz occupied the throne only for three months. Then again between Jehoiakim and Zedekiah, Jehoiachin reigned, and was deposed after three months; those two kings were unimportant men, occupying the throne for a total of only six months. Those kings named reigned for a very long space of time, at the very least for forty years. Consider the period during which this man exercised his ministry. It was during the last period of forty years of Judah's history. Here is Jeremiah, in that period in the history of Judah until Judah was actually carried away, and the mere fact that Jeremiah gives messages delivered after the fall of Jerusalem shows that he himself had been carried away to captivity. He began in Josiah's reign toward the end, or at least when he had been on the throne for thirteen years in that period of reformation. It is well to have that in mind. Josiah had become a very popular young king, and the people were greatly attracted by him. Then the Law was discovered, and he passionately desired to bring on the reformation. Before Josiah started on his reformation he visited the prophetess Huldah and laid open his heart before her and sought her advice. She was a woman of vision, a seer, and she told him to go on, that he was perfectly right in his desire, but she warned him that no permanent result would follow; that in the reformation the people would follow him because they loved him and not because they loved God or His Law. Very frankly she told Josiah what would happen. Nevertheless, he went on loyally, but unsuccessfully. It emerges, if you read Jeremiah carefully, that he saw this service of reformation, and began his ministry in that period.

Then he went through the period under Jehoiakim which was utterly and appallingly evil, when the people returned to every form of corruption and idolatry. Then Jeremiah still went on in the reign of Zedekiah. What was there to say about Zedekiah? Simply this: he was vacillating; in all probability a man of intense vacillation all the way through, and the people already a vassal of another nation. See what was happening. Gradually the national life was passing away entirely, and the people were moving swiftly, rapidly down the steep of depravity that led to ruin and national extinction. The time was approaching when they were carried away into slavery. When we realize that Jeremiah was preaching throughout the whole of that period, we begin to understand what is meant by speaking of the heroism of Jeremiah.

Just for a moment or two look at the man himself. We are told in the opening paragraph that he was the son of Hilkiah. There is a question arising here which I am not at all able to answer dogmatically. Who was his father? You will remember that in the time of Josiah the book of the Law was discovered by the priest Hilkiah. It was at least possible, personally I think it is probable, that Jeremiah was the son of that very priest Hilkiah who discovered the book of the Law. Have you ever thought of the significance of the fact that the book of the Law was hidden, that it was not known about in those earliest years of Josiah's reign when he was a boy? It was hidden in the Temple precincts. And it would appear as if the book were discovered—if I dare use the word—accidentally, and the man who discovered it aroused in Josiah a great desire to bring about a reformation.

We know that Jeremiah was born a priest. That is distinctly declared. Not only the son of a priest, but he was himself a priest and he dwelt at Anathoth. The Book of Joshua,

Chapter 21, gives you a list of the cities of the priests and Anathoth was one. There Jeremiah lived. He was of the priestly order, and a reference he gives makes us believe that he began his prophetic ministry when he was thirty years old. Now you know that at thirty a priest entered into the full office of priesthood. Here is a case in which it was declared from the beginning what was to be his work: the prophetic utterance in the name of God. So we see the man in that way. His call to the prophetic office was one of the most remarkable things on record: "Now the word of the Lord came unto me, saying, Before I formed thee in the belly I knew thee, and before thou earnest forth out of the womb I sanctified thee; I have appointed thee a prophet unto the nations." Here is the man who was foreordained. Before he was born—known; before he was born—sanctified; known by the Lord, sanctified by God, ordained to be Gods messenger amongst the nations, to be a prophet. He was equipped by God and appointed by God. Here the characteristics of the man are very simply revealed.

First of all, he possessed a great simplicity as shown in his answer when the word of the Lord was spoken to him. When the truth of the meaning of his life burst upon him, that it was the divine appointment, he said: "Ah, Lord God! behold, I cannot speak: for I am a child." There is the keynote, and if it is followed through carefully you see it as the music revealing his character always, simplicity. The Lord said unto him: "Say not, I am a child; for to whomsoever I shall send thee thou shalt go, and whatsoever I shall command thee thou shalt speak. Be not afraid because of them; for I am with thee to deliver thee, saith the Lord. Then the Lord put forth his hand, and touched my mouth; and the Lord said unto me, Behold, I have put my words in thy mouth; see, I have this day set thee over the nations and over the kingdoms, to pluck up and to break down and to destroy and to overthrow, to build and to plant." And God gave two signs to him: the sign of the almond tree and the seething caldron. From the very beginning we see the sensitiveness of this man.

The first thirteen chapters of the book are occupied with the story of the process of his training for the full prophetic office. I do not mean to say none of his utterances are recorded during the first thirteen chapters. They are; and yet as we watch, he is being prepared; and again and again we see him shrinking from what he has to deliver to Assyria, shrinking from the sense of the judgment he is bringing and the terror of what that really meant. He is shrinking all the way through, not only in these thirteen chapters. It is found again and again in the book.

Now mark this carefully: wherever you find Jeremiah shrinking, holding back, wishing to escape, it is when he is alone with God. We never find him shrinking when he is confronting the nation, confronting men—no shrinking then! What a wonderful revelation of a man who, overwhelmed with the greatness and the supreme importance of the terrible and terrifying work he is called upon by God to do, shrinks under a sense of his own unworthiness and incompetence: but when he does so, he is with God, and he is talking to God and dealing with God. He was always

conscious that he was a child, but when he heard the voice of God he was no more a child, but a divine messenger. When he came out from the divine presence and faced kings, and rulers and priests and the people, there was no shrinking. He was a singular man, possessing simplicity, sensitiveness, and strength.

And now, after forty years, at the end of his ministry as a prophet of God, knowing that there would be no results (and there were no results from the national standpoint), persecuted, imprisoned, laughed at, scorned, hated, he went through with it. That is heroism. I wonder if any brother in the ministry is depressed, disappointed, after a long time of seeing no results. You have nothing to do with results. You have only one thing to do: preach the word, and deliver the message, and if you are conscious of what that means, you will know what it is when you are alone in the inner chamber with a shut door, trembling in the presence of God, to feel sometimes that you cannot go on. But you will go on. And that is Jeremiah. He went on with his preaching; and when the crash came he went on. He went down, actually down into Egypt, and talked with the people; he still carried on in the presence of danger.

Summarizing in the briefest way what we find here as the message of Jeremiah, we see his persistent denunciations, his persistent lamentations, and his constant proclamations. His discourses all move in these directions.

First, the denunciations. What is meant by that? He was declaring, in spite of the false prophets and the policy of the politicians, that the object of his preaching was God's judgment, which must fall and was about to fall upon them for their sin. He declares the judgment of God. And it is noticeable that he uses a remarkable figure of speech where he speaks of the nation as being a degenerate vine. Again and again he referred to it, showing that the vine must be destroyed. Egypt and Assyria will be set against each other. And Jeremiah stands fast to the fact that in spite of their policies and their clevernesses, God's judgment is about to fall, and it is inevitable because of their sin.

Notice it also running through Lamentations. I do not hesitate to speak of these Lamentations as a revelation of God's suffering in the presence of sin. Listen to this: "Oh, that my head were waters, and mine eyes a fountain of tears." Why? "That I might weep day and night for the slain of the daughter of my people!" But they are slain as the result of the judgments of God upon their sin. That does not matter. That is the heart of Jeremiah. Is it not a revelation of the heart of God? The fulfillment of that according to Jeremiah is long, long after. Our thoughts fly to it when God in Christ looked at Jerusalem and wept over it—doomed Jerusalem, and yet He wept. "O Jerusalem, Jerusalem, how often would I have gathered thee as a hen doth gather her chickens beneath her wings." "I would have gathered ye, and ye would not." The weeping Christ! But it does not interfere with judgment. "Behold, your house is left unto you desolate." Ah, yes, but that was said through tears. "Oh, that my head were waters!" And through all the Lamentations this man knew what it is to hold communion with God so definitely and so honestly that he could tell God his trouble and his shrinking; he so breathed the very spirit of God that in his tears there was revelation, and the Lamentations are a revelation of the fact—the stupendous fact that is difficult for us to understand but which nevertheless abides as a fact—that sin causes suffering to God.

And yet all through you will find proclamations; and if in his denunciations we have the revelation of God's judgment on sin, in his Lamentations we have the revelation of God's suffering for sin, in his proclamations constantly is the revelation of the sovereignty of God. And upon this bedrock of the divine sovereignty he built in hope.

The sovereignty of God! God said to him one day, not "Go to the Temple," but "Go to the house of the potter." A strange thing to send a prophet to a potter's house. But God told him he would see a wonderful thing there. What did he see? The sovereignty of God. The potter made a work on the wheels and it was marred in the hand of the potter. Have you got the music of it? The divine sovereignty and the divine grace. And because of that, Jeremiah was a prophet who proclaimed not only dark, mysterious judgment, wailing messages of sorrow, but such messages of hope. Chapters 30, 31, 32, 33 were messages of the prophet when he was in prison. And when you remember that, notice that in these four chapters, five times over this phrase occurs: "Behold, the days come, saith the Lord." What days? The days of restoration and renewal. And so out of dungeon darkness this daring, intrepid soul sang the great songs of hope which you find in these four chapters. Songs of hope! Aren't you glad that Paul was put in prison? Think of the letters he wrote. Aren't you glad that John Bunyan was put in prison? Out of that prison came *Pilgrim's Progress.*

We need to be a Paul or a Bunyan or a Jeremiah—I do not mean in any greatness but in the littleness and the humility and the fellowship with God that these men had—if we are ever going to be able to sing the Lord's song in the strange land about us. That is what Jeremiah did. This is a wonderful book, with its thunders and its messages of destruction; with its disintegrating forces that plot and blast away individually or nationally, and are lying there unseen—and sooner or later there will be the harvest.

And then this amazing book shows you, as others do, that sin wounds the heart of God. But, thank God, I learn from this great and marvelous ministry that the final victory is going to be, not with sin, but with God.

21. DANIEL, EZEKIEL

We have reached Daniel and Ezekiel. I have put them in that order because the dating of Daniel is earlier than that of Ezekiel. To discover the date of the Book of Daniel, read Chapter 1:1,2: "In the third year of the reign of Jehoiakim king of Judah came Nebuchadnezzar king of Babylon unto Jerusalem, and besieged it. And the Lord gave Jehoiakim king of Judah into his hand, with part of the vessels of the house of God; and he carried them into the land of Shinar to the house of his god; and he brought the vessels into the treasure-

house of his god." And it was at this time in connection with that invasion of Nebuchadnezzar that Daniel was carried captive, so you have the dating there.

Ezekiel opens with these words: "It came to pass in the thirtieth year" [which is undoubtedly a reference to the age of Daniel] "in the fourth month, in the fifth day of the month, as I was among the captives by the river Chebar, that the heavens were opened, and I saw visions of God. In the fifth day of the month, which was the fifth year of King Jehoiachin's captivity." That gives the first note in the dating of Ezekiel. He was carried away under Jehoiachin. Daniel was among those who were carried away under the reign of Jehoiakim; Ezekiel was carried away under the reign of Jehoiachin. It is a little difficult to distinguish between these two kings as the spelling is very similar. You have that reference in Daniel to the period and all the subsequent dates in Daniel are pagan dates, but there is no other date of the kings of Judah, no other date by the history of God's ancient people. Ezekiel was taken into captivity in the reign of Jehoiachin, eight years later. And you will find all the way through the first date is connected with the fact of the captivity.

So really the background of history herein is changed from anything we have noticed before. In dealing with Jeremiah we saw the approach of this period, we saw the last forty years in the history of Judah as a nation, forty years in which Judah was moving swiftly down the declivity to her ruin and the ending of her national life. All that we are looking at now in these prophecies occurred in that period after Judah had lost her national position entirely and become subject and been carried away into captivity.

Thus the Kingdom of Judah as an organized nation is out of sight both in Daniel and Ezekiel. But, of course, the people are not out of sight; they are in sight from beginning to end. There was a period of seventy years in which these people were in captivity until they returned again; and when they did return, I may remind you that they never had a king. There was a certain sense in which they had a constituted national life after they returned, but they never had a king.

Now we are at that period of the captivities, both when we are reading Daniel and when we are reading Ezekiel. In the Book of Daniel (I want to repeat and to emphasize it), the background of history you get is wholly and completely pagan. Using an expression of our own age, you may say that the background of history is that of the great powers of the world at that time. Judah had ceased to become a power in any sense, not only religiously but politically. Judah, God's ancient people, had passed into captivity. The great ruling powers of the world were Babylon, then Media, then Persia. This is the background of Daniel and it is well to remember it.

Daniel himself never seems to be particularly concerned about the nation of which he was a member by birth and by race. Here we see him moving in these great kingdoms in a most remarkable way. It will readily be agreed that Daniel stands out as a most unique man, right from beginning to end, with the most definite relation to the God of his fathers;

never compromising, never lowering the standard of his own relationship to that God. Whether he is speaking to pagan kings or in the general tone and note of prophecy, he stands out as a remarkable man. Then, as you read the story, you notice what is going on before this man Daniel rose to the position of a great minister in these three empires: and as you watch, you will see that in spite of the background of these nations, he rose to his position and influence by reason of his relationship to God and what that meant to him. There is a sense in which there is no more fascinating page in all the Bible than this page that tells of the history of Daniel.

Now when you come to consider his messages, of course the book falls naturally into two parts: six chapters constitute the first part, and six the latter part, and there is a distinct difference in them. In the first six chapters you have Daniels addresses, or perhaps "messages" would be a better word, in chronological sequence, and all are addressed to pagan kings. I cannot help pausing for a moment just to think of all that means. This young man, as he was carried into captivity and almost immediately brought into places where his relationship to his God was being challenged, put himself to a test which was purely material, in the power of his spiritual conviction. And here is this man now standing before great and mighty monarchs. But it is always one of the finest qualifications of the great in certain ways, and of the mighty in certain ways, that God is always limiting, always coming to the end. Make no mistake about that; it is the story of all human history. Yet you see this young man addressing himself to Nebuchadnezzar, then to Belshazzar, and in all his addresses to these pagan kings he brings them face to face with God, and with the fact of God. He does not compromise with them for a moment. He says to Belshazzar in that wonderful sentence that is writ in lines of fire upon the story, having its perpetual application to human nature in its failure, "God, in whose hand thy breath is and whose thou art, hast thou not glorified."

Look at that story, read it again, and think of it. Belshazzar, at the moment drunk, his breath foul with obscenity of every description, carousing in the midst of his leaders, and all of them in the same appalling condition in which they had dared God so far as to use the vessels they had captured from the Jewish people to drink their intoxicating wine. And then we hear Daniel speak, interpreting the writing on the wall. Notice his presentation of God: "The God in whose hand thy breath is." Belshazzar's breath! Why, it is polluted, it is foul. But it does not matter, it is in the hand of God. And the charge against him was that he had failed to glorify that God. Belshazzar knew it. And here was this man standing up and telling pagan kings the message that affirmed the sovereignty and the government of God, and the responsibility of all men to Him, even kings themselves. That is the supreme warning note of Daniel. We have the record of what he said to kings, every one of them having principles of eternal application to the affairs of men. I am so glad in these days that I have nay Old Testament still, and I am watching the goodness of God in human history over all the machinations of men.

In Chapters 7 to 12 you have the stories of dreams and visions. They are not in direct chronological order, as you are told in the reading, because he tells of one happening, and then you come to things which have happened before the one he had already recorded. That does not matter. They constitute revelations of the seers of human history concerning these fallen empires and dynasties, and the great and marvelous consummation. Those who know the Book of Daniel, know full well that this is a very brief and inadequate summary, but it does tell the story of the book in these chapters. If I were to summarize the Book of Daniel I could do it in two sentences: first of all, the messages of Daniel, whether those delivered to pagan kings or those recorded that have been for the people of God, emphasize first the government of God over all kings and all nations; and secondly, they emphasize the fact of the continuity of that government until the consummation in which God's will shall be done, His throne recognized, and the victory be with Him.

I sometimes speak of the Book of Daniel and say that there are two parts of it, the historic note revealed in the first six chapters, and the prophetic light revealed in the last six chapters, in which this man is taken by the visiting angel, the representative of the heavens, and called by him a man "greatly beloved." He delivered the messages of God, he watched the processes of divine government, insisting upon its goodness as a fact. He wrote the story of the process through the ages under the figure of a great image: he told the story that there shall come a stone uncut from the mountains to smash the whole earthly procedure, for the setting up of the Kingdom of God—a truly wonderful picture.

Now, in the date and era to which I have already referred, we glance over Ezekiel. The background of history, as I have said before and repeat again, is wholly that of the captivity. I am looking at Chapter 1:1,2: "In the fifth day of the month, which was the fifth year of King Jehoiachin's captivity, the word of the Lord came expressly unto Ezekiel." That is the first reference to the date. The last is found in Chapter 40:1: "In the five and twentieth year of our captivity." The last date given is in the twenty-fifth year, so that these prophecies of Ezekiel covered a period of at least twenty years between these two dates. If you go through it again and look you will find that no less than seven times he made reference to the captivity, from Chapter 1:1,2 up to Chapter 40:1; in between, he tells the story always relating it to a certain year in the captivity.

So we have that background for Ezekiel as he is seen exercising his ministry in a community of exiles in Babylon at Tel-abib (Chapters 3,15). At the time, the location is marked there very clearly, though there may be difficulty in supposing that now. It does not matter. At Tel-abib on the banks of the Chebar; here is the nation carried into captivity in Persia, living there on the banks of the river Chebar right in Babylon. Evidently they were allowed great freedom, being in a sense self-governing and managing their own affairs, though always under the mastery of their captor. In reading the Prophet's messages and accounts of his meeting with the people, it will be seen that notwithstanding all the discipline of the years of their captivity, these people were falling into the same evil courses that they had followed before they were carried away. Moreover, it is clear that they were sharing the fanatical optimism of the nation that had characterized it during the long period of Jeremiah's ministry. Of course, it will be remembered that Jeremiah was always foretelling judgment to come, that the judgments of God were drawing near. But people did not believe that, and after they were carried away into captivity, numbers of them were still indulging in false optimism, failing to see in their own plight the divine action of judgment. This is the condition.

Now to them this prophet came. He was a priest as Jeremiah was. He was carried away into captivity when he was twenty-five. That is known from the reference at the beginning of Chapter 1 where he spoke of his age. As I verily believe, he was thirty years of age at the beginning of his prophetic work. The city was gone, the Temple was gone, there was no function, but he was called very clearly and definitely to exercise his ministry. He was influenced in his young manhood by Jeremiah. There is no question, as we read the writings, that he had been brought under that influence, and that this fact affected his prophesying. His outlook upon judgment was Jeremiah's. Perhaps if you miss one tiling from Ezekiel which you will find in Jeremiah, it is the tender heart. There is no fountain of tears here, but it is the same message of a man brought up under the influence of Jeremiah. When we say that, we know the deepest truth about him. But something else is true: Ezekiel was a man who evidently had personal dealings with God and personal knowledge of God (the symbolic setting forth of this in Chapter 1 is definite, and it proves that this was so), and in that, Ezekiel was far more than a disciple of Jeremiah.

To summarize: the great burden of Ezekiel is this fact of God, these visions of God, which brought him at last into the place of the ministry. If we were going to compare the prophets—I did it in the case of Jeremiah when I said I thought he was the most heroic of them—I should say Ezekiel had a profounder conception of the facts concerning God than any one of the prophets. His messages were the outcome of visions of God. Chapter 1 proves it. Read again at Chapter 47, and the vision of the dry bones, and others— Chapter 1 ranks with them with that marvelous vision. What a wonderful revelation of God came to him! It is mystic, it is prophetic, admittedly so; and clear as the blazing of the amber. First of all cloud and storm; and then rotating wheels, and then rushing power which he calls the spirit, and then visions, fourfold visions; and then, above all the firmament and seated over all, a man. In the revolving wheels which mark procedure, and in the spirit which marks energy, and in the fourfold presentation left at the heart of it, is the supreme unveiling of God. Four living creatures: one with the face of a man, another with the face of a lion, a third with the face of an ox, and the last with the face of an eagle. Each one had four faces so that whichever way they looked, there was still the face of a man, or a lion, or an ox, or an eagle. Each of them unveils visions of God.

Now it has been said, and I just want to touch upon it in passing, that Ezekiel saw these figures in Babylon, and that these figures typifying life in different forms were to be found in Babylon itself on its temple walls. I am not prepared to deny that. Very likely that is where Ezekiel saw them—I do not know, and no man can prove it. It is one of these suggestions that would seem possible, but supposing it is true? What about it? God, dealing with the Prophet, took these symbols, fulfilling them with might in the revelation of Himself in the eyes of Ezekiel. The face of the man, of the lion, of the ox and the eagle—Babylonish if you like. I am not careful to know, but that is what Ezekiel saw, and seeing it, he saw God.

We are traveling away. We know our Bible. We are in the Book of Revelation, and in that book the Seer is beholding the glory; and he saw four living creatures, exactly the same symbolism, with the same faces of a man, a lion, an ox, and an eagle. Then they typified certain things which came in fulfillment of the fact of God. The *lion* was always the type of kingship and authority and supremacy. The ox everywhere was the type of service and sacrifice. The man was the type of life in its highest form of created manifestation. And the eagle is always the type of *deity* and mastery. These are the things that John saw in Patmos, when gazing upon the glory of the dwellingplace of God and God upon His throne.

And so Ezekiel had visions of God. He saw God, he saw the wheels of procedure, the moving spirit of energy and the unveiling of the personality with the faces of the living creatures. And yet, presently, seated high over all, appeared the form of a man. Ezekiel's understanding of God in His own being and His own nature was more profound than that of any other of the prophets. His supremacy is lowly, stooping, bending to serve, emptying Himself. His revelation of His own nature is seen in a man revealing the mystic marvel of His very Godhead. And Ezekiel saw all these things. He saw that God could act in two ways in the course of prophecy. In Chapter 24 God could act in retribution, in judgment. In Chapters 25 through 48 God is coming to act in restoration. This summarizes the whole message. God is seen acting in retribution because of sin; and on the principles of righteousness His being is supreme. Then God is seen acting in restoration based upon righteousness brought in by the Prophet's ministry. And with mystic visions the whole prophecy ends. All these, simple in their setting, are triumphant in symbolic suggestiveness of wonderful glory. Over the valley of the dry bones the Spirit moves and they come to life. The last thing is the flowing river bringing life wherever it flows.

So the final thing the Prophet had to say was "Jehovah Shammai," "The Lord is there"—the ultimate triumph of God expressed in one of the briefest sentences.

In these two books, with their background of captivity and pagan life, we see God still speaking in spite of human failure, the triumphant Throne of God and its activity in government and yet in grace.

22. HAGGAI, ZECHARIAH, MALACHI

We come to the last of the three books in our Bible, Haggai, Zechariah, and Malachi. And here we find ourselves in some ways in an entirely new atmosphere. In many ways it is the same atmosphere historically and nationally, and yet there is a very marked difference. You will note that the Prophet Haggai and the Prophet Zechariah used dates, but they are pagan dates. They are not the dates of the kings of Israel or of Judah, as we have had them so repeatedly in former studies. As to Malachi, there is no date whatever, and the book can only be placed by deduction.

These three prophecies come at the close of our collection of Hebrew writings. In order to get the background, I think we had better go back for a moment or two and take the history that leads up to the time, and so have clear apprehension of the history behind these three prophets.

It will be remembered that when we considered the historic books of Ezra and Nehemiah we had an account of the return from Babylon, as Jeremiah had clearly foretold. That was the return, not of all the people, for there were many that did not go back, but of a certain section, a remnant. When they arrived there the first thing they did was to erect an altar for worship, and on that altar they offered sacrifices and observed the Feast of Tabernacles which fell due at that time. More than that, they began to build the Temple. How much beyond the foundations were laid I do not know, but they began to build. Then something happened. Opposition was raised against them by the Samaritans, and as a result of that opposition they ceased building the Temple. And that period of the cessation of the building of the Temple lasted for fifteen years. We can imagine that if we start building and get the foundations laid, and begin to build up to a certain height, and then for no reason whatever leave it for fifteen years, at the end of the fifteen years it is overgrown with weeds and possibly covered with rubbish—a ruin.

Now, it was when the Temple was in that condition that Haggai the Prophet arose, and Zechariah. Malachi undoubtedly was later, and to him we will come presently. The people are back. They came back building their altar, offering their sacrifices, observing the Feast of Tabernacles, and setting to work to restore the Temple, the House of God. Then came Haggai and Zechariah, and under the prophetic ministry of these two men the building was resumed, and was completed in five years' time.

Let us look at this wonderful prophecy of Haggai. First of all, bear in mind that this nation which has constituted the background of history over such a long period, all the period of the prophets, is now seen without national constitution. It is a people, but it is no longer a nation; and being without national constitution, it is also without any national power. It has no direct influence in the affairs of the nations surrounding it. It is still a subject people, still tributary to those pagan powers. Their lords and masters are those kings who were in authority, the so-called great powers of the tune. That was their condition. But in those fifteen years they had been wonderfully preserved materially. They were a provident crowd. And those that came back and set to work at once were very successful. If you had been in the city, and had traveled through the streets and along its highways and byways, you would have seen remarkable building going on everywhere. They were getting on, they were doing well. Is somebody asking "How do you know?" Haggai said they were dwelling in ceiled houses, and that meant more than houses with roofs. It is a phrase that marks the splendor of these houses. They were doing marvelously well temporarily. Yet all the while, spiritually, not a hand was lifted to the Temple walls, not a stone added to its structure. The city was full, the houses were ceiled houses of comfort and beauty and luxury; but spiritually they were practically dead, not caring about the house of God. I am not drawing on my imagination. I am speaking from the prophecy of Haggai.

Now for a moment notice his messages. He delivered four in two months and seven weeks. That was the whole period of his prophecy. They are carefully dated all the way through, although it is a pagan dating. He begins his preaching, and almost immediately the people responded. Of course we are not to imagine that in these four addresses we have the only account of all that Haggai said. We have a condensation of the messages that were delivered to these people, and as you follow them through you will see that their spiritual condition was connected with their true position with regard to this very matter of the building of the house of God; because the first burden of Haggai and that of Zechariah who joined him, was to make the people understand their obligation—if they had forgotten, to renew their memory; and if they had never understood it, to understand it now—that that house of God was central to their life; that all their life circled round it, and that as in the days of long ago, so still God was in the midst of them. Remember the history, and how all the national life circled round the central place, that place of tabernacle and witness, the tabernacle of the congregation. I would like both these phrases altered. Not "a tabernacle of witness," but "a tabernacle of testimony": not "a tabernacle of the congregation," but "the tent of meeting." And "witness" there does not mean the witness that we bear, but the place where God witnessed to them of His will and His Law. That was the tabernacle of witness, where God testified.

But it was the tabernacle of meeting, the place where God met with them. He was at the center, enthroned in the august and majestic symbolism of the Shekinah light. They had forgotten all about it. They were neglecting it and living in their ceiled houses, looking very prosperous. And now watching Haggai you will find that before they began to build they raised a protest and their protest was this: "Oh," they said, "it is not the time to build." Isn't that modern? Waiting for the set time! That is what they said. "Of course this Temple ought to be built. We admit it, but it is not convenient. The hour has not arrived. The hour has not yet struck. It is not time to build." Yet they were building their own beautiful houses, but the time had not come for building the house of God. In other words, they were a people with a false content. They were contented with material prosperity and were neglecting entirely the spiritual center of their life.

However, they began to build. Watch that carefully. When they built a little way they paused, they were despondent, and the blame in this case was not upon the younger men, but the older men. Some of them were getting very old by that time. They had been in Babylon many years. As lads, shall we say five, ten or fifteen years old, they had seen the Temple that had been destroyed, and they looked at what was being done now and said, "It is as nothing." They were content to let the house of God alone, and when they began to rebuild they were despondent. The old men were talking, and again I use a modern phrase, about "the good old days." When an old man does that he ought to be sent on to heaven.

Then they went on, and presently they stopped again. Why? Haggai had practically told them that if they would build the house of God and make that the true center of their national life, there would come to them spiritual awakening, and prosperity. But they did not see it coming at once, and they were disappointed. They had false expectations that the results would be immediate upon obedience, and it was not so.

The next stage in their difficulty was wavering through opposition, as revealed in the fact that they began looking at their enemies all round them, those great nations surrounding them, and they were afraid of them. There it is in this prophecy as you go through it; a false content, a false discontent, a false expectation and a false fear. That is the condition Haggai had to deal with, and how marvelously he did it! First of all and fundamental to his teaching was the purpose of the vision that moved him. It was a conviction of the supreme importance of the life of the people, and their well-being, with the house of God right at the center of everything. It was their duty to erect the Temple; and when they talked about the old days, his message in correction was that they need not look back but look on. He told them that the glory of the latter house should exceed the glory of the former. As you read it, you will see that it was not so much the material splendor of the house to which he was referring but to the things that are hidden there; and the glory of the latter house was to be something that was in excess of anything that the fathers had seen in the old house.

And then in a very remarkable way, when they were disappointed because results were not immediate, he uttered to them practically a parable. He showed what the pollution of sin is, and how deep that pollution went, and how they had no right to expect immediate results on the material level. He answers their fear, and assures them, showing that the power of God was greater than all their enemies. In all, he ministered for two months and seven weeks. There were difficulties relative to the condition of the people, but the power of his message is manifested in the fact that they continued in spite of opposition, their difficulties were overcome, and the Temple was rebuilt in five months.

Now we turn to Zechariah and we find the conditions were exactly the same. The messages that Zechariah delivered during the building of the Temple occupy the first part of the book. Then there are the messages he delivered after the Temple was completed, which occupy the second part of the book. It is very interesting to notice the dating, for we see that Zechariah delivered his first message a month after Haggai delivered his second.

Haggai delivered two messages, but we are not told how far they were apart; and then a month later Zechariah came along. The message that Haggai had just delivered, to which Zechariah was a sequel, was the one in which Haggai had pointed the people to the glories of the future. They were lamenting the glories that were departed, and saying this house was nothing after its departed glories. Haggai asked them not to look back, but to look on to the glories that were to come. And then Zechariah came along. I do not know whether what I am going to say may be thought irreverent. I hope not. But I never study these prophecies without feeling that Zechariah felt that Haggai had left something out, and it was most important that it should be put in. Haggai said, "Don't look back, look on and see the glory to be." Zechariah said—and if I put it bluntly I do so in order to be brief— "Look back, and you will find your fathers were not such foolish men as you thought. You are lamenting the lost greatness and the glory. Look back, and in looking back you will see how things were in the past" This is a great message, that first message of Zechariah.

His next vision of the future was delivered two months after Haggai had ended his work, but this man looked on into the future. And he delivered his third message two years later. It was an answer to a question that rose about certain observances. Was it necessary to observe them?

In a wonderful way he showed them that the feasts some of them were observing were not God-ordained feasts. That is the last message of Zechariah during the building of the Temple. Then there is no message for two or three years, till we come to the last movement, in which is contained what I have sometimes called for my own study and thought the Apocalypse of the Old Testament. It is the most remarkable piece of prophesying uttered in that period. Notice it falls into two parts: first of all, in the land of Hadrach; and then concerning Israel.

Now that uttered in the land of Hadrach is difficult of exposition, and I am not at all prepared to say anything very definite about it. Personally, I am inclined to think that at the time Zechariah was in the land of Hadrach. Of course, there was a time when people said there was no such place, but we have been digging up and we know now that there was. And Zechariah foretold in a most remarkable way events that had not transpired. See what he had to say of the coming of Alexander—he described it so completely. He also described the period following that, which we speak of as the period of the Maccabees. Then he clearly saw the coming of the Romans. He described the great successive movements of this period, the period when Alexander came, and the period of the Maccabees, that remarkable family—or race as they came to be—who resisted the power of Judaism. It was in that period that the Pharisees were born (and Pharisee simply means "protests"). The Pharisees were the Puritans of that age, those who will have nothing to do with the conformity of the nations around them. The Maccabean period is a wonderful story. And with the ending of that period came the Roman power. Trace that movement through in order to lead to the one supreme matter that he had to reveal. Follow these things: Alexander, the Maccabees, the Roman power— and in that period, and under that dominion, the true King would come and would be rejected. You have it all in this book. And that is the story of his messages which begin in the land of Hadrach.

Next he comes to the last part, the great Apocalypse of the Old Testament, in which he sees beyond the rejection of the King under the Roman authority and power, to the coming and the crowning of the true King, rejected and yet reaching His crowning. It is apocalyptic—much of Zechariah is. The visions in this book are all such, all symbolic and suggestive.

These two men, Haggai especially, Zechariah helping him in the early part of his ministry and then continuing some of his ministry, brought about the building of the Temple and its completion. That is the last until you come to Malachi.

In Malachi the conditions are revealed through the messages delivered and the way the people received them. I said at the beginning that the book is undated, but may be dated by deduction from the conditions. If you study Malachi, you will see that there were three things against which he protests, and with vehemence. The first was a polluted priesthood. The second was the fact of mixed marriages. And the third was the fact that the people were failing in their duty to God because they were not bringing in the whole tithe. Now if you go back to Nehemiah, and study the conditions obtaining when Nehemiah paid his second visit to Jerusalem and became so magnificently iconoclastic, these were exactly the same conditions, and the things that Nehemiah protested against were the very things Malachi protested against: polluted priesthood, mixed marriages, neglected tithes. (Malachi came some time after Nehemiah had done his work and passed on, and it is interesting that Malachi does not refer to either Ezra or Nehemiah.) But the conditions had gone on, in spite of Nehemiah's great wrath, and when he visited the city a second time, the people had returned to a priesthood polluted, had formed mixed marriages with the surrounding nations, and had failed to bring in a full account of tithes. That is a very unfortunate translation: "Bring ye all the tithes." The Hebrew word is not "all the tithes," it is "the whole tithe," which is a much profounder thing. You can bring all the tithes without bringing the whole tithe. The tithes are very mechanically accounted, a tenth of everything. And you can bring it—but unless that tithe you bring is the representation of the attitude of life and spirit, it is not the whole tithe, not complete in what it ought to be. And these people were revealing the looseness of their relationship to God by the fact that they had not brought the whole tithe. From beginning to end Malachi is dealing with that situation, and the whole condition of the people at that time can be summarized by saying they had become entirely formal. Here is the keynote of Malachi. You do not find it so clearly in the Authorized Version as you do in the Revised Version. Seven times over the prophet charged the people with certain things and every time they answered with that one word—"Wherein." It was the keyword. Mark it in your Bibles. Malachi said, for instance, "You have robbed God." They said, "Wherein have we robbed him?" It is only one illustration. They were doing all the external things— bringing their tithes, offering their sacrifices, attending the services of the Temple—but Malachi said they were doing nothing. They answered him, "We do not see it. Wherein? wherein? wherein?"

That was their condition, and Malachi's message was set first in stem denunciations of that formality. But he did not finish on that note. His message ended with enunciation of a coming day, the day toward which he was looking, and he described it in its twofold aspect. It shall be a day that bums the heavens, a day of destruction; but a day with Christ at the center, rising with healing in His wings, a day of restoration. He was looking on to a day fire-destroyed, but also to a day of healing sunlight. "They that feared the Lord spake one with another; and the Lord hearkened and heard, and a book of remembrance was written before him… They shall be mine, saith the Lord of hosts… in the day when I act."

"When I act." And Malachi saw the day.

Then you remember how it ends: "Behold, I will send you Elijah the prophet before the great and terrible day of the Lord come. And he shall turn the heart of the fathers to the children, and the heart of the children to their fathers; lest I come and smite the earth with a curse."

I do not think anyone can escape the significance or suggestiveness of the fact that when you have read all the literature of the Old Testament, the very last word is "curse." Yes, but it is not a malediction. It is a warning note: "Lest I come and smite the earth… It is an interesting fact that according to instructions, rabbis, whenever they read Malachi, never ended with that verse. They do not today. They read to that point, and then by instruction they go back and end with the fifth verse, "Behold, I will send you Elijah the prophet." At any rate, it is perfectly clear that the curse was not pronounced, but that it was possible. And there was a warning against it, and a declaration of a new day to be ushered in by the coming of Elijah, the prophet; of turning the hearts of the fathers to the children and the children to their fathers. There was a prediction of the new day. And it all ends with the solemn warning.

23. WORLD CONDITIONS AND THE OLD TESTAMENT[1]

---

[1] This chapter, a lecture delivered March 31,1939, is included for two reasons: it is a link in the chain of harmony that Dr. Morgan is forging, and it is illustrative of the warmth and informality with which he delivered the lectures (the chapters of this book) to his congregation at Westminster Chapel, London. The times of which he speaks are not so different from our times, after all; the

Before passing on to the New Testament books, I want to make a survey of our teaching on the Old Testament. The use of the word "survey" rather than "summary" is intentional on my part.

I have been challenged as to what is the difference between a summary and a survey. There is a sense in which they may both be used in this connection; and yet, strictly speaking, a summary is a gathering up of things done and statements made. If I were making a summary I should go over the whole ground rapidly. Strictly speaking, a survey is a looking over the ground. I am not attempting to go over it again even in the briefest fashion; but having gone over the ground, we want to survey what we have done, and that in one particular, which is this: "World Conditions and the Old Testament."

We begin with world conditions. What are the world conditions, or how shall I speak of them? The newspapers constitute a mirror into which we look to see the world. I admit that very often one can get a very distorted view of world conditions from the newspapers. I suppose some of you have looked in those curious mirrors, some concave and some convex, and gazing at yourselves have said, "If I look like that, God help me!" But then, you are not like that. And our newspapers do that very thing every morning, and the evening editions are worse than the morning editions. I grant you that. But on the other hand, there is a great deal of value in the newspaper because in it you do get news of world conditions.

Now let us bear in mind that our approach to world conditions as Christians—for all of us, and certainly for myself—is Biblical. How often we are reminded of John Wesley's great dictum, "I read my newspaper to see how God is governing the world." I quoted that one night in an American city, and a good man said to me afterwards, "I am rather surprised John Wesley said that. Newspapers must have been far better in his day than they are today." But think of what newspapers were in John Wesley's day, and by comparison our newspapers are changed too. Wesley read them to see how God was governing the world, and John Wesley never read his paper until he had first read his Bible. I do not say that literally he never read his newspaper before he read his Bible, but I certainly say that for more than fifty years I have never opened a newspaper before reading the Bible. That was true of John Wesley, generally speaking; and the man looked at the newspaper with the light that was flashed on it from the Book, and saw how God was governing the world. That is still true. I think half the restless, panicky outlook that I find among Christian people today about world conditions is due to the fact that they do not read their Bibles.

Now, if we look at the world as we see it in the newspaper, there are three great facts revealing a threefold need.

There is the fact of *sin*. You cannot read your newspaper without coming face to face with it. It is almost absurd to stop and argue it. I declare to you dogmatically that there is no man or woman who will quarrel with that statement. The condition of the world reveals sin everywhere. I pause long enough to say that you may not see the word "sin" very often used in newspapers, but you see that which it represents recorded very graphically there. Sin is there—headlines may vary, but the fact remains. The Greek word translated "sin" so constantly in the New Testament means simply, "missing the mark." If you study Greek literature you will find this word used for an arrow which, being shot from the bow, does not strike the target. It misses the mark. Or again, it is employed concerning an orator whose foundations are not in harmony with his terms, and if you had been listening you would have said, "That man is missing the mark." It has been said about some of us preachers before now: "He is missing the mark." You may say it does not sound so dreadful. Yet it depends on what the mark is that is missed. You remember Hamlet said, "The time is out of joint." That is right—"out of joint," missing the mark, dislocated. It means, further, failure. It is the word which is written over all. What is the mark the world is missing? The divine ideal for humanity: individually, socially, nationally, internationally. Wherever you look, you will see that. Sin! I do not care what paper you take, you cannot read the paper any morning without being brought face to face with this.

But why is the divine ideal missed? Again I am not going into any theological arguments, but declare that which is a great theological fact. Humanity has missed the mark because it has definitely rebelled against that mark, and rebelled against the Kingdom of God. That is the story we see everywhere as we survey world conditions.

And the very revelation of the conditions is at the same time a revelation of a need. What does the world need? And just as I used a rather old word, sin, I use a rather old word, *salvation.* That is, some way of deliverance, something that will readjust the dislocated life of the individual and of society and of the nations, something that will bring bone to bone and sinew to sinew so that the dry bones shall live again. You can read it in the Book of Ezekiel. What is the something that shall do that? What does it mean? Humanity needs a way back to God, and I think one of the encouraging signs of the hour in which we live is that *that* has become almost a commonplace. We are hearing it as we did not hear it a few years ago. But this is the fact—world conditions of sin, and humanity sighing for some way by which it can get back to God—often with no language but a cry, but a cry that is understood by the One who supplies; and what is needed is salvation for every man! Whether you speak personally, or whichever way you use the word, man needs a way by which he can be brought back to God.

Next, as I look out over world conditions, what strikes me is really a sequel to the first, a corollary which follows necessarily and inevitably. What is it? *Anarchy.* This world today is characterized by anarchy which is the direct result of sin; it is patent. It may be remembered that there are places in the world where there is no anarchy, those countries where

---

conditions he describes as obtaining then are still with us; with only a slight change of date he could be speaking of us, today.

The Publishers

the people are compelled to do what they are ordered to do. You cannot see any anarchy there.

That great statesman, General Smuts, has described conditions in some countries as that of armed anarchy. He was perfectly right. A dispensation that produces obedience, but does not carry the consent of the governed, is a dead failure and inevitably must prove itself so. There is not a land that appears to be ordered today under the compulsion of autocracy; there is not a land which is not liable at any moment to break out into blood-red revolution. Not one of them! Seething underneath is the discontent of humanity, not daring for the nonce to express itself, but it is there. That is not a condition of order but of anarchy; and wherever you find it you will see that the result of that kind of supposed order is injustice, cruelty and suffering. Where you have injustice, cruelty and suffering, these are the symptoms of lack of authority, conditions of anarchy.

What does this world need today? I have said, salvation. So it does. But what else does it need? *Authority*—authority which is based on righteousness, which acts in justice, which produces order. In other words, what the world needs is the Rule of God recognized, yielded to, obeyed. In obedience to that there is no injustice, cruelty is abandoned, suffering is brought to an end. The rule of God in this world means the absolute monarchy of the Cross. World conditions: anarchy. And the need: authority.

Once more I look abroad in the world, and I am impressed first with its sin, second with its anarchy, and finally with its appalling *ignorance*, humanity's state of "not-knowingness." Can you really say that this is a day of much enlightenment? Knowledge, enlightenment everywhere, everyone being educated, and you speak of ignorance! Assuredly yes. Let me do it in this way. To me humanity today looks on, and of course knows nothing of the future; it is entirely hidden. And as within its philosophies new light is breaking forth upon the mists that lie ahead, yet we are entirely ignorant of what we may read in the newspapers tomorrow morning. Of course we are. I am stating a fact. And then again there is ignorance—not of the future only, which of course is necessary in a way by reason of our finite minds, but ignorance of the present humanity, not understanding the conditions in the midst of which it is living, and looking back, misinterpreting history. Is there anything more appalling than humanity's seeming inability to read the lessons of the past? 1939? Yes, and in 1918 we thought we had learned our lesson. And we had not learned anything. Nothing has resulted from those bitter and appalling experiences through the world. There is confusion among rulers and those who are supposed to be ruled, confusion everywhere. Oh, the ignorance of humanity!

And here again, for the last time, what does the world need to confront this appalling widespread ignorance with regard to present conditions? What does it need? *Interpretation*, based on absolute knowledge. No interpretation is to be trusted which is the result of the examination of conditions that had existed or do exist or will exist. Here is a trite, commonplace illustration. It is said that two and two make four. Do they? Are you sure? It depends on what are the two and the two. There are two men walking down there, and two donkeys going down there. Two and two make four. Four what? It breaks down. All these commonplace things do break down. "A point is a position without magnitude," they taught me. What absurdity! You cannot have position without magnitude. They taught me as a boy that a line is length without breadth. It is wrong. You cannot have length without breadth. We are all in ignorance! We want an interpretation of man, using the word individually or generically, that is based upon absolute knowledge, intelligibly expressed, that can only be found in God, that can only be provided through revelation. There is no salvation (I do not wish to be irreverent) unless God takes a hand. There is no authority that is not vested in God, and the eternal Throne. Humanity needs to hear God speak.

That is the value of the Old Testament From its first page, through all its historic sections, along the line of all those didactic books, seers, psalmists, prophets, it is forever revealing the need created by sin, of salvation. We can hear the sigh for the priest, a priest to stand between God and humanity, and to put his hand upon it and bring them together. And that is what the world is asking for today. Through all the Old Testament I can hear the sigh for the king; and as I watch them and see them breaking down and failing until I see a kingdom ending in the most appalling anarchy and disruption, I can hear the cry for the king. The world is still crying for that king. In all the voices of the teachers, in the records that have been preserved for me, I am conscious of the necessity for some word that shall be final, that shall interpret. No, the Old Testament does not provide the priest or the king or the prophet, but it reveals humanity's need of priest and king and prophet. The years have rolled away and have merged into decades and centuries since that Old Testament literature was written, but I affirm now that it is as alive as it ever was. And there is nothing in your newspaper tomorrow morning that is so much up-to-date as to the revelation of humanity and its condition and its needs, as is to be found in that literature that is the Old Testament. "In divers portions and in divers manners" God spoke in the past

And now we are going on to come to God's answer to that need. Remember, He has answered. And, of course, that creates the deepest condemnation of the condition of the world today; the condemnation very largely of the Church in its failure. But He has answered. The Priest is found, the King is given, the Prophet has spoken. In these last days He has spoken in His Son, and the Son is the Priest, and the Son is the King, and the Son is the Prophet. Ah yes! This Old Testament is wonderful literature! Many voices are speaking. They are all clear, although not one complete, and the whole of them not complete: "Divers portions and divers manners."

What I think of the Old Testament, I think of the New Testament. When I attempt to survey both in this way I think of the last book in the New, and the final vision of our Lord and Saviour granted there to one of His own in Patmos Isle. What a vision it was! I am only concerned for one moment with one thing that John tells us about that vision. He said His voice was as the voice of many waters. And oh! the waters there are in the Old Testament. They are flowing, they are not complete. But when the Son spoke, all the flowing tones and cadences and values of the voices of the past merged in Him. His voice is as the voice of many waters. In other words, to put it very simply and plainly: world conditions are patent, but the supply has been granted by God, and there is no other healing of the world's wounds, or righting of its wrongs, or articulation of its vast dislocation, but the provision that God has made.

And reverently, we are going on to look over some of the literature that reveals God's supply.

PART IV

THE PENTATEUCH OF THE NEW TESTAMENT. GOD'S SUPPLY— THE LORD HIMSELF

24. MATTHEW—THE KING

Commencing now the study of the second part of our consideration on the general theme of the harmony of the Testaments, we must remember that in the previous chapters we have gone over the Old Testament, not so much to consider in detail the contents of the varied books or even the individual messages which they bring us, but rather seeking to discover the full value of the literature of the Old Testament.

Turning to the New Testament, we shall consider it from that standpoint. It is important to repeat that. We are not attempting to consider the books in detail as to their content, or even as to the nature of the respective messages contained in these books, but rather getting the impression of their value. To repeat, we may summarize the harmony of the Testaments and the relation of the Old and the New by saying that in the Old Testament we have a revelation of human need, and in the New Testament we have the revelation of the divine supply, the supply of that which humanity needs.

In a brief backward look: we considered the Pentateuch, and then the Historic books from Joshua to Nehemiah, then the Didactic writings and the Prophetic books. And what we have claimed for them is this: that in the Pentateuch the supreme value is that we hear the sigh for the priest; in the Historic books, the cry for the king; and in the Didactic books we follow the quest for the prophet. But neither the priest nor the king nor the prophet has been found in the Old Testament. If you take the section dealing with the priest, the central figure is Aaron, but however great his service for the nation, from the standpoint of the priesthood he was imperfect. If you take the period of history of the kings, I shall instance two as reaching the highest revelation,

David and Hezekiah, and in each case from the standpoint of kingship we find failure. If you take the Prophetic books, it is difficult to make a selection, but for the sake of argument we will take the two great books, the one Isaiah, and the other Jeremiah—and when we look at them we find that the wonder is there, but only partially and not complete.

THE PENTATEUCH OF THE NEW TESTAMENT
"Both Lord and Christ"—Acts 2:36

THE PENTATEUCH OF THE NEW TESTAMENT: THE LORD HIMSELF	OFFICIAL		
	Matthew King	*Mark* Priest	*Luke* Prophet
	I. His Coming From God to Man Of Man for God	I. The Outer Court Service Sacrifice	I. Preparation by Spirit Babyhood Childhood Manhood
	II. His Campaign Initial— Life Teaching Works Final— Judgment Suffering Death	II. The Holy Place Resurrection Commission	II. Power of Spirit Teaching Offering Rising
	III. His Conquest Resurrection Commission	III. The Holy of Holies Ascension Cooperation	III. Proclamation Through Spirit Preparing Witnesses
	ESSENTIAL		
	John The Logos I. The Eternal One The Word— Wisdom Speech II. The Temporal Fact Tabernacled— Grace Truth	III. The Unveiling Life—"I AM" Light—I Am Holy Love—Full of Compassion	
	MEDIATORIAL		
	Acts The Lord of the Church: The Head and the Body I. The Lord Between God and Man a. The Kingdom The King b. The Will The Prophet c. The Fellowship The Priest	II. The Spirit Between the Lord and His Body a. Kingship "Jesus is Lord" b. Prophecy "He shall teach you" c. Priesthood "Not orphans"	III. The Church Between the Lord and the World a. The Enthronement Proclamation b. The Ethic Enunciation c. The Evangel Evangelization

In the Old Testament the sigh for the priest is first revealed; then the cry for the king, and finally the quest for the prophet. When we come into our New Testament, we find not the priest at the beginning, but the king. Matthew reveals the King: then the Priest is seen in Mark: and the ultimate Prophet in Luke. There are those who very strongly believe the Gospel of Mark was written first. I think personally that it was, though I do not think it has ever been proven. Of course, some may say, "Why not put that answer to the cry for the priest first?" I do not know and I am not prepared to tell you how it was decided what order should be set up in the New Testament, but I am sure it was under divine guidance. Whether those who arranged the canon and put Matthew and then Mark and then Luke and John, understood what they were doing, I do not know: but no man ever knows or feels his need for the priest until he has stood in the presence of the king, and measured his life by the king's requirements. That is why if I were meeting some very young folk who might say to me, "How shall I read this New Testament?" I should say, "Read it as it is." There was a time when I advised people to begin with Mark, but I do not do so now. Take Matthew and read it until you see what it says about kingship, and you will be driven to Mark to find the priest, and so forth throughout. There is remarkable orderliness from the spiritual standpoint in this arrangement. We get in Matthew the King—His standards and His requirements; in Mark, the Priest—His redemption and His restoring power; in Luke, the Prophet—the final and inclusive word of God to man about men; and in John, the Person Himself in glistering omnipresence.

You cannot take up any one book in the Bible with an open mind, no matter how many times you have read it before, without feeling there is something about it that you have never known before, never felt before. That is where the Bible is different from all other literature. The standard of Shakespeare! You cannot exhaust the Bible. Although we have been over this ground again and again in different ways, we can come to it once more and take this Gospel according to Matthew. It presents the King. I do not think I need stay to argue that It is so self-evident from beginning to end. The word "kingdom" occurs no less than fifty times in this Gospel. It is often "the kingdom of heaven," sometimes "the kingdom of God," sometimes "the kingdom," standing for the same fact; but it is preeminently concerned with the King and His Kingship and His dominion.

What does it tell us about the King? First of all it tells us how this King came into human history; then it describes His campaign in human history, and finally leads you to the revelation of His conquest. Sang the ancient poet, as he surveyed the tumult of the nations, "Why do the heathen rage, and the people imagine a vain thing? The kings of the earth set themselves, and the rulers take counsel together, against the Lord."

God was saying "Yet," and that "Yet" is so significant. This is its meaning. Instead of the tumult of the nations and the clamoring of the kings and the rebellion of the rulers, "Yet I have set my king upon my holy hill of Zion." That was written hundreds of years before Jesus came, but that singer, with singularly fine vision and clarity of understanding, saw some King anointed by God, and saw that the anointed King was the Son of God. Now the centuries have run their course since that song was written, and we follow through the appalling history of the Hebrew people, and the breakdown of the idea of kingship all the way through. We are here in the New Testament, and you could write as a caption to this new book, with perfect accuracy, the words, "Behold, the king we were told about is come into human history, and into the world." I prefer to put it that way, because we have been tracing across history and seen these failures, and the need of humanity for a king, and the King is here. Let me express what I want to in this way: Who is He? What does He tell us about the King?

He tells us first of all that He is come from God Himself. The will and the act of man have been impotent, and have never been able to provide a king. Now, by the will of God and the act of God, the King is born. I am stating the truth that we are thinking perhaps in other words. It is just as well sometimes. Of course, the story in Matthew opens when this Person was born into human history of a Virgin, as told in the prophecy of Isaiah. Mark the significance of it. No will or act of man had been able to develop a human being that was fit to rule over humanity. And because of that entire breakdown, God is seen breaking in upon human history in the fullness of time, and bringing into human life and human history His King—developed, born, not of the will of man but of the will of God, and not of the act of man but by the act of God. A passing word! If you get rid of that, then you have got rid of Christianity. The moment we are in doubt about that we are in doubt about the whole superstructure. Everything depends upon that, and you have no final hope in the authority of Jesus except upon the basis of that tremendous fact. The King is of God, and from God to man.

Turn that little sentence around, and the King is seen as coming to man for God. He is from God to man, He is come to man for God. If you press me as to what I mean by that I shall answer it in two sentences: He is come to man for God revealing God. He is come to man for God to rule in the place of God. That summarizes a great deal more than the first chapters; it takes up the whole outlook, and not only the whole outlook of Matthew but of the New Testament.

The King is seen. Every one of mans best kings was finally defeated, even Hezekiah, the highest and the best and the noblest in intention and endeavor, leaving his kingdom in tumult: Hezekiah, with all the fineness of his reign, breaking down and failing. But now the King is come. Forgive the repetition of this sentence. I think that is worth everything. He is come from God to man. Man has not produced Him. God begat Him in the Virgins womb, and so introduced Him to humanity and to human history.

And He is come in order that God may be revealed: in His holiness, that God by no means looked upon sin: in His compassion, that God by no means forgot or forsook the sinner. He is come to rule for God, to express to men the authority of the eternal Throne.

That is the story of Matthew.

As you read it and follow right along, you find first what I have described as His campaign. It is revealed to us as one of interpretation first, and then executive activity. The King is seen by interpretation, and that in three ways: His teaching, His works, and His life of interpretation—interpretation of God, interpretation of the One He has come to reveal, and of the authority and rule and reign of God which He has come to reveal, and of the authority and rule and reign of God which He has come to establish in the world in interpretation of His teaching.

The teaching runs all through. I must, I suppose, to be intelligible, use an old and hackneyed and foolish description, "The Sermon on the Mount." Don't be anxious. I am not gibing at the thing but at the stupid name of it. Sermon! After the sermons I and many have preached! Dr. Oswald Dykes, as I have often said, in his great book gave us a very fine title, "The Manifesto of the King." And that is exactly what it is. In that Sermon on the Mount—as we call it—that great ethical enunciation, that manifesto of the King, the laws of the Kingdom of God for man, individually, socially, nationally, racially are all found. We have not outgrown it. We have not begun to grow up to it even in the Christian Church.

Then again, to tarry for a moment with outstanding things: in Matthew 13 are the great stories, or parables as I should prefer to call them, of the Kingdom. Parables of the Kingdom in which, from the standpoint of the divine understanding of God and of human nature, He shows what the processes will be that He has come to enunciate and of which His disciples, at least those of His Church, are supposed to be the agents. If you pause there briefly for a moment you will find three set discourses of Jesus in Matthew. In Chapters 14 and 15, that marvelous prophecy Jesus uttered in which He surveyed the ages that fell before Him which He had come to elucidate. He surveyed them from three standpoints: the Church, the Nation, and, of course, the Kingdom. And it is wonderful to read that great prophecy, and see how all through He is talking as One with authority, whose authority is final and will be, in the last eras when humanity passes before Him for the fixing of destiny as the result of their life and their relationship to Him in the world. He is interpreting Kingship, but He did this also by His works. In Chapter 9 He moves amid the delirium of humanity, coming into contact with human failure, and in every case showing His mastery of dereliction and His ability to deal with it. Whether it is in the material realm or the physical, whether it is in the mental or in the moral realm, always from the spiritual standpoint you will see Him healing spiritual disease, casting out demons, and giving man his restored balance, forgiving sins and sending people away to sin no more: always the spiritual is supreme. We see Him, I repeat, as master of every form of human dereliction, and moving amongst those who are derelict, restoring, healing, delivering. Then, if I stand back and look at Him, I find His final interpretation of the Kingdom is not in His teaching, it is not in His workings, but in Himself! Through all the vicissitudes of His life He reveals the glory of the divine ideal for men. So I see the King of the ages, come from God to men. He is come to men for God! And I find Him interpreting in His compassion, in His teaching, in His works and in life.

But that is not final. His final and great revelation is in His executive action. He warns the rulers of the failing nation, and then there comes the solemn moment when He tells them He was compelled to pass sentence on them for instability and against evil; He says to them that the Kingdom is taken from them and shall be given to a nation bringing forth the fruits thereof. Oh, yes, that is the King speaking—rejected of men, but by God already in purpose set upon His holy hill of Zion.

And then, the infinite wonder and mystery of it, that which we celebrate on Good Friday; when violence has seemingly done its worst He is still King, and

> Death by dying slew,
> And hell in hell laid low.

He is the King who went to the Cross of rejection, and turned it into the very center of the rule and realm of God.

Of course, that is all there is to say about it. Conquest! This was a conquest over all the forces producing anarchy in the world. And the King has gained a victory. In that tremendous statement of the Apostle in one of his Letters, speaking of the underworld of evil, and speaking of how they came against Him in the hour of His agony in Gethsemane and on Calvary, Paul says He made a show of them, openly triumphing over them in His Cross. A Victor!

I turn to Calvary, "He bowed his head and gave up the ghost." A head "bloody but unbowed!" That is popular braggadocio. "He bowed his head and gave up the ghost," in final authority and kingship, and because of that, God highly exalted Him and gave Him a name that is above every name.

We listen to Him, the Risen Lord, saying words—how well we know them, how often they grip us—"All authority is given unto me in heaven and on earth. Go ye, therefore, and disciple the nations." And Paul says, "He must reign until he hath put all things under his feet." The King! The King!

The cry for the king. Behold the King! Oh, what wonderful dramatic incident. Matthew does not record it, but without apology I go to John and borrow it, very simply, in a few sentences. Jesus and Pilate are talking. And without comment, I just want to give it to you in that dramatic form:

Jesus said, "My kingdom is not of this world."

Pilate: "Art thou a king then?"

Jesus: "Thou sayest that I am a king."

Here is the authority provided for the world in its anarchy—and the world will never escape its anarchy until it bows before the thorn-crowned and the glory-crowned Son of God.

25. MARK—THE PRIEST

We now consider the Gospel of Mark. When we were dealing with the Old Testament we saw very clearly in the Pentateuch the need for a priest, a mediator, one who (to use the language of a later writer in the Bible) would lay his hand on God and man, that man might be brought back again to the God against whom he had rebelled. Of course, in the Old Testament we saw the priest, a great priest in very many ways, Aaron; but you cannot read the story without feeling that the deep need of humanity is not met in Aaron. He is a promise, a foreshadowing, not a fulfillment; and what applies to Aaron applies of course to the whole system, that initial, preparatory, necessary system of the law. That is what the writer of the Letter to the Hebrews meant when he said the law made nothing permanent, and in that it failed. Or again, in a later passage in the Hebrews, speaking of the law in contrast to Christ, the Old Testament system in contrast to the New, the writer says it taketh away the first that it may establish the second.

And in Mark, we have the Priest. I must go back once more. In Matthew we have the revelation of the King. If you study that Gospel and listen to His teaching or watch Him at His work, or supremely observe Him in His person, you are reduced to a sense of utter hopelessness and helplessness. His laws are impossible of obedience. This is a sentence easily uttered, but it runs counter to a good deal we are hearing today.

Forgive me if I reminisce for a moment. I have in mind a great preacher of long ago who said to me one day, "Morgan, do you mind if I say something very definite?" I said, "Of course not. You are an old man in the ministry and I will be glad to hear it." And then he said, "You are talking too much of the Cross." I looked at him in astonishment and perplexity as he continued, "You know the Cross is really a very difficult subject and none of us knows what it means. People are not interested." I said, "What am I to preach?" He said, "The Sermon on the Mount." It was a good while ago, fifty years at least, and I did things then because I was younger and therefore perhaps a little more overbearing; I said, "Tell me, have you ever read the Sermon on the Mount?" He was a little annoyed, I suppose naturally: "Read it! Of course I have read it." I said, "I did not think so." "Why?" "Because it is the Sermon on the Mount that drove me like a frightened, hunted beast; and I never stopped running away until I struck the Green Hill with its Cross, outside the city wall." Forgive that little reminiscence, but it abides true. Preach the Sermon on the Mount? Set the people to obey it? What is the use? You cannot do it. Its outlook is too great and bright, the atmosphere too rare. It is far beyond the snowline. You can take little bits of it and say, "I agree with it." (I refrain from quoting.) But you read it and your soul is naked, bare, knowing that the searching eyes of God are upon you. You cannot obey it. But that is not all the story. You *can* obey it, for it drives you to the Christ, and you have His redemption and His regeneration and His renewal and His new life.

To stand in the presence of the King and His requirements as revealed in Matthew is to know condemnation, to be hopeless and helpless. What shall we do? Read Mark and you will find the secret. Here our Lord is revealed too. It is the same Person, no stranger. No man or woman here or in any country, or of any religion, brought up and reading the New Testament for the first time, having read Matthew and going on to read Mark, will make any mistake. It is exactly the same Person. That is self-evident. I am not taking time to argue that. But the difference between the two Personalities is profound. In Matthew you see the King, wearing the purple of royalty, standing in magnificent autocracy. When you come to Mark, He is stripped of royalty. You read it there. Oh yes, He is the King, but that is not the impression. When you read Mark first, it is not the kingliness of Jesus that will impress you. All the way through—I repeat the phrase—He is stripped of royalty, girded like a slave, forever active. Have you noticed that there are more geographical places named in Mark than in any of the Gospels, signifying the constancy of the journeyings of Jesus, never resting? That is the characteristic that strikes you. Why? Mark tells you why from the beginning.

Now Mark opens in a very remarkable way. Take your Bibles once again. I am going to be very technical for a moment: "The beginning of the gospel of Jesus Christ, the Son of God. Even as it is written in Isaiah the prophet, Behold, I send my messenger before thy face, Who shall prepare thy way" (1:1,2). Does it strike you that there is anything unusual about that? What is peculiar about it? It is not written in Isaiah the prophet, it is written in Mark. "The voice of one crying in the wilderness," it goes on. That is not in Isaiah. What is the matter with that? There is an old phrase I think I learned from Dr. John A. Hutton: I will take my courage in both hands. This is one of those phrases in which I want to say the punctuation is entirely wrong. Don't imagine that I am interfering with the integrity of Holy Scripture. Every tyro knows that in the Greek manuscript that bit is not punctuated at all, but the punctuation was inserted by some perverse souls. Instead of a full stop after the word "God," I would put a full stop after the word "prophet." Now then, listen: "The beginning of the gospel of Jesus Christ, the Son of God, Even as it is written in Isaiah the prophet."

Of course, if you are looking at the Old Version, it does not say that at all. "Prophet" is an accommodation made by the translators because they did not know what to put. This is the title of the book in verse 1. This is what it is about. It is like many an author who has written his title, and then put in a quotation from another book suitable for the whole thing.

"Behold, I send my messenger before thy face, Who shall prepare thy way." Now he is starting. Verse 4: "John came... Mark is telling you distinctly that he is going to write the story of Jesus which you have in the Prophet Isaiah. That is the key of the book.

I cannot resist another pause for it is distinctly necessary for those people that tell us Mark never mentions the Virgin Birth. No, but he opens the books and refers to Isaiah to show you what he is writing about—and there you will see the story of the Virgin Birth. So Mark draws attention to it evidently.

What a wonderful opening: Jesus, the name of His Humanity; Christ, the title of His mission; the Son of God, the testimony to His nature. If I am really puzzled as I read that, I go back to Isaiah and there we have the revelation of the Servant of the Lord. It is a great revelation, the very heart of the Gospel. Take the passage: "Ye... that publish good tidings, that preach us the gospel of peace." "The gospel"— the same word that Mark uses; and from that point on all the way the Servant of the Lord is described until you reach Chapter 53 in which the Servant of the Lord is seen suffering and triumphant. What for? "He was wounded for our transgressions, he was bruised for our iniquities; the chastisement of our peace was upon him; and with his stripes we are healed." What this Gospel of Mark is intended to do is to show us the Servant of the Lord stripped of royalty, girded for service, and that is how He is presented.

There are only three places in the Bible where the Son of God is referred to as the Servant of God. One is in Isaiah. One is in this Gospel, and the other is in Paul's massive summary: "Christ Jesus, being in the form of God emptied Himself, and took the form of a servant"; the Servant of the Lord, the Son emptying Himself of deity and of all sovereignty and taking the place of a servant. And as a

Servant therefore He became the Priest, the great Mediator between God and man; and that is the great revelation of this Gospel.

Let me get off to another angle for a moment. Just refresh your memory about the Tabernacle in the wilderness. You remember it. I am not talking about the Temple—the Temple is an accommodation to human weakness from the beginning. I am talking about God's pattern for worship in the national life, the Tabernacle. Get the background. There is the great Court of the Tabernacle itself. There is the Outer Court in which the burnt offering was made, and at one end there is another section in which you pass within the veil, and then you stand in the Holy Place. There is the Outer Court, the Holy Place; and in the Holy Place the table of shewbread, the incense and the golden candlesticks. Softly and reverently go through, and you reach the Holy of Holies, with the Ark and the overhanging cherubim and the overshadowing Shekinah glory. The Outer Court: the Holy Place: the Holy of Holies. Then I ask you to remember that in this Gospel Christ is presented first in the Outer Court, then in the Holy Place, and passing at last into the Holy of Holies.

At first, He is seen in the Outer Court of service, and that takes the greater part of the Gospel. It begins right there and runs on to 14:42. We are watching Him in the Outer Court, that Outer Court still within the Tabernacle; and the last words recorded of Him in the Outer Court give an account of Gethsemane, until He says, "Arise, let us be going." We have the service in that Outer Court, but not in detail; that, of course, is impossible.

First of all we see His dedication to His work. I quoted just a little at the beginning, and I stopped abruptly at the words, "John came." Look at 1:4, "John came," and run down to verse 9 and you have an equally particular word, "Jesus came." John came foretelling; Jesus came. He came in obedience for dedication. He dedicated Himself to the sacred work for which He had come as the Servant of the Lord, that of Prophet and Mediator between God and man, a Prophet of redemption for men on behalf of God. He came.

With almost blunt brevity Mark tells the next thing. It is only a few words: He was attested as the Son of God. Instantly you see Him in the wilderness, tempted of the devil. All that is part of His dedication to His work. He is in the wilderness, and you watch Him from that period to His public ministry. It has three movements. The first is a lonely period; and then He called four men and went on again; then He called twelve to be with Him until He sent them forth; and last came the moment when He is sending them forth. I summarize that section by saying this: as we watch Him we see His apparently restless activity—no one thinks I am speaking irreverently when I say "restless." He was restless in activity. He was so beset by His work that His mother thought He was mad and tried to persuade Him to go home to quietness and rest. Read the Gospel through. Follow Him all the way. Mark the words falling from the lips of Jesus, "Verily the Son of man came not to be ministered unto but to minister." A beautiful word that, "minister." Yet it misses the bite of this declaration. I am going to change it: "The Son of man came not to be served but to serve, and to give his life a ransom for many." That is the ceaseless story. That is all I can say about it. You will find it better summarized in Acts where it says, "Jesus went about doing good." Jesus' life was a life of unremitting toil.

You remember in the fourth chapter that little phrase, "They took him in the boat as he was." There is only one meaning—tired out, wearied with His work: and when they took Him in the boat, at once He lay down and He was fast asleep. Unremitting toil! Mark tells us that He was so busy that He had no leisure so much as to eat. That is the character of the first part: the Priest at the brazen altar serving, serving, serving.

Then, at that very verse, there begins what I am going to describe as a great parenthesis. A parenthesis does not mean something unimportant, but of supreme importance. In the activity of the priest, once a year he left the Holy Place, the Holy of Holies into which he went once a year, and he had to go outside the Court, to pass through the camp until he reached a place beyond. What for? To offer sacrifice. That was not offered in the Court, certainly not in the Holy Place, not in the Holy of Holies, but outside. The priest had to go there, and after he had offered the sacrifice there, he came back and bore it with him from the Court, from the Holy Place, into the Holiest of Holies, the blood of the sacrifice, and He sprinkled it upon the Mercy Seat. It is all symbolical. But here Jesus passes outside the place of service in the ordinary sense of the word. He went outside the Court. That is what the writer of the Letter to the Hebrews means when he says Christ suffered without the camp, outside the organizations of nature, outside the place of service, alone. That is the great parenthesis: betrayed, condemned, slain. He said, "It is finished." But what happened? There is no more dramatic sentence in all the Bible than this, "The veil of the Temple was rent in twain from the top to the bottom " They buried Him. He suffered without the camp. He served to save.

And what then? The Resurrection, and in that resurrection the Priest is seen passing beyond the place of service in which He had served for three years, passing through the Outer Court into the Holy Place; and you see Him in the Holy Place during those forty days, the Holy Place where was the golden candlestick shedding its light, and the table of shewbread of communion with God, the place of intercession. Mark all His conversation during that period, mark all His interests. He is seen sharing in the golden candlestick in the shedding of light; setting the table of fellowship by the pattern of God; and you have the road of access to the altar of incense for intercession.

Then, says Mark, He "was received up into heaven, and sat down at the right hand of God." The Priest has entered into the veil, into the Holiest of all. Yes, and again I quote Hebrews: "Within the veil; whither as a forerunner Jesus entered for us, having become a priest for ever after the order of Melchisedek." And again, a little later on: "Christ entered into heaven itself, now to appear before the face of God for us."

That is how Mark ends. The Priest and the Outer Court of service, and the Holy Place of light-bearing and fellowship, into the very Holiest of all. What for? To appear in the presence of God for us. Yet Mark tells you something else. That He entered into the Holy Place, and sat down at the right hand of God. And then there came a ministry. Listen! "The Lord working with them." During the period of His own service He has been training others for service, and He has gone into the Holy Place. Ah, but He has not left them! He is still working with them. Such is God's supply.

We have heard the cry for the king, and the King has come, revealing the ideal but condemning failure. We listened to the sigh for the priest, and the Priest has come, able to deal with failure and make possible the realization of the ideal.

> Where high the heavenly Temple stands,
> A house of God, not made with hands.
> And there our great High Priest our nature wears.
> God's Supply. The Priest is found.

26. LUKE—THE PROPHET

We come now to the revelation of the Prophet: the same Person throughout, Jesus, the King, the Priest, and the Prophet. It is a wonderful quest, that quest of prophecy which we find in the Old Testament. There we have glanced at messages of God to men, but partial and incomplete. It was a very significant word that Moses uttered to the people in those early days of national history when he said that God would raise up unto them a prophet from the midst of them, unto whom they should hearken.

And that great word of Moses was cited by Peter and applied to our Lord. It was also cited by Stephen in his apologia. And the fulfillment of the Mosaic prophecy is found in our Lord Himself. There had been a partial fulfillment or answer to the quest of the prophet through all the ages when, as I have said, God was speaking, but He was not speaking completely, fully, finally. Now our minds inevitably are leaping away to the New Testament to another writing from the pen of Luke. (I am referring to the Letter to the Hebrews; but as to whether Luke wrote it or not, I am not going to enter into argument just now. Any student of Luke, comparing his Gospel and the Letter to the Hebrews will discover significant similarities.) We are thinking of the words in the Letter to the Hebrews, "God, having of old time spoken unto the fathers in the prophets by divers portions and in divers manners, hath at the end of these days spoken unto us in his Son." In that we have the fulfillment of all the messages of God in the past; we find their complete fulfillment in Jesus.

After Luke has done his story and he has written about Jesus, he writes the preface to his Gospel and names the One of whom he has been writing; he calls Him "the Word" (1:2). People do not notice this title of our Lord. They read it, of course, but they do not take time to recognize it. Why not? Because the translators spelled "Word" with a small "w." If you turn over to John, you find he says, "In the beginning was the Word, and the Word was with God, and the Word was God… And the Word became flesh, and dwelt among us." Every time, in that translation, "Word" was spelled with a capital letter. There is no more reason for capitalizing the word 'Word' in John than there is in Luke's preface. It is exactly the same word: in John, the Logos; in Luke, the Logos—the Word. He is the One Luke has been writing about—

But I am not dealing with the preface now, though I want you to notice he says that "many have taken in hand," to give their account of things accurately from eyewitnesses. They were what he was not, for he had not seen Jesus. But from the stories of those who were eyewitnesses and servants of the "Word," he uses that great name there as his final finding personally concerning whom he has been writing. Now I claim that in that very fact there is evidence that the real value of the book is that Jesus, as we see Him named, is indeed the speech of God to men. John uses it in another application and another relationship: "The Word was made flesh and tabernacled with us." In Luke, the supreme emphasis is that He came to speak, to be the Word uttering the finality of truth from God to men; and let me say at once, *about* men.

Now when Peter was writing his Letter, he referred to these past writings. He gave us a very remarkable account of how they came to be. Let me quote to you. In his Second Letter he says, referring to the past: "Men spake from God being moved by the Holy Ghost." It is a great sentence. I hate to seem hypercritical. I never feel the word "moved" really gives the significance of what Peter wrote. You really want a phrase to interpret that word: "Men spake from God being borne along." Being caught up and carried over and borne along by the Holy Ghost—what a wonderful account Peter gives of the ancient writings.

In all the messages that came to men from the prophets, these were men who spoke from God, and they spoke as they were caught up and borne along and sustained by the Holy Spirit. It is well to remember that the Holy Spirit has ever been the medium of divine communication. This is true all through Old Testament history and all through the New.

Now we have come to this story of our Lord, and whereas it may find no harmony with the story that Matthew tells and the story that Mark tells, it has one particular note and emphasis that we must not forget: it shows how this One called the "Word" by Luke, at the end became the final Prophet, the complete revelation of God's humanity. John shows how He became the full and final and complete revelation of God. Luke reveals Him as having authority of the deepest truth concerning God's humanity. The old question is being asked still: "What is man? What is man?" It is as old as the psalmist who says: "When I consider the heavens… what is man that thou art mindful of him, and the son of man that thou visitest him?" This was the deep inquiry of recognition of something in man that was uncountable, so small beside the sun and the moon and the stars and the cosmos; and yet God visited him, and God was mindful of him. That comes away back out of ancient writings. What is man? And you have no answer to it in history, no answer to it in the Old Testament. You have got wonderful records of men in the New Testament that stand out as great mountain peaks of personality, but there is no one who answers your inquiry, "What is man?" Every one of them fails, every one of them breaks down. Every one of them grovels sooner or later and denies the pure light of majesty and infinite possibility. What is man? Do you want to know? Do you want to know in this age when men are still arguing about it? What is man?

You will find the answer in this Man Jesus, and you will find it portrayed perfectly in this great Gospel of a Greek. Notice always how fitting is the human instrument God employs. You talk about the majesty of His deity, and the story is written by a tax collector who kept accounts. Then you have Mark, just one of the common folk, who never seems to have had much discipline, and who worked among the fisher folk and caught their tricks of speech. Listen: it is "Straightway, straightway, straightway," all the way through. And here you have a Greek; brought up in Greek philosophy, knowing that the quest of the Greek was the perfecting of personality. And Luke says, in effect—I know he would forgive me if he were here—"Behold, the perfect Personality, Man as God meant him to be when He said, 'Let us make man.' " All the full and final message of God to men about His intentions and purposes in humanity is found here.

Let us notice one thing. I have remarked that Peter said that men spake by the Holy Ghost. I have declared further that the Spirit is always the medium of divine communication. Luke's Gospel emphasizes in a very remarkable way the relation of this Logos, this Word, to the Spirit. What is Luke's teaching? It is that Christ was prepared by the Spirit, was in the power of the Spirit, made His proclamation in the Spirit and accomplished His mission through the Spirit. Let us look at the Spirit working through the various periods of Christ's life.

See it first in His birth. There is, first of all, the presence and work of the Holy Spirit in the birth. "Mary... thou shalt conceive in thy womb, and bring forth a son. The Holy Ghost (Spirit) shall come upon thee, and the power of the Highest shall overshadow thee; therefore also that holy thing which shall be born of thee shall be called the Son of God" (Luke 1:30-35). Oh, yes, there is the biological difficulty here, with its long controversy. It is difficult for many Christians to understand. We must remember that it was Mary herself who first raised this biological question, so we need not be ashamed not to understand. Read Luke! He goes into detail, on the story of the Virgin Birth.

Matthew tells the same story in another way, and his story is a great chapter of the Christian tradition. The Christ Child, Virgin born, stands forth in human history as Something, Someone, entirely new; we stand in the presence of an infinite mystery as we stand in the presence of the birth, but we also stand in the presence of a demonstrated fact, for there can be no accounting for Him as we see Him and hear Him everywhere save that He came begotten of the Holy Spirit and the human Virgin.

See it again in His childhood. There is a short, simple statement about the childhood of Christ, in Luke: "And Jesus increased in wisdom and stature, and in favor with God and man." This, and the short story of Jesus in the Temple with the doctors—this, and nothing more. He had his bar mitzvah, or Hebrew confirmation, almost certainly in Nazareth. Through the years of childhood, Luke tells us, the Spirit guided Him in training for His Father's business.

He was anointed. How? The Holy Spirit descended in the form of a dove, bodily, upon Him. The *Spirit* anointed Him, and it was attested by the divine voice which said, "This is my beloved Son, in whom I am well pleased."

He went into the wilderness with the Spirit; when you read the story of the temptations, remember that He did *not* face those temptations alone. He did not overcome them with any merely human strength; He overcame them as a man filled with the Holy Spirit. That was the way God planned it. Man failed, in Adam, because he could not avail himself of fellowship with God through the Holy Spirit. But Jesus went down to face the underworld of evil in the strength of that Spirit, and where Adam failed, He conquered. He went down filled with the Spirit, and He overcame.

He came back from the wilderness in the power of the Spirit. He had been born of the Spirit, nurtured all along in the Spirit, was anointed with the Spirit, and now He set about His work in the power of the Spirit. He went home to Nazareth, stood up in the old synagogue pulpit and read from the Book, "The Spirit of the Lord is upon me." Presently He selected twelve men, trained them, walked the roads of Galilee with them, ministered with them, lived and died with them. With them He revealed that Word of which He was the full and final consummation: "When the days were well-nigh come that he should be received up, he stedfastly set his face to go to Jerusalem" (Luke 9:51). "Received up." What does that mean? The reference of this passage is to the Transfiguration, in which man came to a full realization of the meaning of humanity: "He was transfigured." Luke takes great care to explain this: He was metamorphosed, changed. If Jesus had had no mission ahead of Him, no redeeming purpose, no word concerning redemption to be given to man, He might have left the world right there on the Mount of Transfiguration, for He had fulfilled His mission *up to that point*. But He had a mission ahead of Him, and a redeeming purpose to fulfill, and there on the Mount of Transfiguration, as He came to the full glory of His humanity and was exalted, He prepared Himself to walk from the Mount to the Cross. *Then* he became obedient unto death. At birth He had been made "in the likeness of man." Now He showed humanity the full, high glory to which humanity could rise, and only after He had done that did He set His face to go up to Jerusalem—and Calvary.

Must I trace that journey? We are all familiar with it. "He, through the eternal Spirit, offered himself without blemish unto God" He was crucified. He died. They put Him in His tomb. He rose by the Spirit.

Think of those men whom He had gathered, who were to be His witnesses, and to whom He said, "Ye are witnesses of these things." If you ask me, "What things?" I will tell you, as He told those men, "All [the] things which were written in the law of Moses and the prophets and the psalms concerning me"

Behold, the Priest is found, the King is found, the Prophet is found, and the great message He has delivered to men from God is the interpretation of humanity in Himself, in God's ideal man.

And it is infinitely more than that. He has proclaimed to men the message of redemption, and the way of deliverance; we see Him as the final and complete Prophet, revealing not only His holiness and His righteousness but His grace and redeeming love.

Thus does Luke reveal the Prophet.

27. JOHN—THE LOGOS

In the Gospel of John we have a revelation of the Person through whom God is supplying humanity's need.

I sometimes feel that if someone took up these writings and read them over for the first time honestly, he would discover the King in Matthew; he would be conscious of the marvelous work of the Priest in Mark, and he would be conscious of the matchless revelation of the Man Jesus portrayed for us in Luke. And having read these three books I think he would have a sense of mystery and amazement and astonishment.

The authority of the King is of such a nature that one is filled with amazement; and the stupendous service of the Servant of the Lord who is the Priest is astonishing; then again, the dignity and the grace of the great Prophet, forbidding all familiarity, would truly possess the soul if the Gospel of Luke were studied carefully. In other words, I am inclined to think that the reading of these three Gospels would lead someone to say at the end, "Who is this? Who is this King whose note of authority is so final, this Priest whose service was so complete in sacrifice? Who is this Prophet who has revealed humanity to us in a way that, apart from that revelation, we never could have understood our own human nature as to its possibilities? Who is He?"

Who is this, so weak and helpless,
Child of little Hebrew maid?

"Who is this?" The Gospel of John answers that inquiry. It is a full and final answer. There is a Sense in which we have found the answer before we read John. We found it in Matthew in the King and how He came; we found it in Mark's prophetic announcement of His coming in Isaiah; we found it in Luke's account of the being of this Person. It is Jesus. They all of them, directly as in Matthew or John, or by indirect reference as Mark, tell you that He was born of a Virgin by the will and the act of God, not by the will and act of man. Yet somehow I want that explained. Yes, we know that, and have read these three accounts, and yet we want to know more. We want to know—if it is possible for our finite minds to apprehend—who is revealed in the Gospel according to John.

Now, this Gospel may be summarized by saying that John presents this Person and he begins with that which is eternal.

Then he proceeds to that which is temporal, and through the whole writings he shows us the things that were revealed of that Person who is at once eternal and temporal, the great unveilings that come through Him.

We begin at the beginning. You remember the opening sentence: "In the beginning was the Word, and the Word was with God, and the Word was God." That is the opening sentence of this story from the pen of John.

What is meant by "the Word?" I take the question into the realm of the ultimate simplicities and ask you, "What is a word?" What do you mean by a word? Take up your book or newspaper—nothing but words, words, words! Well, what is a word? A word is a shrine of truth. (Must I amend that? I know it is possible to lie, but I am speaking now of a word in its essence.) A word is always something which is spoken, but the thing spoken is a vehicle in which a supreme idea is conveyed. Now, if you take this word "Word" as it is used in the New Testament, what is a word? It is wisdom in essence, but it is more than that. The New Testament word is the Greek word Logos, and that which we have here in John is exactly coincident with the Hebrew word. I am not going to deal with that, but the Latin equivalent for *Logos is R*and that means "reason"; and that means simply "truth."

Now here we have this—shall I say this commonplace—word, raised to the highest altitude of sublimity: "In the beginning was the Word." That is wisdom, that is truth in essence, in the beginning. And here, in the simplest way, let me remind you that the opening verse of John 1 antedates completely the opening verse of Genesis 1. Genesis 1 says, "In the beginning God created." When you get beyond that, you will find that wisdom was there; it existed. That can be said in a simpler form: Thought preceded anything concrete, the idea, that which results in visibility, the Word. I lift these simple things of speech to the ultimate strength of possibility: "In the beginning was the Word." Wisdom existed in essence at the beginning, Dr. Joseph Parker once said, "That dateless date, In the beginning! that date upon which high rising and deep falling centuries are but tufts of foam flung up into its vastness"

Wisdom and wisdom made known—these two ideas belong to each other. The suggestiveness of the one is never absent from the other. "The Word" always means "truth," but it always means "truth uttered."

I am going to make an excursus into the Colossian Letter where Paul is writing of the glories of Christ, that marvelous Letter in which he says—I quote one little sentence only—"He is the image of the invisible God." Not "He was"; not "He became"; but the eternal "is." The reference here is to that Person, for we are bound to use words, in the mystery of the Godhead, who was always the medium through which God revealed Himself.

So that "the Word" means the essential truth, and that essential truth as uttered. It does not become the Word in the full sense as simply being in God or existing in the mind of God. It becomes the Word when that which is in the mind of God is expressed.

John, beginning this story of Jesus, introduces Him thus: "In the beginning was the Word." And the sentence reveals the pre-existence of the King, Priest, Prophet. We have been looking at Him as pre-existent ere time begins. It says, "He was with God." That marks perfect fellowship between this wisdom and this wisdom uttered of God: and he climaxes everything by a tremendous declaration, "The Word was with God," of the very nature of God. Then, if you leap over that introduction, from verse 1 to verse 14, you have the next thing immediately: "The Word became flesh." Here is the secret of the authority of the King. Here is the secret of the victorious mediation of the Priest. Here is the secret of the finality of the revelation that came from the great Prophet. He is, because He was.

The final question, the central question, is, "Who is this Person? Who is He?"

At Caesarea Philippi, when He took His disciples up there and challenged them, that was His question. He did not ask them what men were saying about His miracles. He did not ask them what men said about His teaching; but "Who do men say that the Son of man is?" Who am I? The supreme question. When you realize that, you understand the truth as Peter did not learn it until afterwards, although he confessed at once the supreme conviction that had come to him—and I think to the rest—"Thou art the Christ, the Son of the living God."

That is the secret of His authority; the authority of the King named Jesus is God's authority. That is the secret of His mediatorial victory. The secret of the victory of the Cross is the secret "that God was in Christ reconciling the world to himself." The secret of His complete, final revelation of the meaning of humanity to humanity is that God spoke to men concerning Himself, and He Himself now spoke to men concerning humanity. That is the supreme revelation. Who is this that by His word and His authority engages in this sacrificial work which is the wonder and the glory of this revelation? Who is He? "In the beginning was the Word, and the Word was with God, and the Word was God." So everything of value in the presentation of the Person and the work of our Lord leans back on that. I do not want controversy, but if you rob Him of that you have destroyed vital Christianity both in your own soul and in the work of the holy Church and in the world itself. Who is He? John tells you at the beginning. He is the eternal. And when you have done with the eternal there, it runs all through the Gospel.

I want to go on to what I call the temporal (and please mark that I say temporal and not "temporary"). By temporal I mean, of course, that which He did with time, and time is entirely a thing of humanity. Yesterday, with all its beginning, is a temporal relationship. While we are considering this, that Man of Nazareth is at the right hand of God, highly exalted, and remains with that great central Word of truth, the truth revealed to angels and principalities and powers and men, and whatever other creations there may be in the vast far-flung splendors of the universe of God. Temporal? Yes. But not temporary, not something that came and passed. What was this? "The Word became flesh"; that is, took human nature, was incarnate in human life, pitched His tent—which is really the meaning of the word "tabernacled," a beautiful word. "The Word became flesh, and pitched His tent among us," lived where we lived, tabernacled among us—the same Person who is in the creation. It is the Word that becomes incarnate. But it is the Word in new manifestation such as humanity had never had before, such as I venture to say the heavens had never known before—that essential wisdom, and that wisdom in utterance of human form and human frame, tabernacled in flesh. And John says, and what a significant thing it is, "We beheld," the same Person, but now adapted to human apprehension and understanding. And men had said, even though they had not beheld, that they had believed; and their belief deepened as they believed in the one God. And the great underlying statement of their philosophy was always this: "The fear of the Lord is the beginning of wisdom." They started with wisdom and they believed that wisdom dwelt in God. A reading through Proverbs shows that they had never seen wisdom. They had some measure of intellectual conception of the great fact that there was some way of its manifestation, and John says, "We saw and beheld him"; we beheld Him, the Word, in a new manifestation and adaptation of humanity's capacity, something that men could look at and listen to and handle.

Let me speak as a witness rather than dogmatically. I find that in the Gospel according to John I get nearer to the human than I do in either of the other Gospels. I wonder if you will understand that. Do not dream for a moment that I am denying that the essential and final and divine revelation of Him is divine. Yet mark how closely these things are knit together. It is in John that I am conscious of the humanity. In Matthew is the King, and I am overawed. In Mark is the Servant by sacrifice. In Luke is perfect Humanity revealed, and that frightens me. In John I have the real humanity, and don't misunderstand me if I say I never read John without feeling I can do exactly what John did—put my head upon the bosom of Jesus. It was John who did that.

A little technicality may help us. It is John who all the way through gets one face to face with the human Name of Him as no other writer does: Jesus. Now the technicality of that is this, and I will use the Authorized Version. If you read Matthew, you will find he calls Him Jesus 170 times. If you read Mark, you will find he calls Him Jesus 99 times. Luke calls Him Jesus 100 times. John uses the name of Jesus 276 times. If you read the Revised Version, you will find a very slight difference because the revisers, in some cases, have made the slight difference of using the name "Jesus" in some places, and "he" in some places, and the number is as follows: in Matthew we have the name Jesus 149 times; in Mark, 42 times; in Luke, 80 times, and in John, 246 times.

I want to take another mechanical illustration. There is a Greek pronoun which stands for "I," exactly the equivalent of the Latin ego. If you follow the Greek Testament through, it is very interesting to see how often Jesus is recorded as having used that "I" in common human speech. How many times does Matthew tell you Jesus used that word? Only 29. Mark, who is presenting the Servant, gives it 17 times. Luke only uses it 33 times. How many times does John tell you Jesus said "I"? One hundred and thirty-four, speaking of Himself. And yet you never read that Gospel of John and feel that you are in the presence of a person who used the first person singular in the way of braggadocio. Never! And yet He is always using it.

I have often drawn attention to the fact that in John you have no set discourses of Jesus until you come to the great allegory of the vine. He is always discoursing, always discussing in the presence of those who inquired of Him or asked Him questions—mostly His enemies—but in all these you find He uses that pronoun no less than 33 times. In other words, while you are impressed with the human as it is revealed and illustrated by the constancy of the use of the name "Jesus," you are impressed by the most august majesty and deity as He uses that personal pronoun in the first person singular so constantly and so amazingly.

So, in the human there is the divine, the Word made flesh. Beyond that I cannot go. Take the whole Gospel from that standpoint and consider it. We must keep sight of this commonplace and yet good thing to say: as you read the Gospel you will find 8 occasions upon which our Lord uses the words "I am." Search them out and don't miss one: "Before Abraham was I am." Then look where He puts the "I am"—against things that symbolize and illustrate and help to interpret God always.

When you go back into ancient history to the moment in the desert when Moses saw the bush that was burning and not consumed, you remember that he heard a voice saying, "Put off thy shoes from off thy feet, for the place whereon thou standest is holy ground." And you go near with Moses, and presently you ask, with great and holy daring, the name of the One who is speaking; and the answer is given in a remarkable way—"I am." Read it as if for the first time, and wait eagerly and anxiously to know what follows. "I am": and He does not say anything but it rolls back upon itself in majesty: "I am that I am."

And centuries run their course until this present saying, "The Word was made flesh, tabernacled"; and John takes the great divine revelation and declaration "I am," and focuses it and links with it all he had to relate, all the simple things that interpret the Godhead. This is the Gospel of John.

Consider the great key words of John's writings, whether in the Gospels or in the Epistles or even in the Apocalypse. What are they? Life and Light and Love. In every incident recorded and every discourse that you read, you will see Life is the burden, and Light is shining, and Love is pulsing. Yes, he laid his head upon the bosom of Jesus, and I have no doubt that when John's head lay upon that bosom not only was he conscious of the beating of the human heart, but he became conscious of the beating of the heart of the eternal passion.

John finishes by giving you this account in his own writing: "Many other signs therefore did Jesus in the presence of the disciples, which are not written in this book: but these are written, that ye may believe that Jesus is the Christ, the Son of God; and that believing ye may have life in his name."

Who is He?

Peter was right. I sometimes think that when John wrote the little addition at the end of Chapter 20, before he added the postscript of what we call Chapter 21, he was thinking of Peter, as if he were saying to you that he had written all this to prove to you that Peter was right, when at Caesarea Philippi he said, "Thou art the Christ, the Son of the living God."

But you do not wait there, for in that same chapter he records the climacteric conviction as it came to a man like you, like me, like many, perhaps like most of us—wavering, wondering, puzzled even by the resurrection, and hardly believing, not daring to believe it—and then when he stood in the presence of Jesus and saw those hands and that side, he said to Him, "My Lord and my God."

So God has supplied human need Himself, in the Person of His Son, incarnate in human flesh with all the authority of the Godhead and all the fullness of redeeming Love and all power of revealing Truth to humanity.

This is He.

The Word made flesh.

28. ACTS—THE LORD OF THE CHURCH

We reach now the Book of the Acts and we realize that we are in the presence of the same Person we have seen in the Gospels. It is still Jesus, all the way from beginning to end; but there is a tremendous difference between the Person as we saw Him in what may accurately and Scripturally be described as the days of His flesh on earth, and the way in which we now see Him. We call to mind the great soliloquy of our Lord which Luke recorded, when one day in His earthly ministry, in the midst of all the limitations created by the conditions of humanity, He said, "I came to cast fire upon the earth; and what do I desire, if it is already kindled? But I have a baptism to be baptized with; and how am I straitened till it be accomplished!" One of the most arresting words there is the word "straitened." Our Lord said to the men who were His disciples—and among the crowds were many foes and friends—I have come for a purpose, and there is no passion in My heart so great as the accomplishment of that purpose. Would that it were already kindled, but I am straitened. I cannot fulfill that purpose yet. There is only one way in which it will ever be fulfilled: "I have a baptism to be baptized with."

Now in the Acts He is beyond that baptism, and He is no longer straitened in Himself. I think it must be said in passing, He was even then straitened in His people, and He has been ever since. But in Himself He was no longer straitened, and it is thus we see Him as we read this book. This book may be called an account of the beginning of the bringing of Gods supply to humanity to meet its need. All intelligent people know that this book is not correctly titled. It is not the acts of the apostles—it is some of the acts of the apostles, and some acts not done by apostles at all. It is something much bigger than that. I am not attempting to give it a new title, but I am attempting to interpret it. It is a page of history, and it gives the account of the beginning of that movement wherein and whereby God's supply of His human need is brought to humanity. The great mediatorial mission which is also kingly and prophetic is revealed here in new power; the Lord Himself at the center, no longer straitened. As we read, we see first of all the Lord mediating between God and man. The baptism accomplished, the victory won, the power of death broken, the Lord Himself ascended to the right hand of eternal power and authority. He is seen here as the Mediator, the One mediating between God and man.

Then, if you look again, you will see that there is a Mediator between the Lord and His people, and that is the Holy Spirit. Finally, you will see that the Church is revealed as mediating between the Lord and the world. I do not mean by that you can divide the chapters, so many for one thing and so many for the other. I am rather gathering up the ultimate values of the book, and if you will do so you will see all the way through there is unanimity in its need. Here is the marvelous supply God has provided to meet humanity's need, and here you have the account of how that supply is placed at the disposal of humanity. First, The Lord Himself, the Mediator between God and man. Then, as we look at those whom He is gathering to Himself in unstraitened power, we see the Holy Spirit of God mediating between the Lord and all those who are His. Finally we see the Church ideally presented as going out into the world, the instrument mediating between the Lord and the world with all its need.

To explain further: first of all, we see Him as mediating between God and man. Listen to the story of His ministry. We saw Him as King, and we heard Him at last say, "All authority hath been given unto me in heaven and on earth." We watched Him in sacrificial service completing the mediatorial work by which He became the one final and sufficient Priest, mediating between God and man; and we saw Him as the Word, the incarnate Word according to Luke, revealing to humanity the meaning of human nature in all the glorious perfections of His humanity. Now it is the same Person, but He is seen at the center of—what shall I say—the Universe? He is central to the universe, at the center of all human history, and all human life, and all human affairs. He is seen as King, as Prophet, and as the Priest, representing all the divine authority. During all His public ministry He preached the Kingdom of Heaven, or the Kingdom of God, interchangeable terms. But it was the Kingship of God He came to proclaim. Now all the authority of Kingship is seen vested in Him, and the supreme note, as we look at Him there, is that of this very authority which is absolute and final. There is no appeal from His authority. It has pleased the Father that in Him should all the fullness dwell, even corporeally, on the human level. But now God has exalted Him above all things in heaven, and things on earth, and things under the earth; and in the Acts we see that all the way the supreme Lord represented in His authority, the absolute authority of God, the Kingdom of God.

There is no account of any words that He uttered in this book. No great discourse is recorded as falling from His lips. You have certain things He said at the beginning before His ascension, and ever and anon something He said to individual souls under differing conditions; yet all the way through His teaching—yes, let me use that word—is concerned with the will of God, just as it was in His lifetime; but now His interpretations are accepted by those whom you see passing before you in this book. The complete philosophy of life, the complete wisdom, the complete Word has been given. The quest is no longer a quest It has become a conquest, because He has been found. Heaven and earth may pass away, as He Himself did say, but His words can never pass away. So we see Him mediating between God and man in Kingship, and in the revelation of the will of God to men and by them. How wonderfully we see Him as the great Mediator bringing men into fellowship with God. How? Sin is put away. Holiness is made possible. Peace is realized. It is the One we looked at in Matthew, Mark, Luke and John, but no longer limited and straitened. The Passion baptism is fulfilled, and He is now in the center of human history, the One Mediator between God and man. If the God whose holiness has been insulted, whose justice has been condemned, whose love has been trampled under foot, if He is to reach man, if man the rebel is to find his way back to God, he must do so through Him. He is the Mediator between God and man, and that is the great fact of this Book of the Acts.

Then, of course, if that is the first value, perhaps it is not the most impressive. The most impressive thing in the Acts is the revelation it gives to us of the Holy Spirit, and the relationship of the Holy Spirit; the Holy Spirit is seen as the Mediator between the Lord and all those who are His. We have two Intercessors. The One is Jesus Himself, at the right hand of God. The Other is the Spirit within us. Christ before God forever pleads our cause. The Spirit within us forever pleads the cause of Jesus Christ; and that is the whole wonderful story.

Take it in application to the three things we have referred to that we find vested in Christ, His Kingship, Priesthood and Prophetic teaching. What relationship does the Spirit bear as to man's attitude towards Him as Lord? I might say a good deal about that. I prefer to quote and make the Apostle Paul speak: "No man calleth Jesus Lord but by the Holy Spirit" A very remarkable and startling and searching declaration, to abide for all time true. Oh yes, you and I may say, "Lord, Lord." We may even give force to the saying: "Lord, Lord, did we not prophesy in Thy name, and in Thy name do wonderful works?" And yet He may be saying, and will say, "I never knew you." Saying with the lips that Jesus is Lord is one thing, and may have no value at all. It may have great value, but it may have none. To say "Lord" means the complete Submission of the soul to His mastery, the yielding completely to Him as Lord; and that is the first work of the Spirit in the soul of a man. When man, hearing the great evangel, turns his face toward Christ, directly he does so with inquiry, with quest, with desire, the Spirit is there to enable him to call Jesus, Lord. The Spirit mediates between the human soul and the Lord, giving the light and the life that enables that human spirit to call Him Lord.

The Spirit moreover is the Mediator between Christ and His teaching to all His people, and again I prefer to quote. This time I am not quoting from Paul but from the Lord Himself, when here in the days of His flesh among the early disciples. Hear it as though you had never heard it before. What did He say about the coming of the Spirit? "He shall teach you all things, and bring to your remembrance all that I said unto you." Which means this among other things: If you read the Sermon on the Mount; if you read the great parables, the parabolic discourses principally; if you read the Olivet prophecies, if you may so name them; if you read the Paschal discourses, you never can understand them save as you have the interpretation of the Holy Spirit as you read. You can make a wider application of that, seeing that what Peter said is true with regard to the Old Testament, to Him all the prophets give witness. But the supreme Witness is the Spirit; and the only way of rightly understanding the prophetic utterances and the historic meanings of the Old Testament as well as of the New is that of complete dependence upon the Spirit. Did not Jesus also say, "When he is come, he shall guide you into all the truth"? It is the Spirit who gives you power to call Him Lord, the Spirit who interprets to me, day by day as I walk my way, the things Jesus said.

Oh! but He said so little. Yes, as to bulk, very little. To use an old and homely illustration of my own that I have used often when talking to young people: if you take the trouble some day to write out for yourself all the words which are recorded as having fallen from the lips of Jesus, do you know you cannot fill a small exercise book? So little, yet so much; enough to cover all the necessities of human need individually, socially, nationally, internationally, and racially; so that if humanity does but get back into the presence of His teaching, there is the solution for all our problems. How shall we go about it? "He shall guide you into all the truth." Here you see in this book how He was doing it. A little further on in the epistles comes the enlarged conception of the Master Himself that growingly came to those early followers, under the teaching and inspiration of the Holy Spirit. That Spirit is not withdrawn. You say that you are waiting for the Spirit! Nothing of the kind. It may be the Spirit is waiting for you. Do not tell me you are praying for His baptism of power in ministry, and proof that you have the Spirit. You will never receive it; and if you do, you need to be very suspicious of it. The Spirit is *here*. No, you are not waiting, we are not waiting for Him. How often He is waiting for us, and He is persistently saying within us, "Jesus is Lord," and enabling us to say it; and He is persistently and growingly willing to lead us on and on, to more perfect understanding of the matchless teaching of this one great, full and final Prophet.

Within the veil is the Lord Himself. The ascension of Jesus was the great hour—forgive me if I use an expression that seems applicable to earthly things, and use it in a heavenly sense—it is the great hour of His coronation, and He passed within the veil. Luke relates at the end of His Gospel the last attitude in which the disciples saw Him. He lifted up His hands and blessed them; and those lifted hands were priestly hands, and the blessing was the benediction of His perfect Priesthood. Presently one of His earthly witnesses was dying, dying as the brutal stones were hurled upon him, lacerating the flesh, bruised and broken; and as the life was ebbing away, he said he saw Jesus standing; He was ascended to the right hand of the Father, and sat down—that is the place of authority—but if a child of His is suffering and suffering for Him, He is the Priest, He is seen standing, ministering to the deep necessity of that suffering child. Yes, He is the Priest within the veil, and yet in fellowship with His own. Listen to Him, "I will not leave you orphans, I will not leave you desolate"; well, what will happen? "I will come unto you." How did He come? He came in the Holy Spirit, and He came with the Spirit to abide with them for fellowship to disannul orphanage, to cancel loneliness. The Holy Spirit is the great Instrument, the Mediator at the beginning, giving power to call Him Lord through all the days, bringing to mind the things He taught, and interpreting them; and forevermore canceling the loneliness by making Jesus a living, bright reality to the soul on its pilgrimage.

And then of course, ultimately, we see in this book the Church of God between the Lord and the world. That is the vision! I am not saying it is more important than the others; it is dependent upon the others. The Church can only fulfill that great and high and holy and mysterious and marvelous and majestic and mighty function as she knows what it is to be brought nigh to God through Him; as she knows what it is to be filled with that Spirit of interpretation and revelation and power. But these things being granted, then Gods medium of communication between the world and Himself through Christ by the Spirit, is the Church.

What has the Church to say to the world? The first work is that of proclaiming His enthronement. But her second work is that of enunciating His ethic, or moral standards; and her final, ultimate ceaseless work is that of heralding His great evangel. Every one of these is important; but I still say that the first thing we have to do is to proclaim the enthronement of Christ. Take a little glimpse from this Book of the Acts. These people came to Thessalonica. Read the story of the Church there and the coming to Thessalonica, until hostility was stirred up against them, and certain people laid a charge against them. What was the charge? They declared that contrary to the decrees of Caesar these men are saying that there is another King, one Jesus. That was the message the Church went forth to give, and that is the message we are still called upon to deliver first—first before the evangel. A man never comes to the sense of need for the evangel until he has stood in the presence of the King. It is when I stand before Him and see His regal dignity, His final authority, His matchless beauty and spotless purity that I put my hand upon my lips and say "Unclean, I am a leper. What shall I do to be saved?" Now is the time for the evangel, but we must first call men to measure their lives by His Kingship. The enthronement of Jesus is the first note in the message that the Church is bearing to the world as she mediates between the world and God through Jesus Christ.

In the matter of enunciating His moral standards, we hear Jesus saying to Peter, as representative man, "I will give unto thee the keys of the kingdom." The keys never were the symbols of priestly office. They were the symbols of the work of the scribes. In those days they knew that perfectly well when He talked about keys, and He said in effect, "What you bind is bound, and what you loose is loosed." In both cases the binding and loosing means the declaration of what is obligatory on human life, and what is optional. If you consult the writings of the Rabbis you find this teaching. Hillel binds that, and some other teacher looses it. Hillel says it is obligatory and this other teacher says it is optional. That is the phrase. Our Lord has sent His Church out to bind and to loose, to set up the moral standards, and declare them; and they must be the moral standards that are based on the authority of the King; first the enthronement and then the laws, but we are sent out to proclaim those laws. We have no right under any circumstances, for the sake of supposed convenience, to modify the law of Christ in any detail.

Then, of course, thank God for the last thing. If we proclaim His authority, and pronounce His enthronement and ethic, then the sense of need is created. Then, blessed be God, we have an evangel, the good news that men may rise, the good news that the fetters can be broken, that liberty can come to the enslaved, that by the mystery of His Cross and passion there is redemption, full and plenteous. That is the great commission. These are the things that flash and flame through all this Book of the Acts.

The wonder of this book grows on me! What is it? It is a page in human history. It is the account of about a generation in human history, about thirty-three years, just about the length of the life of Christ. It is a picture of the Church and her Lord. Remember this, taken purely as a piece of history, in it you have the account of the initiation of an entirely new era in human history. That is the marvel of the book. It tells how God's supply for human need has been provided, and how it is made available to humanity, and there is none other name given under heaven among men whereby we must be saved but this one Name. And there is no hope for humanity, sighing for its priest, crying for its king, questing for its prophet; but there is every hope in Him, who is at once the King, and Priest and Prophet.

PART V

THE EPISTLES: GOD'S SUPPLY— THE INSTRUMENT OF THE LORD

29. ROMANS, GALATIANS, THESSALONIANS

We come now to the section of the Letters of the New Testament. They are all, strictly speaking, letters. Most of them are actual letters. Some of them were perhaps just pamphlets, but we speak of them as "Letters" in the New Testament, or Epistles. Of these we have twenty-one, and I want immediately to emphasize that they were all written to the Church and for the Church, not for the world or for outsiders. When you come to examine one or two of them, you will see how important it is to understand that.

For instance, one of the Letters deals fully and completely with salvation and is written to the Church. If a soul says to you or to me, "What shall I do to be saved?" we would not answer that person by saying, "You will have to read the Letter to the Romans and you will have that question answered." It is perfectly true that the question is answered, or rather explained, in Romans. But we would say to that man, "Repent toward God and believe on the Lord Jesus Christ, and thou shalt be saved"; and when he is repentant and believing and born again, then we can give him the Letter to the Romans and he will find there the true meaning of his experience. That is a distinction I always feel inclined to make.

THE EPISTLES

"All scripture is given by inspiration of God, and is profitable"—
II Timothy 3:16

THE EPISTLES: THE INSTRUMENT OF THE LORD	FUNDAMENTAL	*Romans, Galatians* *I, II Thessalonians, Hebrews, I, II, III John*	
	Resource		Responsibility
	I. Salvation by Christ Justification, Sanctification, Glorification		I. Dedication Romans 12:1, 2
	II. Liberty in Christ The Gospel Charter, The Law of Faith		II. Steadfastness Galatians 5:1
	III. Life with Christ Work of Faith, Labor of Love, Patience of Hope		III. Fidelity I Thessalonians 4:1
	IV. Authority of Christ The Final Speech of God The Full Truth for Man		IV. Obedience Hebrews 12:25
	V. Fellowship Through Christ Light, Love, Life		V. Fear I John 5:21
	EXPERIMENTAL	*Philippians, Philemon* *I, II Peter, James, Jude*	
	Resource		Responsibility
	I. Joy Triumphant In Christ, Over Circumstances, Toward Finality		I. Rejoice in the Lord Philippians 3:1
	II. Love Triumphant In the Slave, In the Master		II. Willing Obedience Philemon 14
	III. Life Triumphant Established in Christ, Established Through Processes, Established Against Foes		III. Conflict in Communion I Peter 5:8, 9
	IV. Faith Triumphant In Conflict, In Conduct, In Character		IV. Demonstration by Works James 2:24
	V. Loyalty Triumphant To the Lord, Over His Enemies		V. Fear in Love Jude 21
	VOCATIONAL	*I, II Corinthians* *I, II Timothy, Titus, Ephesians, Colossians*	
	Resource		Responsibility
	I. Temporal a. Church Unifying Spirit, Unfailing Law, Ultimate Triumph b. Ministry The Minister Himself, The Minister and the Church, The Minister and the Truth		I. Temporal a. Church At Work, I Corinthians 4:58 b. Ministry At Work, II Timothy 2:15
	II. Eternal a. Church The Heavenly Calling, The Earthly Conduct b. Christ His Personal Glory, His Instrument		II. Eternal a. Church The Worthy Conduct, Ephesians 4:1 b. Christ The Worthy Conceptions, Colossians 3:1, 2

Another preliminary word. I am not taking the Letters in the order in which they occur. I suppose it is generally believed that Thessalonians were the earliest written, but I do not believe that for a moment. I am perfectly certain that Galatians was the first Letter Paul ever wrote. They do not appear in the New Testament in the order in which they were written, so I am violating no supreme value if I take a letter out of order in consideration.

I have graded them under three headings: the Fundamental Letters, the Experimental Letters, and the Vocational Letters. By the Fundamental Letters I mean those pertaining to the great foundation truths of our holy faith. By Experimental Letters I mean those letters which deal with experiences of those who have this faith and have entered into relationship with Jesus Christ By Vocational Letters I mean letters that deal with the Church's vocation and the minister's vocation and the responsibility of the Church. Of course, this grouping is not intended to be final or dogmatic. It is merely suggested. I am not saying that in the list I call "Fundamental" that you have doctrine only and no experience—for experience is in the vocational and the fundamental writings. But the main purpose and value of them is rightly stated under the headings I have suggested.

One other word by way of introduction. You cannot read these Letters without seeing in them that all the writers (of course thirteen of them came from the pen of Paul, and if you count as his the Letter to the Hebrews, fourteen) see and emphasize the relationship between doctrine and deity, creed and conduct, truth and triumph in life. We find two main divisions, the part dealing with the resurrection of the believer, and the part dealing with the responsibilities of the believer. It is tempting to emphasize the truth of this because it is so important.

Two great mistakes have been made, that I can see, with respect to an interpretation of these New Testament Letters. One is that of men who say the supreme thing is the doctrine, and that if you have the doctrine nothing else very much matters. The other mistake is that of saying the supreme thing is the deity, and that if you have the deity the doctrine does not very much matter. You cannot divorce them, they lie close together. All deity depends upon doctrine, all conduct is based upon creed; all triumph in the Christian life is the outcome of truth sanctifying that life. And these things run all through these Letters.

To summarize the three Letters we are about to consider: in Romans we have the supreme document of Salvation; in Galatians we have the Magna Charta of Christian life; in Thessalonians we have a very remarkable conception of what the Christian life ought to be, based upon doctrines.

Beginning with the Roman Letter: it must be noted that we have no account of the founding of the Church in Rome. It certainly was in existence before Paul went there. As you read in the Acts, among the companies that were gathered on the Day of Pentecost who shared in the Pentecostal effusion of power, there were sojourners from Rome who, no doubt, went back, and as the result of their going back, the Church was founded there in Rome. At that moment when Paul was writing to them he had not been able to go. He wanted to go, and he did go at last, though not in the way he thought to go. But he went, and the account of his ministry there is full of wonderful power. When he wrote to them, he felt there might be something that needed stating clearly to the Church in Rome about salvation which he and others were preaching and proclaiming in the name of Jesus. Therefore, he wrote this Letter to these Christians at Rome, and began in the most remarkable way by tracing the background that proved the necessity for salvation. This he does in the first three chapters, and in the third chapter there is a Summary of the whole thing in verse 23: "All have sinned, and fall short of the glory of God." That is the Apostles summary of world conditions, and the things we looked at as illustrated and revealed in the Old Testament, he has summarized. Remember Paul has dealt with the facts under the two main heads: he begins with a Gentile world. He then passes to the Jewish nation, and summarizes and brings them all under the same condemnation, showing that all are involved in this supreme and appalling necessity.

To me it is always wonderful. With clear, daring and intrepid eyes Paul looked into the facts of human life. At the Gentile, holding down the clear light upon his unrighteousness and proving his indecent action; at the Jew, condemning the Gentile and yet practicing the same thing while professing to hold a better creed. He saw the whole world brought into condemnation. That is the background only.

Then follows that marvelous section in which he deals with salvation provided in Christ for humanity whether Gentile or Jew, whether barbarian, bond or free. To go through it carefully is to find that this salvation is dealt with as having three qualities, or three phases. (I am almost afraid of another word lest I seem to be minimizing.)

What is the salvation that God has provided to every man? You must come down to the individual and leave out the racial problem. Now I think of the individual, and the first phase of salvation is justification. How boldly this is dealt with. And the second phase—and here is where I do not like my word in case I am using one with two meanings—is sanctification; and the final phase in this great work is glorification. As we go from Chapter 3 on through the fourth and then to the eighth, that movement is seen. Justification is infinitely more than forgiveness. Justification is that act of the righteous God in righteousness whereby He places righteousness at the disposal of sinning men. Justification puts the sinner back into the place as if he had committed no sin. That is the first thing, and that has to do, of course, with the essential nature of man which is spiritual. Justification has to do with the spirit relationship with God—the spirit which is the essential thing. I need not argue that. The mind is essential, the body is not essential. Neither one nor the other is final, and neither is a complete personality without the other. But the deep center of human personality is spiritual and there salvation begins. It takes the man or woman, youth or maiden, brings them back into right relationship with God, and sets that soul into place with

God, justified freely by His Grace in response to the soul's faith in Christ Jesus.

Sanctification is a process that has to do with the man's conscience, the voice bringing him into harmony with Christ. And the final thing will be that glorious day for which we are all waiting, when the body will be transformed into the body of His glory. There are tenses of salvation. Past? Yes, I was saved. Present, progressive? I am being saved. I am in process of salvation. Future? I shall be saved, for now is my salvation nearer than when I believed. That is the great doctrine, and that is where the Roman Letter sets forth these values of salvation.

Glorification refers to the time when the body shall be changed and there shall be a new personality. This is the redeeming work which began with the spirit, continues through the mind, and will be completed in the glory of the resurrection. Such is the resource.

Then the responsibility: Paul writes the tenth and eleventh chapters and then says, "I beseech you brethren, by the mercies of God." I halt there. What are the mercies of God? We think of the mercies of God by which we are surrounded: life and health, food and raiment, and the sun shining; but Paul was not thinking of these things. The mercies of God were justification, and sanctification and glorification—these three fundamentals which He gave us in salvation. "I beseech you therefore, by the mercies of God, to present your bodies a living sacrifice, holy, acceptable to God."

Notice the psychology of that I am not fond of that word but still it is right—the Bible is full of psychology, but it is Bible psychology. So Paul was talking: "I beseech you… present your bodies." What does he mean? All you have in your body. It is personality, which means the central and essential fact of personality, which is spirit. I beseech you, spiritual entities, present your bodies. Oh yes, you can do that, you are responsible for it. The responsibility is finite, but it is definite responsibility. By those mercies of God— which are the marvel of this salvation, by the eternal wonder of what has been done by God in Christ in glorifying, by these mercies placing these things at your disposal—present your bodies a living sacrifice, holy, acceptable to God, which is your reasonable service.

If in Romans we have the document of salvation, in Galatians we have the Magna Charta of the Church. What a Letter it is!

I often sit down to compare for myself the Galatian Letter with Philippians. My dear and honored friend, Dr. Rendel Harris, once said to me that the Galatian Letter was Paul's high explosive. It certainly was. He was angry, really angry. He was satirical when he wrote it. Some of the satire in Galatians is very biting and acid and searching. It was the Galatian Letter that was Martin Luther's thunderbolt out of which the Reformation came. That is general. What is the background of the Galatian Letter? A peril that was threatening the invasion of the Church. And what was it? No, it was not false doctrine in a sense; it was not heresy in the way in which we use the word today. It was heretical, and it was acute and it was a peril—a peril created by Judaising

teachers. Who were they and what were they doing? These teachers were going forth superemphasizing that certain rites and ceremonies were necessary to salvation. Judaism! Yes, in other words, these Gentile Christians especially were being told, "Yes, you can be a Christian, but you must go through the Jewish gateway and submit yourself to the rites and ceremonies of the Jewish faith." In other words, salvation was dependent not fully, not only, upon faith, but upon rites and ceremonies. This stirred the anger of Paul to the very deeps, and I am not going to take back a word. He was angry, and was capable of being angry, even with Peter, withstanding him to the face because he was to be blamed. This Letter is vibrant with the hot anger of a man who saw the whole Church in peril by this wicked idea that something was necessary to salvation. That is the background, and that is all we need to say about it because the Letter itself puts it fully and clearly.

What does Paul insist upon with illustrious argument in this Letter? The liberty of those who believe in and through Jesus Christ. Faith in Him means complete emancipation from every yoke of bondage. Now you understand what I meant when I said it was Martin Luther's great dynamic. We still need it. We are still in danger of superimposing certain rites and certain ceremonies upon faith as necessary to salvation: baptism, the Lord's Supper, and so on. All right and proper in their place, but not one of them was necessary to salvation. There is perfect liberty from every yoke of bondage and rite and every other incubus that rested upon the soul of man in his attempt to gain salvation.

And yet you cannot read this Letter without seeing how careful Paul is to point out that liberty is not license. Faith has its law of requirements, and the law of such requirements is severe and searching. You are not to say that because of faith you are set free from certain obligations that abide and are binding. All the resources of Christ, *and* perfect liberty— *within* the law, the law of His mastership and His leadership.

And then Paul comes to the responsibility. And what is it? "Stand fast… and be not entangled again in a yoke of bondage." Stand fast in your liberty, but *stand*. Let nothing move you from that freedom. It is yours in Christ. Don't let yourself be entangled with rites and ceremonies necessary to salvation, but appreciate your liberty in loyalty to your Lord.

We turn to Thessalonians. There are two Letters. The second, as everyone knows, was written to correct a mistaken idea that possessed the Thessalonian Christians about something Paul had said about the second advent of our Lord in his earlier Letter. The second Letter is most valuable, but I am concerned with the great teaching which is fundamental in the first Letter and by implication runs through both Letters. In these Letters you have the most remarkable conception of what Christian living is. In Chapter 1:2 Paul says, "We give thanks to God always for you all, making mention of you in our prayers; remembering without ceasing" …what?… "your work of faith and labor of love and patience of hope." That is Christian living.

We read in 1:9: "For they themselves report concerning us what manner of entering in we had unto you; and how ye turned unto God from idols, to serve a living and true God, and to wait for his Son from heaven."

By placing words from verse 2 by words out of verse 9, you will find that all the argument of the Letter revolves around that conception of Christian living:

Verse 2   *Verse 9*

The work of faith............ You turned to God from idols

Labor of love................. To serve the living and true God.

The patience of hope...... To wait for His Son from heaven.

There you have all the Christian life and experience, the work of faith. That is where it begins. You will remember what our Lord said one day when He was asked what the disciples should do: "This is the work of God, to believe in him whom he hath sent." The work of faith—that is turning to God from idols, That is where your Christianity begins, or else it never did begin. Having turned to God from idols, what is the issue? The labor of love. What is that? To serve the living and true God. While serving, after turning, what is our attitude? The patience of hope. Hope for what? To wait for His Son from heaven.

And these three words show all the story of the life of our Lord, in His ministry and His mighty work. He wrought, when He came, that in which I can believe; and believing in it, I turn through Him to God, from all idols. He did that in order that I might become His, and that I might—all through the processes of my life—know what is the labor of love. All the while, and nothing is more remarkable in this Letter than this, there is shining upon the pathway of those who have turned from idols to serve the living and true God, the light of the second advent of our Lord. The outlook of the Christian is always to be the second advent of our Lord. If you are trying to find out when it will be, you are not looking for it. It is a great mistake, a persistent peril. We are not intended in know. We are intended to live ready always in the light of the second advent.

What is the Christian conception of life? It is the life of faith in Christ in which we turn from idols to serve the living God in complete surrender. That is what faith means. This is forevermore the labor of love, to serve God to whom we turn. And whether the way is hard or easy, or whether monotonous or over hills and through valleys; all the way to move onward toward the sunrise and the glory and the consummation—that is the patience of hope, to wait for His Son from heaven. The great responsibility which is taught in the Letter is that of our fidelity to our Lord.

These are the three foundation documents of our faith: the salvation which God provided for humanity; the liberty which Christ creates for those who trust Him; and the life that such are called upon to live on the way.

30. HEBREWS, I JOHN, II JOHN, II JOHN

We have come to Hebrews and John. And I summarize first by saying that in Hebrews the theme is the authority of Christ. In the first of the Letters of John the subject is fellowship through Christ. As we shall see, it is fellowship with God in Christ, and it is fellowship with God through Christ. (The second and third Epistles following are personal and local illustrations of the great principles revealed in the first Letter.)

I wish to refer to two things in the background of this Letter to the Hebrews: first of all, the remarkable anonymousness of the Letter; and secondly, its great certainties. (I do not mean the certainties declared in it, but the certainties of the Letter.) Nobody knows who wrote it. That may be a shock! I have a strong conviction, but I do not know, and you do not know—and that is one of the of the Letter. Some people are sure that Paul wrote it; certainly it was written in that period of the history of the early Church. Another school is sure that Apollos wrote it, and there are those who think that Priscilla wrote it (it is acute enough to indicate a woman did write it, but at the same time, I do not think it is proved). I think myself that Luke wrote it, and that he wrote it under the influence of Paul—but I cannot prove it. There is nothing in it that gives any clue as to the time when it was written. It is anonymous as to its recipients—we do not know to whom this was sent. It is noticeable upon reading it that it has not the form of a letter. There is no address at the beginning as there is in other letters, and there is no mention at the end of any names which can mark it in any way. So we do not know for whom this Letter was written or to whom it was sent.

Now as to the certainties about the Letter. The first is this. It was written to Hebrews. You cannot read it without seeing it was intended for Hebrew Christians. Moreover, we can detect evidence all through the Letter that it was written to some particular community. It was not a general letter in the sense in which John's Letters were. It was written to some community on the subject of persecution. One of the earliest beliefs—I do not know that it was right for there are no proofs—was that this Letter was written to the Church in Jerusalem. There are many evidences with which I cannot deal here. But it is certain that the people to whom it was written were in great danger of apostasy. There were those who were falling away through persecution and abandoning their Christian faith; and it is evident that this particular danger was created for these Hebrew Christians by the tremendous lure of the splendor of the Hebrew religion and ritual. They had been born in the midst of that religion; they had known its splendors. As you read it, you can see what probably they were thinking. They were thinking of the simplicity that there is in Christ and the freedom from all ritual Then probably these people had seen the Letter to the Galatians. I think that Galatians was the first Letter from the pen of Paul preserved for us. Luke would see the great argument against Judaism and Judaising teachers, and I can hear what Paul said as I read this Letter to the Hebrews. I can hear the Hebrew saying, "Our faith was brought to us by angels. What have we in Christianity compared with that? Moreover, we had a great leader, a law-giver, who gave us the whole system of our life and our religion. What has

Christianity to offer us in comparison with that? Moreover in the hours when we marched into this land we had a great leader named Joshua, and we had a priest, Aaron, and a priestly order." And they challenged that Christianity, and succumbed to the temptation to return, from the simplicity in Christ, to submit themselves to the old form of religion. Now, all this is in the Hebrew Letter. I have not imagined these things, this is exactly what the writer is talking about: Moses, Joshua, Aaron—that is his first line of argument. As I have said, these people were in danger of apostasy by the lure of the splendor of the Hebrew life and religion and literature. That is the background. To these people, in these conditions, this letter or pamphlet was sent.

And what does it say? We can summarize everything when we declare that the writer tells these people that while it is true God had spoken to their fathers, mat day had passed away. "God, having of old time spoken unto the fathers in the prophets by divers portions and in divers manners, hath at the end of these days"—that is, in the days in which that was God's method of revelation—"spoken unto us in his Son... It was the great declaration, and Christ is revealed as the final speech of God to men. God has said nothing to men since then, and God has nothing to say to men other than that which He said when He spoke in His Son. That does not mean that we have understood it all. It does not mean that we have plumbed the depths or climbed the heights of what God said when He spoke in His Son. But it does mean that He has nothing else to say. It is the final speech.

This is exactly what Hebrews shows. It is as if the writer says, "You are right, God did speak to the fathers but He has spoken in His Son. You are right. Your whole system was ministered to you by angels, but the Son is greater than the angels. You are perfectly right. Your great leader, Moses, led you out, but he could not lead you in. The Son has led you out and is leading you in. And you may say Joshua led you in, but he could not give you rest. The Son has not only led you out, but has led you in and brought you into the place of perfect rest."

Ah! But they say, "We had a priesthood, we had Aaron." So they did, but there was nothing permanent; but the Son has a glory greater than that of Aaron and is become a Priest forever after the order of Melchizedek. The finality of the Son—greater than angels, greater than Moses, greater than Joshua, greater than Aaron! If you look for this word "better" in the Bible, you will find it occurs no less than thirteen times.

And as Christ is revealed as the final speech of God, He is revealed as the final truth for men; and the truth about Kingship, the truth about Priesthood, the truth about the Prophetic dynasty unveiling the will of God is found in Christ. The Letter to the Hebrews reveals the authority of Christ as being absolute! Such are the resources referred to.

In view of these resources, the writer refers to the subject of responsibility. It is all gathered up in Chapter 12, in this sentence: "See that ye refuse not him that speaketh." I would suggest that you put this verse by the side of Chapters 1,2, and 3. Listen! "God has spoken unto us in his Son"; "How shall we escape if we neglect so great salvation?"; "See that ye refuse not him that speaketh." So the whole Letter is gathered up in the grand appeal which is made by the glories that are revealed and the absolute finality of the authority of Jesus; and the necessity for recognizing it, obeying it, seeing that we refuse not Him that speaketh.

I turn for a few moments to John. What is the background of this Letter? It is catholic. I mean this in the true sense of the word. It is often called the General Epistle of John, and rightly so. It is not directed to any particular Church named or to Christian people by name, but evidently to Christian people under certain conditions. My own personal opinion is that John wrote this Letter in Ephesus; there is no doubt John was there in Ephesus for some considerable time. That is shown in the general Ephesian atmosphere. I do not mean Christian—the Letter is written to believers in Christ who are in the midst of pagan surroundings, and it is written specifically to show them what their Christianity really means.

Now, you have the declared purpose toward the conclusion of the Letter. Read those words in Chapter 5:13:

"These things have I written unto you, that ye may know that ye have eternal life." He does not mean so much an intellectual demonstration as an experimental demonstration. All he has written, he has written as a test, so that you can find out all those who really have eternal life at all.

The closing declaration of this Letter may be linked with what John wrote at the close of his Gospel. What did he say after he had penned his Gospel? "Many other signs therefore did Jesus in the presence of the disciples, which are not written in this book: but these are Written, that ye may believe that Jesus is the Christ, the Son of God; and that believing ye may have life in his name."

Now the Epistle: "These things have I written unto you, that ye may know that ye have eternal life." The Epistle is a sequel to the Gospel, interpreting it. Let me put it in this way. In the Gospel, the way into life is declared and illustrated. In the Epistle is given the interpretation of the life you find when you believe in Jesus as the Son of God. The Gospel is written that you may believe, and believing have life. The Epistle is written that you may test your experience.

I quote from Chapter 1:3, "Our fellowship is with the Father, and with his Son Jesus Christ." The life that we live when we believe that Jesus is the Son of God is a life that becomes a life of fellowship with God and His Son.

"Fellowship" is a wonderful word. The word that John used that we find in all his writings is the Greek word, which we have translated sometimes "fellowship, agreement, partnership, partakership." A common word? Ah it is! If you want to catch what our word "fellowship" means, go to the Acts of the Apostles, and you read where the disciples had all things in common. That is the root—all things in common, and all resources of God at my disposal, all my resources at His disposal—as they ought to be.

That is the whole theme of the Letter of John. And that fellowship is re-examined in this Letter in two divisions, sharp, clear and final. What are they? There is one in the first chapter: God is light. You will find one in the fourth chapter: God is love. And you will find them amplified in the fifth chapter, "He gave unto us eternal life, and this life is in his Son." You must know if you study John at all, if you read his Gospel or his Letters, these are the great words—Light, Love and Life: the essential things of God brought to men in the Son of God. God is Light, and light for men is in Christ. God is Love, and love for men operates through Christ. Life is in the Son of God, and this life is in His Son. And that is what John is after. Now do we know that Light, and are we walking in it? Do we know that Love and are we obeying its impulses? Do we know such Life and do we yield entirely to His claim and His power? If we do, then we are in fellowship with the Father and with His Son, our Lord and Master. And so we ought to know by these tokens whether We have life at all. If we lack them, we may make loud professions and sing hymns and do all sorts of good works, and yet not have life.

"These things are written that ye may know that ye have eternal life." And the responsibility is ours, as John declared in the last sentences of that first Letter: "My little children, guard yourselves from idols." Anything that stands in the place of God to you; anything that stands between you and God; anything—even that by which you are attempting to realize your life—if it comes between you and God is to be swept out if you would know what fellowship with God is, directly and immediately. What is it? It is walking in the light, answering the love of God, realizing the power of the life of God.

31. PHILIPPIANS, PHILEMON

We are now beginning to consider the second group of Letters, the group I have described as Experimentals; by which I mean the group of Letters in which we have revealed what experience of Christianity means. What are the facts in Christian experience?

Let us first remind ourselves of the fact that in all of these Letters the Church is seen facing the pagan world. I have insisted before, and I repeat now, the Letters are for the *Church* and not for the world. Every Letter was written to Christian people and is intended for their consideration. But the whole of them were written to people, members of the Church, who were facing the pagan world. Of course, that is true of the whole of the New Testament literature. The story of Christ is the story of Christ in the pagan world. The story of the Church is the story of the Church moving out into the pagan world delivering its message, that pagan world upon which, as Matthew Arnold has very brilliantly said, dark lust and deep loathing had fallen.

Now when we come to these Experimental Letters and the study of them, the dominant note in all of them is that of a Church facing a pagan world. I have no sympathy with people who tell us today that these are the darkest days the world has ever seen. The days in which we live are appalling, but they do not compare with conditions in the world when Jesus came into it. Historians talk of the *Pax Romana* and make much of the fact that there was peace everywhere, the Roman peace. Do not forget that the Roman peace was the result of the fact that the world had been bludgeoned brutally into submission to one central power. There have been many attempts since then to repeat it. It never has succeeded and never will. There will never again be a world hegemony until He shall come who shall represent peace and reign over all the earth.

Notwithstanding the prevailing conditions, the dominant note of these Letters, revealing the experience of the Church, is a note of triumph. The dire and dread facts and conditions are never lost sight of—indeed, they are there all the way through. The people are seen going out and facing these facts—and suffering because of these facts—but we never see them depressed and cast down, we never see them suffering from pessimistic fever. They are always triumphant. That is the glory of Christianity. If ever I am tempted to think that religion is almost dead today, it is when I listen to the wailing of some Christian people: "Everything is wrong," or "Everything is going wrong." Oh, be quiet! Think again, look again, judge not by the circumstances of the passing hour but by the infinite things of our Gospel and our God. And that is exactly what these people did.

We take Philippians first. What is the background here? Philippi. Remember that Philippi was a Roman colony, and that does not mean what we mean today by a colony. But a Roman colony meant in every case a city established exactly on the pattern of the Roman Empire, an outpost of Empire always. It had the same order, the same laws, the same methods of enforcing those laws. Philippi was an outpost of the Roman Empire, a colony in that sense. Then Philippi is interesting to us because it was at that point that Paul crossed over into Europe. What has resulted in Europe for Christianity began there, with Paul entering into Europe. We have the story of the beginning. The vision of the man in Macedonia, and how Paul straightway went to Philippi and there began the Christian movement in Europe. "And the Lord opened the heart of Lydia." Through the open door of a woman's heart, Christianity marched out of Asia into Europe beginning the great campaign in Europe.

Notice another thing. When you read the story of Paul coming to Philippi, you will notice Christianity began to face a new kind of opposition; an opposition that it had not known in the East began when it marched toward the West. Commercialism! Oh, perhaps you do not hear that word, but that has characterized western opposition to Christianity ever since. The opposition of the East has been religious, mystic, occult; but when Paul came to Philippi something happened, and you will notice how the hostility worked out against Paul and his message when a source of gain was gone. Christianity began to interfere with commercial enterprise, and then the European opposition began. And it is still going on.

What happened to Paul because of the opposition? He was soon found in prison. A matchless story! And then the jailor, a brutal man, wishing to keep safely his prisoners, Paul and Silas, was not content with putting them into an ordinary prison but thrust them into the dark, dank dungeon; not content with that, he fastened their feet in the stocks, and their backs probably were bleeding and sore from the Roman lictors. And having done that, he locked the door on them. You note I have called him "brutal"; and if you say to me, "What makes you think so?"—when he had done that, he went to bed and went to sleep. He had no feeling of compassion in his heart.

Now the significant thing is what happened in the night. Paul and Silas sang. They sang hymns, they hymned God and they worshiped. Think of it! Feet in the stocks, backs bruised and bleeding and sore, in agony from those rods in the dank, darkness of the inner dungeon—but they sang. I do not know what sort of voice Paul had nor what the voice of Silas was like, but I do think it was such singing that all the prisoners were listening. I think they sang heartily, and you know the result. I need not tell the story. I am emphasizing just the background of this Letter. The Church in Philippi was born then and there. The first Church member was that brutal jailor. And before the night was over his brutality had vanished and he was washing their stripes and taking them into his home and caring for them. Christianity had come to Philippi and the Church was founded. And now years have passed away and Paul is in prison again, this time in Rome. This Letter was certainly written, in my own judgment, in the first imprisonment, not the final one. Paul is in prison, and that is the background of the Letter: the Church formed by the singing of hymns in prison, and now a man in prison is writing to the members of that Church. And how he loved them! You may have noticed that this is really a singing letter, a love letter. You cannot read it without seeing how Paul loved these Philippians and how they loved him and ministered to his necessity now and again. There was a great link of love to the man who writes from prison this singing letter. Sin is never mentioned in the Philippian Letter. Have you noticed that? The flesh is only mentioned to be dismissed, and there does not seem to be a ripple of any kind, except just a reference to two women in the Church who had not been getting on very well, Euodia and Syntyche; some of the people did not like them because they did not agree, and Paul had to beseech them to be of the same mind, and the others to see that they treated them with brotherliness. But that is the only little ripple. It is all singing from beginning to end.

What does it all mean? Epaphroditus had come from Philippi bringing gifts to Paul, and just on the human level that was the occasion of the writing of this Letter. And what a letter it is! There are things in this little Letter to the Philippians so sublime that nothing else can reach the same height in all the Bible, from Genesis to Revelation. There are unveilings of truth concerning our Lord in Colossians and Ephesians, but how different they are to this, though written at the same time. In this Letter Paul writes of the mind of Christ, and he gives us a description of the mind of Christ by way of an injunction to these Philippian Christians: "Have this mind in you, which was also in Christ Jesus." Then follows: Who being in the form of God, did not make that equality a thing to be snatched and held for His enrichment, but emptied Himself, stepped from sovereignty to servitude, took on Him the form of a servant, passing all the high hierarchies of the heavens, He became a man; and "being found in fashion as a man," having come to the fulfillment of the meaning of humanity, He still "humbled himself, becoming obedient even unto death"; and when He came to death, He did not die as many have died, surrounded by loved ones, their passing soothed by the ministry of such— "yea, the death of the cross."

What does this Letter do for Christian experience? I have already shown you what it does. It shows all the way through the joy of the Christian. Since imprisoned in Philippi, Paul is still writing a singing letter a generation after. It is joy from beginning to end. How do you account for it? What is the source of joy as revealed here? Paul and Silas had all the meaning of joy in the familiar word, "To me, to live is Christ." And the secret of that joy was to have in them the mind of Christ, to share the mind of Christ, and the mind of Christ was the mind of a great self-emptying. Paul knew what it was to have a string of the lute that only uttered praises and love, broken and flung away. He knew self-emptying, and therefore he was filled with joy. If you would learn to know the measures of his joy, read again in Philippians his autobiography. How much we know of Paul through his own writings! But nothing is so revealing as that passage which he writes in this Letter. Don't forget he was a prisoner. I may say in passing that the word he used in this Letter, and used in Ephesians, Timothy, and in Thessalonians is "prisoner." He spoke of himself as a prisoner, but in all of them it is as "the prisoner of the Lord, of Jesus Christ"— never of Nero. Nero was out of sight, banished. A prisoner! Roman soldiers about him, Nero's manacles on his hands? Nothing of the kind, said Paul, "My Lord is Christ and I was manacled as a prisoner of Jesus Christ." But he does not use that word here. He refers to "my bonds" four times, and you see in that reference to his bonds he uses a note of triumph over them. Indeed, on one occasion he says his bonds have turned out for the furtherance of the gospel. There he is, a prisoner, rejoicing, and writing to these people, telling them of the secret of this joy. The Christian life is pre-eminently one of joy, and triumph. And you see how his joy is working toward finality when you read the third chapter. He is looking on, he is pressing toward the mark.

I have no doubt many of you have noticed this, and heard it said before, but it is worth repeating: when this man was Saul, before he became Paul, he was persecuting the Church of God. You remember what he wrote in this Letter: "One thing I do, forgetting the things which are behind: I press on toward the goal"; and he has been writing of his persecution of the Church before that. It is the same Greek verb used for "press." It is the same idea. The very passion that Paul had put into the business of persecution, he is now putting into the business of accomplishing his purpose and fulfilling his life, until he shall be transformed into the very likeness of His Lord. He is triumphing all the way through. And that is the responsibility of a Christian.

In the third chapter he says, "Finally, rejoice in the Lord." Then he gives that very marvelous story of himself. And again in the next chapter, when he gets nearer the end, he says in verse 4, "Rejoice in the Lord always: again I will say, Rejoice." He would show it is the privilege of the Christian to rejoice. Paul did not add it is the duty of the Christian to rejoice: it is commanded, and that is what Paul means when he says in effect, "I had better repeat that again. I will say 'Rejoice.'" And that is the privilege of the Christian. It is the true experience of the Christian. And the measure in which you and I fail to rejoice and to know joy triumphant is that measure in which there is failure somewhere in our relationship to Christ.

There is so much in this Letter! "Work out your own salvation in fear and trembling." It is God worketh in you. Work it out, and if you do not work it out, then the joy of the Lord will cease. Oh yes, this Letter is a well-spring of joy. "I will draw water out of the wells of salvation," said the prophet long, long before. And here is the picture. Do not forget: the pagan world, the persecuted Church, the prisoner at Rome, and the writer, and joy is triumphant. That is the normal, not the abnormal, Christian experience.

Let us consider Philemon. What a wonderful half sheet of paper it is! What is the background here? It is first of all Paul, a prisoner. He is still a prisoner, and there is no doubt that this little Letter to Philemon was written at the same time that Paul was writing to the Colossians, the Ephesians and the Philippians. You will find in Colossians that he sent Onesimus down and Tychicus to carry the Letter to the Church at Colosse. And you will notice that when Paul wrote the Letter, he did not write only to Philemon, but to "the church in thy house." I imagine Philemon receiving the Letter and looking earnestly at it, and then at the man who is handing it to him, Onesimus, the slave who has run away. And I can imagine Philemon reading it quietly on one side, and then he finds Archippus is named, and he says to him, "Archippus, you must listen too." And Archippus came. And then he called the household, because the Letter is to all of them, to a fellowship.

And there was the runaway slave. I am going to say something dogmatic: I think that Onesimus was Philemon's brother. I cannot see why commentators dodge this. When Paul says that Onesimus was a brother to Philemon, not only in the spirit but in the flesh, he means it. You say, "He was a slave." Do not forget the conditions at that time. Relatives were sold into slavery. And I have no doubt that Onesimus was a slave to his brother, Philemon. There he was, a slave. He had run away from Colosse. I do not know how long he was on the journey or where he went, but somehow or other he got to Rome, and he found Paul was in Rome. He knew about Paul; perhaps he had seen him in Philemon's house on some past day. He went to Paul and he was born again. Said Paul, "I have begotten him in my bonds"

There is the background: Paul a prisoner, that Christian household at Colosse, and the runaway slave. You know the story, but notice what you might pass here. Love triumphant, first of all—Philemon's love for the Lord Jesus, and Paul begins by recognizing that. Secondly, Paul's love for Philemon in Christ. Thirdly, Onesimus's love for Paul as the one through whom he had been led to Christ, and to whom he wanted to minister and had been ministering there in the prison. Love everywhere. But the manifestations of the triumph of love are the outstanding facts of this little Letter. Paul's triumph of love is seen in that he sent Onesimus back when he did not want to. Of course, he wanted to in the deeper sense, but, "I fain would have kept him with me for ministering." No doubt Paul did not want to do without Onesimus. His love for him was great. But it was a love that pointed out to him that, in order for the perfecting of the character of Onesimus, it was necessary for him to go back, and as far as possible make restitution for the wrong which he had done.

Paul also loved Philemon. He wanted to give Philemon—he tells you so—an opportunity for the exercise of his faith in love. Oh yes, Paul sent Onesimus back and love triumphed. And love triumphed in Onesimus. He went back because of love for Paul, if you like, but also for something more than love for his leader—love for the Lord of his leader, as Paul had interpreted it to him. It was not an easy thing to do. According to the law under which they were living, his life was forfeit. It was perfectly legal for Onesimus to go back and for Philemon to have him put to death. But he was going back, and there is only one thing strong enough to make him tramp a journey like that. It is love. And then, of course, there is the victory of the love of Philemon, when he received the Letter. We are not told what he said. But, oh yes, we are. Paul was sure that Philemon would receive Onesimus as he asked him to do, no longer as a slave but as a brother beloved. Love is seen triumphing in Paul and in Onesimus and in Philemon.

The responsibility of love is revealed in one little phrase in which Paul says he is sending him back. He wants Philemon to receive Onesimus "not of necessity, but of free will"; not merely because Paul asks him, but because his life is mastered by a love that forgives and forgets and receives and restores the soul to its new inheritance in Christ Jesus. Love is seen radiant in that little Letter, triumphant from beginning to end.

So there are these two Letters, Philippians and Philemon, triumphant in joy. It is a great thing that Elihu said when he was talking to Job: "He giveth songs in the night." And history proves the truth. About midnight, Paul and Silas were singing. And all that followed came out of the fullness of their experience in and through Jesus Christ. On the darkest night we are told to sing, on the most perilous journey we are told to sing. So we ought to do. It is a command laid upon us to rejoice, and if we never do, there is something wrong with our relationship with our Lord. Love never fails. I think no more beautiful thing was written in the Old Testament about love, perfect love, than Zephaniah wrote: "He will be silent in his love. He will joy over thee with   singing. And there the two great things merge, love triumphant and joy triumphant. God will rest in His love, as we lean on it. The English of the Hebrew word there is a perfect picture of motherhood, the Motherhood of God. You see the mother with her baby, watching it, silent in love, until silence ceases and singing begins. What a thing to say! He will rejoice over thee with singing. And you and I can have that love of God, and know the love of God, and know the joy of God. And the men to whom Jesus could say, under the shadow of the Cross, that He bequeathed to them His joy, will know the triumph of joy over all circumstances, and the triumph of love all the way along.

32. I PETER, II PETER, JAMES, JUDE

We are going to consider Peter, James and Jude in the Experimental group, which is now our subject. We have already considered Philippians and Philemon, and I want just to summarize in a phrase only: Philippians is the revelation of the Christian experience as Joy triumphant; Philemon is the revelation of the Christian experience as Love triumphant.

We come now to the Letters of Peter. There are two of them and they breathe the same spirit of triumph exactly, and consequently we need not enter into any discussion. We shall, of course, have to see why they were written, because it is very important; but as to where Peter was when he wrote these Letters and when they were written, we need not argue.

The background of the first Letter of Peter is revealed in its introduction: "Peter, an apostle of Jesus Christ, to the elect who are sojourners of the Dispersion in Pontus, Galatia, Cappadocia, Asia, and Bithynia." This was written to the elect, who are the sojourners of the dispersion. That word "dispersion" was a well-known word. You will find it used in James also, and in the Gospel according to John in a remarkable connection when Jesus spoke to the multitude about going away, and that they should not see Him: and then they began discussing and asked, among other things, "What does He mean? Where is He going? Is He going to those of the dispersion?" That is exactly the same phrase used which Peter has written: and mark very carefully, he is writing not to the members of the dispersion but to the elect, to the Christians who are members of the dispersion. "Dispersion" was a collective term in common use at the time among the Jewish people, and it referred to the Jews who were scattered over Asia.

Now Peter is writing to those who he says are elect, and then tells us what he means by elect. I pause because it is important. "To the elect in... Bithynia according to the fore-knowledge of God the Father, in sanctification of the Spirit, unto obedience and sprinkling of the blood of Jesus Christ: Grace to you and peace be multiplied." There you have the actual background. This Letter was written to Jews, but to believing Jews—in other words, to Christian Jews. At this time, the very name of "Christian" was held in contempt by the pagan world. The rulers not only disliked, but positively hated these Christians. And these Christian Jews scattered all over Asia were facing at this time—I quote a verse from the Letter—"fiery trials."

This is the Letter, and these were the people to whom it was written. I want to call to mind that it was really Simon Peter who was talking. Oh, the matchless wonder of our Lord's method! Simon was positively sure that he would not deny his Lord even if everybody else denied Him. And he was sincere, but he did not know himself. Our Lord knew him. And He told him what was going to happen, and in that connection He said this: "When thou art turned back again, stablish thy brethren"—you are going to deny Me, going down into the depths, Peter; but "when thou art turned back, stablish thy brethren." Now just for a passing moment look at this Letter at Chapter 5:10: "And the God of all grace, who called you... strengthen you." And the purpose of Peter in writing this Letter was to do that very thing that his Lord had told him—to stablish them and strengthen them, these people passing through fiery trials, knowing what slaughter and persecution meant, their confidence and their faith in peril as happens with people always at such times.

What is the whole theme of this Letter? You have it all here in the beginning: "Blessed be the God and Father of our Lord Jesus Christ, who according to his great mercy begat us again unto a living hope by the resurrection of Jesus Christ from the dead, unto an inheritance incorruptible, and undefiled, and that fadeth not away, reserved in heaven for you, who by the power of God are guarded through faith unto a salvation ready to be revealed in the last time." That is the summary of the truths that Peter was insisting on. He goes on: "Wherein ye greatly rejoice, though now for a little while, if need be, ye have been put to grief in manifold trials, that the proof of your faith..."

There is the starting point. What is Peter showing them? Just this: that they were begotten by God to a living hope by the resurrection of Jesus Christ, and that being thus begotten by God, they are guarded unto a complete salvation that is to be revealed. And in another Letter he tells them that they shall be perfected after a little while. The great theme of his Letter is that the Christian life is a life of triumph. The Letter stresses life triumphant in conduct; life triumphant in character; life triumphant in conflict. These people are Christians: they are elect, they had been begotten by God, guarded by God to a hope and held by God for the ultimate glory; and their faith being tried, he is writing to stablish them.

In view of this life—begotten by God, guarded by God, kept by God—they have been brought into relationship with the living Christ, and they are partakers of the divine nature. What is their responsibility? Read Chapter 5:8: "Be sober, be watchful." The effect of this life and its abundant possibility of power is not to make them careless but careful. But why? Because their supreme enemy is not to be found in the persecuting emperor, or the persecuting pagan world, or the persecuting Jews; but there is a power behind with which they have to deal: "your adversary, the devil, as a roaring lion, walketh about, seeking whom he may devour." They were to mark the predicated force of the power that was opposed to them, and to remember that it was a spiritual force of wickedness—the devil as a roaring lion, ever seeking for the

Weakest link, the least guarded door, the place where he could break in and attack the citadel of the soul.

And then Peter uses this phrase—I do not know whether this grips others as it always grips me—"Knowing that the same sufferings are being accomplished in your brethren who are in the world."

What are we to do? The word is individual. We are to trust the life that is ours, and act in its power, allowing it to have full dominion over us. We are to be vigilant, watchful, sober; and we are to fight and withstand, remembering that each one is not alone in the fight. The same afflictions are being accomplished in our brethren in the world. You see what an incentive this is, for if I break down I am affecting the whole band. If I am true and faithful and sincere in the power of this life, begotten in me by God, then I strengthen the whole of the people. That is our responsibility.

Now turn to James, and the background is the same as that of the Letters of Peter. Read verse 1: "James, a servant of God and of the Lord Jesus Christ, to the twelve tribes which are of the Dispersion, greeting." He is writing to the same people and their background is the same. Notice from this Letter that these people are experiencing manifold temptations. It is evident—though it is not stated here—that one great danger threatened these people while they were thus suffering from manifold temptations: they were becoming content with their faith as an intelligent concept having no bearing upon conduct. We are all familiar with the fact that there are those who say that Paul put the doctrine of justification by faith in contrast if not in opposition, to James with his doctrine of justification by works. Now it is an arresting fact that so great a soul as Luther ruled that James contradicted Paul's doctrine of justification by faith. Now it is a very daring thing to differ from a man who has been dead a long time, and moreover from so great a man to whom the world has owed so much as to Luther. But Luther was wrong and mistaken. Yet I think you can understand him when you remember the background and the conception in which Luther lived and the awful degeneracy of Christianity against which he protested, with its indulgences and so forth. To him, faith and its concept was everything that mattered. It did seem to Luther that James was giving away the citadel. If you look through James, you will discover that there is no letter more mighty in its evidence for faith as a principle than this Letter of James. It is eloquent in a remarkable sense, with allusions to the Sermon on the Mount (there are more references to it in James than in all the Letters of the New Testament put together). James was the brother of our Lord Himself, and I have no doubt that all through his early years he was critical and wondering. I do not think he or his brother Jude came into anything like intimate connection with Jesus until after the resurrection. And yet it is perfectly evident that he followed and listened to Him and was impressed by His ethical teaching and His moral demands. These things show all through his Letter. Now then, what is he doing? He is showing them that faith assures the victory. If there is no victory their faith is worthless. Their faith is of no value if they still have lust and war, one with another.

That is the great message. He is not denying faith, he is glorifying it and interpreting it. He is showing the tremendous effect of faith that produces conduct and action according to righteousness. In other words, he is showing that the result of faith is triumph.

And if you look at Chapter 2:26, he summarizes everything by saying, "For as the body apart from the spirit is dead, even so faith apart from works is dead." And does any man imagine that Paul would have quarreled with that? I think I could turn to Paul to show that he was just as insistent upon the importance of work as was James. No, James is not correcting Paul; he is correcting a false concept of faith which looks upon it as an intellectual thing and fails to see it as producing definite and positive and ethical and moral results. That is the great message.

We read in Chapter 5:7: "Be patient, therefore, brethren, until the coming of the Lord. Behold, the husbandman waiteth for the precious fruit of the earth, being patient over it, until it receive the early and latter rain. Be ye also patient; establish your hearts: for the coming of the Lord is at hand." There is the question of responsibility. The husbandman is patient. What for? Fruit. Faith without works is dead. But faith, if it be a living faith, is triumphant and produces results in character and in conduct.

Let us turn to Jude, that One wonderful chapter. What is the background of this Letter? "Jude, a servant of Jesus Christ, and brother of James, to them that are called, beloved in God the Father, and kept for Jesus Christ: Mercy unto you and peace and love be multiplied." This Letter is not merely for those of the dispersion but for all Christians, for those who believe in and keep themselves in the Christian religion.

One of the most interesting facts about this Letter is that he did not *mean* to write on the subject in the Letter. He had a purpose but this was not within it. What do I mean by that? If you will read the Letter, he says, "While I was giving all diligence to write unto you of our common salvation, I was constrained to write unto you exhorting you to contend earnestly for the faith which was once for all delivered unto the saints." He was intending to write about one subject and then something happened and he had to write about another subject. I remember hearing that poet-preacher of Wales, Mr. Elvert Lewis, preach out of Jude. Said Mr. Lewis, "I cannot say dogmatically, but I think the Holy Spirit knew that there was no need for him to write a treatise on our common salvation, because St. Paul was doing that in the Letter to the Romans; but there was something important. What was it? What was the purpose of this Letter? It was written undoubtedly because through the atmosphere of the pagan world, and through violence and persecution and trial, the people were in danger of breaking away from the Lord and Saviour Jesus Christ."

And that is the whole point of the Letter, to save them from that appalling peril. Jude refers to it in the fourth verse: "…denying our only Master and Lord, Jesus Christ." And he is writing this Letter urging them to have absolute loyalty, and in triumphant loyalty to give complete cession to the Lordship of Jesus Christ.

I close by asking What is the individual responsibility? Jude conveys it in verses 20,21: "But ye, beloved, building up yourselves on your most holy faith, praying in the Holy Spirit, keep yourselves in the love of God." Be very careful not to miss the meaning. It does not mean you must do things that will keep you in the love of God; but, being in the love of God, keep there. It does not mean you must do the things that will make God love you—you cannot do anything that will make God cease to love you—but respond, act in accordance with it and "keep yourselves in the love of God, looking for the mercy of our Lord Jesus Christ unto eternal life."

So, in Jude, we have a revelation of the way of loyalty, and the triumph of loyalty.

I will summarize these Experimental Letters in this way: remember the experience of Christian life is that of joy triumphant, of love triumphant, of life triumphant, of faith triumphant, and of loyalty triumphant. Or to quote Paul's great word in his Roman Letter, it is possible for us to be more than conquerors over all these things through Him that loved us.

33. I CORINTHIANS, II CORINTHIANS, I TIMOTHY, II TIMOTHY, TITUS

By way of introduction to this chapter, I want to remind you that the Church is not an end but a means to an end. I think it is very important that we should remember that, and we are greatly in danger of forgetting it. I have but to recall to memory words that we have pondered together in other connections, the great words written by Peter, "Ye are an elect race, a royal priesthood, a holy nation, a people for Gods own possession, that ye may show forth the excellencies of him who called you out of darkness into his marvelous light." And taking from that great declaration the simple central truth revealed, it is this: Ye are… that ye may." "Ye are"—and he described the Church; "that ye may"—and he tells the purpose of the Church. The Church is the instrument of illumination, the vehicle of vision, the method of manifestation. Consequently, it is at once seen that the Church has a vocation. That is what I mean when I speak of the Vocational Letters, the Letters that are especially concerned With the Church's great vocation.

I have placed these Letters in two groups, again not intending that the grouping shall be in any sense dogmatic or final, but suggestive: First, I and II Corinthians, I and II Timothy, and Titus, the Letters dealing with the temporal, or present, vocation of the Church, the vocation of the Church in time; and second, two Letters, Ephesians and Colossians, dealing with the eternal vocation of the Church, the vocation of the Church in the ages to come.

We take now the first group, and here, once more, let me make a division between these. In Corinthians we have Letters which have to do with a Church. In Timothy and Titus we have Letters having to do with the ministry within the Church. I divide them in that way, and I am condensing greatly because there is a good deal to see in these Letters.

In I Corinthians we have positive teaching, and II Corinthians is an addition to the First; I am not proposing to tarry with the Second Letter but will concentrate on the First. It has often been said by expositors that this Letter to the Corinthians sets forth true Church order. I am not quarreling with that, but I am inclined to say it does not go far enough. What is the Church set in order for? And there we reach the deepest note—service. It is the Church at work, and the Church fitted for work, and the things that hinder the Church in her work that are largely apparent in the Corinthian Letter.

Now let us take the background of this particular Letter. We have to remember the particular Church we have here, the Church of Corinth. In Paul's day Corinth was the virtual, if not the actual, capital of Greece. It was a rare and wonderful city, famous for its wealth, for its magnificence, for its theosophic dissertations. There are two words coming to us from that time. One is a phrase that refers to "Corinthian words"; and by Corinthian words was meant a form of eloquence and ability in speech. Great orators uttered Corinthian words. There is another equally revealing phrase that gives us an emphasis on the times of Corinth: "They lived as they did in Corinth." And whenever you find that anywhere in Greek writings, you know it refers to a state of corruptness and lasciviousness and unbridled passion to which men were giving vent. At the same time they were discussing philosophies, the wisdom of words. Ah! there is a phrase you have noticed in reading the Letter. Paul said it was wisdom of words, eloquence in discussion, philosophy. And there you have the background of this Letter.

The story of the founding of the Church of God there is very simple and very beautiful. Paul came there from Athens. He had crossed over into Europe, coming to Philippi, moving on to Thessalonica. There had been difficulties there and some of the brethren (I think because they felt that he was somewhat tired and weary and oppressed) sent him away from Thessalonica to Berea, a little town off the highway of Caesarea; and it always interests me to find that Paul went to Berea but did not stay long, although he found the Bereans who listened more noble than those of Thessalonica. Do you remember why? Because they searched the Scriptures to see if these things were so.

It is often said that those Bereans did not want argument, but just received what was told them and believed it without any question. That is exactly what they did *not* do. They listened to Paul; and then they searched the Scriptures to see if he was right. That is the duty of everyone when listening to any preaching. But Paul did not stay in Berea. They got him away to Athens. You know the marvelous story of Athens. Then he left Athens and went on to Corinth where he found two people of the same trade as himself, and he went on with his trade and his preaching. The Lord appeared to him in Athens and said a remarkable thing that I never read without feeling the thrill of it: "I have many people in this city"; this city where you would have expected that there would not be any. But men were tired of the discussion of clever men and were waiting for some authoritative message, Paul stayed there and so the Church was founded.

Now to come to the boundaries of Corinthians. In the first chapter, after a general statement, Paul makes the great pronouncement in verse 9: "God is faithful, through whom ye were called into the fellowship of his Son Jesus Christ our Lord." That is the great fundamental affirmation Paul makes at the beginning of this Letter and which colors everything that runs through it. Now where is the end of the argument? We have it in Chapter 15:58: "Wherefore, my beloved brethren, be ye stedfast, unmovable, always abounding in the work of the Lord, forasmuch as ye know that your labor is not vain in the Lord." There are the boundaries. The verse begins, "Wherefore." I am greatly interested in the struggle expositors have had with that "Wherefore." Some say it is immediately connected with the great resurrection chapter. They are wrong. That is not the final thing. You put these words close together (they are close together in value and intention) and what do you have? "God is faithful, through whom ye were called into the fellowship of his Son Jesus Christ... wherefore... be ye stedfast, immovable, always abounding in the work of the Lord."

These are the great boundaries of the Letter, a fundamental and final affirmation, and everything between bears witness that these Christian people have been put into fellowship with Christ. God will be faithful, and the ultimate appeal is that we should be faithful, stedfast, always abounding in the work of the Lord.

Now between these boundaries you will find that the epistle written to these people has to do with things that are interfering with their fulfillment of their mission and their responsibility. It is very interesting to notice that this Letter is an answer to a letter, or letters, Paul had received. And you notice he never gets to the answer until the seventh chapter and there he says, "Now concerning the things whereof ye wrote." And then he begins to answer the questions they had asked him. Evidently they were faced with certain difficulties and had written to him about them; and he received the letter and sat down to dictate, or write, his answer. These later chapters are our divisions, and are occupied with other matters, but they all have a bearing upon their questions.

What do you find in his answer? Take the first part. He is dealing with intellectual difficulties that had sprung up and had caused schism where they ought to have been united. Paul is showing them the folly and futility of such divisions. Then he has to deal with secular matters, for there are moral derelictions permeating the Church of God. And then he comes to the seventh chapter and deals with the difficulties about which they wrote. I need not now enumerate them, but we can put them all together briefly by saying that the Church had become infected with the spirit of the city. How constantly that has been the difficulty! Indeed, I have been told sometimes and have heard it said that the duty of the Church is to catch the spirit of the age. A thousand times, *No.* The duty of the Church is to correct the spirit of the age, and in proportion as a Church becomes infected by the spirit of the age or the spirit of the city, she loses her power to do her work. Her work is to be in fellowship, in partnership with Jesus Christ and to do His mighty work. Paul is dealing with the intellectual discussions of those who say, "I am of Apollos; he is the more eloquent"; and others who say, "We do not agree to that; we are of Cephas who is the principal apostle and we are following him."

Then there are those moral derelictions to which I have referred, and Paul was dealing so far with the things of carnality which were causing divisions, and paralyzing the Church. Then he comes to Chapter 11, and he says, "Now concerning the spirituals." Not, as in our Version, "spiritual gifts." That is a great mistake, and has not the thought of gifts in it. The Greek word may be rendered "spirituals." He had been dealing with the things that hinder the Church. "Now," said Paul, "we come to the spiritualities, to the things that equip the Church for her service." What are they? First, infinite truth that makes all one; second, infinite law, which, being obeyed, there can be no schism and no weakness; and finally, the ultimate triumph of resources. So you see here how Paul has put one opposite the other:

Divisions—the unifying spirit.

Derelictions—the law of love.

Difficulties—the ultimate triumph through Christ.

Such is the great Letter. The Church is to fulfill her function, her relationship, her partnership with Christ.

What is the final appeal? Read Chapter 15:58: "Be ye stedfast, unmovable, always abounding in the work of the Lord," doing things with Jesus. God has put you into partnership with the Lord. You are to be faithful. That is the Church's function; and the Church is fitted for the fulfillment of her vocation as she masters the carnalities in the power of the spiritualities.

Now let us look briefly at these three little Letters, two to Timothy and one to Titus. What is the background of these Letters to Timothy? Ephesus—wealthy, almost beyond the computation of wealth, the capital of the Ionian confederacy of States. When Paul lived at Ephesus, there was the Temple of Diana, one of the wonders of the world for its beauty, that Temple which was the banking house of the merchant men, and was—of course—the center of worship. It was the home of necromancy and the black arts. And in the midst of such conditions was a Church, a company of believers, a company of the followers of Christ, united to Christ. Timothy is there in over sight, watching over and caring for the Church in the interest of the city of Ephesus.

What were his resources? In the Second Letter, Chapter 1:12,13,14, we read: "For which cause I suffer also these things: yet I am not ashamed; for I know him whom I have believed, and I am persuaded that he is able to guard that which I have committed unto him against that day. Hold the pattern of sound words which thou hast heard from me, in faith and love which is in Christ Jesus. That good thing which was committed unto thee guard through the Holy Ghost which dwelleth in us." Here, once more, I am going to join issue with a most common and popular interpretation of it. Paul says, "I know whom I have believed... guard." Guard what? I read from the Revised Version: "that which I have committed unto him" Did you notice the marginal reading? The marginal reading says, "He is able to guard that which is committed unto him." Now which is right? They cannot both be right. As a matter of fact, neither of them is correct in strict translation, and consequently there may be room for both meanings. Let me translate literally. What does it say? "I am persuaded that he is able to guard my deposit." Ah! that may mean something Paul had deposited with Him. That is how it is usually taken. But it may mean that He, God, is able to guard that which He, God, hath deposited with Paul. Personally, I am sure that is what he meant: the thing which God gave Paul for which he is responsible. And he goes on to say, "that good thing which is committed unto thee." Paul had a deposit, so had Timothy a deposit. It was a deposit of truth. Paul says, I know God is able to guard it, but do not forget, you are responsible too. You have got to guard it, to guard that which He has committed unto thee through the Holy Ghost which dwelleth in thee. But there is a reference to Ephesus, to the deposit to the Church, and Timothy, the minister, is responsible for that deposit: to make it known to the Church, to apply it to the Church, so that the deposit of truth may be revealed, flashing its light upon Ephesus. It is so difficult not to stop here. What is this truth committed? Go back for a moment to the previous Letter and you will find it—the Church of the living God, which is the pillar and the ground of the truth—"And without controversy great is the mystery of godliness; He who was manifested in the flesh, justified in the spirit, seen of angels, preached among the nations, believed on in the world, received up in glory." That is the truth, and the minister is responsible for that truth. It is his deposit. I do not want to be uncharitable, but any man in the ministry who fails to show that has been false to his ministry. So far as the truth itself is concerned, the deposit committed to the minister of God is to be kept and guarded, and the minister is to have his responsibility. I think that all students of the ministry should be compelled to make an intensive devotional study of I and II Timothy.

If you want a revelation of what the ministry in the Church really means, turn to Titus. In essential teaching it is linked with the Letter to Timothy. The background is Crete, and what a background it is! What has Paul to say about Crete? He says it to you by quotation: "A prophet of their own said, Cretans are always liars, evil beasts, idle gluttons. This testimony is true." That is the condition. What is the background? Even there you have a company of believing souls: and if you read it carefully you will see one thing; that the Church had become disordered through false teachers, and Titus was sent to set things in order. He called them together for an understanding of their position in Christ. Paxil charges him to be careful about sound doctrine. This is only a letter to Titus, but it summarizes in a most remarkable way the whole truth concerning the Christian fact and enterprise. Read Chapter 2:11, 12, 13 : "The grace of God hath appeared, bringing salvation to all men, instructing us, to the intent that, denying ungodliness and worldly lusts, we should live soberly and righteously and godly in this present world; looking for the blessed hope and the appearing of the glory of the great God and our Saviour Jesus Christ."

After the advocation of sound doctrine, the second duty of the Church is to live soberly, righteously, godly, forevermore looking for the second advent. And this Letter recognizes that Titus is responsible for teaching the responsibility laid upon every man who is called into the sacred ministry. Thus, the Church is seen in the midst of darkness, for the sake of that darkness, that the light may shine.

The minister is the servant, not of the Church, but of Jesus Christ for the sake of the Church—the one in oversight who is seen watching over the Church that its shining may be clear. The Chinch that is in business for Jesus Christ, let her be stedfast, unmovable, abounding in the sacred and holy work because Corinth needs it—and the world needs it. And those who are called into the ministry of watching over the Church shall be having authority, which is the authority of the truth itself made known and applied to our lives and the things of the time and the age.

34. Ephesians, Colossians

We consider here the two Letters to the Ephesians and Colossians which I have already described as dealing with the eternal vocation of the Church. From the standpoint of systematic teaching, unquestionably these two Letters constitute the ultimate in Pauline teaching. I am not dealing with the time of writing; I am thinking of the whole of Paul's writings which have been preserved for us. The system of his teaching unquestionably begins with the Roman Letter, the fundamental letter dealing with the subject of salvation. And on and on, in differing ways, we may follow as Paul gives interpretation to one to whom was committed the stewardship of the Church, until we reach these two Letters. Of course, in common with the Letter to the Philippians, these Letters were also written from prison. Without doubt they are Letters of the first imprisonment, as was also that to Philemon.

The supreme note of these Letters is the eternal note transcending time. I do not mean that either of these Letters deals merely with heaven. The present is clearly seen in both of them, but the present is set in a remarkable way both in Ephesians and Colossians in the light of the ages to come, and the ages that have gone by. As I have studied these Letters again, reading them and pondering them, I have felt that somehow all they say stands between the eternities and reveals the relationship with those eternities, the past and the future.

I prefer to reverse the order in which these Letters appear in our Bible, taking Colossians first and Ephesians second. There has been a good deal written as to the order in which Paul wrote these Letters; I am not going to enter into such discussion for the order does not matter. For the purpose of this survey I prefer to take Colossians first and then Ephesians.

Here we can deal simultaneously with the background of both because their general background is the same. They were written to men in the very pagan world as represented by the Roman Empire. The first Letter we are to consider was written to people of the Church in Colosse. In the margin of the Letter three places are mentioned, not only Colosse but Laodicea and Hierapolis, and the Letter is sent to this group. Some one has well said that they could have been three mission stations. At any rate, Colosse was the central and influential one of the three. Colosse of that time may be dismissed very briefly. All that is necessary to note is that it was a residential city rather than a commercial one. Ephesus was commercial and wealthy. Colosse was characterized by a very great beauty: and the Church was there. It is only necessary to read this Letter to see plainly that the Church was in danger through philosophic teaching which degraded the Person of Christ. Every one of the Letters reveals that in all of these Churches there was that special danger. Unquestionably what is known as the gnostic heresy had invaded the thinking of the Church. To accept the teaching of the gnostics and thus be influenced by that gnostic heresy was to degrade the Person of our Lord and Saviour Jesus Christ, removing Him from the height to an infinitely lower truth. The great purpose of the Colossian Letter is to set forth the glories of the Christ, to correct false thinking about Him.

Turn from the city of Colosse to Ephesus, and there arises the question of the scholars as to whether this Letter was ever intended for Ephesus or for a group of Churches. If to a group of Churches, certainly Ephesus was one, and Ephesus was the central one. The story of Ephesus is very interesting. Timothy came to that city and John came; to know more about the city we can turn to Revelation and read the Letter the Lord sent to Ephesus.

In Colossians the theme that fills the mind of the Apostle supremely is the glories of Christ. What are the glories of Christ referred to? First creation, and secondly resurrection, and finally peace through Christ. We begin with the glories of Christ and see His glories in creation: Paul calls Him the first-born of all creation. Then we come to the glories of the resurrection: He is the first-born from the dead. And then follows the issue, that in all things He should have the pre-eminence, and that all things should be summed up in Him, having made peace through the blood of His Cross.

The first-born of Creation! That does not mean first in order of procedure, but first-born in the sense of being very high and supreme in the realm of creation. Paul makes it perfectly clear by what he says—that all things have been created by Him, and in Him all things hold together in creation of which He is the origin and the sustainer. He is the revelation of God, the glories of Christ. Those philosophic thinkers, those gnostic teachers who were putting between men and the ultimate truth, intermediaries, indulgences and so forth, are told by Paul that there is no need for any of these because of the glory of the origin of creation and the glory and the sustenance of that which is created is in Christ Himself.

Take these two phrases and see how wonderful they are! First-born of creation: in Him all things agree, in Him all things consist; all the power and the wisdom and the beauty of the glory of God are seen as resident in Him and in Him all the fullness dwells corporeally, bodily. And first-born from the dead: life won out of death, a new beginning growing out of ultimate disaster. We see Him not only as the originator of all the wonders of creation and their sustainer, but we see Him in a great mystery stopping death, coming out of it, first-born, taking pre-eminence in the lonely splendor of His victory. And on the basis of it, through Him peace is yet to be established.

Then go on with the Letter to find this wondrous thing, that all these things of infallible glory are at the disposal of the Church. Read in Chapter 1, starting at verse 24: "Now I rejoice in my sufferings for your sake, and fill up on my part that which is lacking of the afflictions of Christ in my flesh for his body's sake, which is the church; whereof I was made a minister, according to the dispensation of God which was given me to you-ward, to fulfil the word of Cod, even the mystery which hath been hid from all ages and generations: but now hath it been manifested to his saints, to whom God was pleased to make known what is the riches of the glory of this mystery among the Gentiles, which is Christ in you, the hope of glory: whom we proclaim, admonishing every man and teaching every man in all wisdom, that we may present every man perfect in Christ." In Chapter 2 he goes on to say: "For I would have you know how greatly I strive for you, and for them at Laodicea... that their hearts may be comforted, they being knit together in love, and unto all riches of the full assurance of understanding, that they may know the mystery of God, even Christ."

That is an imperfect reading. There has been much more, very much more, that we might have read, but this selection was intentional. I wanted to stress repeatedly that word "mystery." "The mystery of the church"; go a little further, and read again, "this mystery... which is Christ in you, the hope of glory"; until we come to the ultimate, "the mystery of God, even Christ." It may be wise to repeat something that is very well known to some and very commonplace: the word "mystery" in the New Testament never means what it does today. In the New Testament the word "mystery" always means something that cannot be discovered by the intellect but which can be revealed; and which, being revealed, can be apprehended. A very great distinction! We read a paper today and see something that is in it, and say, "That is a great mystery." We mean something we do not understand. That is not what "mystery" means here. Here it is something that could not be discovered by the thought processes of a philosopher but which can be and has been revealed; and a thing revealed is a thing manifest.

Here, in this Letter, Paul is talking about the mystery of the Church, and then he stresses that to the ultimate—the "mystery" of Christ in you, the hope of glory. Very reverently, take those things and put them in the other way from which Paul referred to them: the ultimate mystery is Christ; the second great mystery is that Christ is formed in the human soul; and the resultant mystery is the Church, the glory of the Church, the mystery of it in its glorious place.

These—I say it reverently—are at the disposal of the soul in whom Christ is. And these glories are at the disposal of the Church for her fulfillment of her great vocation in the world. The summarizing declaration is that in Chapter 2:9, 10 "For in him dwelleth all the fulness of the Godhead bodily, and in him ye are made full, who is the head of all principality and power." All fullness is in Him, and we are in Him filled to the full All the resources and the glories of Christ are at the disposal of His Church.

With that general idea of the Colossian Letter we turn to the Letter to the Ephesians, the subject of which is the eternal character of the Church. We see the Church, as in Colosse, as being at the disposal of the fullness that is in Christ. Now at Ephesus we see the Church and its ultimate meaning, its ultimate vocation. The first subject is the eternal character of the Church, and it may be said that this is the whole theme of the Letter. To read the first part is to find that the Church was, according to the plan of God from eternity and past ages, to flash a light upon the present. Remember the words, "before the foundation of the world"—the plan of God. Go on, and read that that Church is now made nigh, in the power of God in time. The true revelation of this Ephesian Letter always seems to me to be that the purpose of God in eternity is to be fulfilled by the Church in the generations of the age and the ages. Ephesus stretches back before the foundation of the world, and looks on to the generations of the ages, and the great inclusive age of that marvelous description that must forever baffle us, as all these references to the ages will. We make a tremendous mistake when we attempt to express it in some words of our own thinking. For instance: our translation of "forever" is really an absurd poetic suggestiveness, an imagery. Have you ever sat down and tried to dream—it may be a very foolish thought but I have often done it—of the ages to come? Have you ever tried to peer into the future through the spheres—or to look back? We can look back no further than the Bible takes us and the Bible does not take us very far. But for a few moments, let us roll history back and see age succeeding age, each having its own value and leading to a great movement. On the basis of the intellect, try to imagine the generation of the age of the ages. I know a little about them. Then the age I am living in, how is it going to end? (I do not know when it is going to end, but I know how.) I know beyond this age there is yet another. I have some gleams of things beyond, but I do not know. But I do know this: the vocation of the Church lies out there ultimately and finally.

Now Paul tells us two things about the vocation of the Church in these ages: the first is found in the second Chapter of the Ephesian Letter, in verse 4: "God, being rich in mercy, for his great love wherewith he loved us." And in verse 7: "That in the ages to come he might show the exceeding riches of his grace in kindness toward us in Christ Jesus." I will dream my dreams about those ages, knowing nothing about them, reverently peer into them and think about them, age succeeding age; but I believe that in all those ages, those undying ages, the Church is to be the central witness of the

grace of God by reason of His kindness to us. The eternal vocation!

Glance at Chapter 3:10 and mark the resulting thing, the immediateness: "To the intent that now unto the principalities and the powers in the heavenly places might be made known through the church the manifold wisdom of God"

The thing is absolutely overwhelming. I do not say inexplicable, because I believe it. The ultimate vocation of the Church—and I hope the words will not be spoiled by putting them in a different form—what is it? To be a light out of the ages. And what is the Church to do in the ages? To reveal to those ages the grace of God: not to preach the Gospel, but to reveal the grace of God. Have we ever considered the meaning of our redemption? You and I individually, presently the whole Church, will pass out into those ages to reveal the grace of God as it can be revealed in no other way. That is a tremendous thought, and yet how true! Do you know there are songs that we can sing that no angels have ever sung or ever will sing? I am not thinking of our hymns but of songs recorded here in the heavenly descriptions. I will tell you what the angels will never be able to sing: "Unto him that hath loved us and redeemed us by his precious blood."

The undying ages! Of ages to come and new movements I cannot say, but this I know: the Church will be telling her story of redemption and showing the grace of God, not to the ages only but to the angels, those unfallen spirits that desire to look into this world and its redemption.

Now hear the appeal: "I beseech you therefore, that ye walk worthy of the vocation wherewith ye are called."

PART VI

THE APOCALYPSE: GOD'S SUPPLY—THE VICTORY OF THE LORD

35. REVELATION—THE CONSUMMATION

We have come to the last of our studies in the general subject of the harmony of the Testaments. I have been thinking once more of the quaint lines of George Herbert— I am almost inclined to say the lines of quaint George Herbert—I quoted in my "General Conspectus":

Oh! that I knew how all thy lights combine,
And the configuration of thy glory.
Seeing not only how each verse doth shine,
But all the constellations of the story.

That is what we have been trying to do, and as we come to the end I feel as I have many a night when I have gone out and looked at the heavens. I have seen them. But how much have I seen? The question would be more appropriate if I said, "How little have I seen?" Yet I have seen enough of the heavens to be conscious of all that lies there.

May we be equally conscious, in our study of the Scriptures, not only of "how each verse doth shine," but of the constellations in their glory.

THE APOCALYPSE
"On his head were many crowns"—Revelation 19:12

THE APOCALYPSE: THE VICTORY OF THE LORD	GRACE: CHRIST AND HIS CHURCH 1-3	
	The Lord Himself 1:1-18 I. Inclusive "The Faithful Witness" —Prophet "The First-born of the Dead"—Priest "The Ruler of the Kings" —King II. Particular Priest—"Unto Him . . ." Prophet—"A Great Voice . . ." King—"The Son of Man . . ."	The Lord and His Church 1:19-3 I. Inclusive Ministry The Seven Stars Church The Seven Lampstands II. Particular The Letters "I know" "I will" "He that hath an ear"
	GOVERNMENT: CHRIST AND THE KINGDOM OF THE WORLD 4-20:6	
	The Central Facts 4, 5 I. The Throne ONE Four Four and Twenty II. The Executive THE LAMB The Book The Songs	The Conflict 6-16 I. Seals II. Trumpets III. Bowls The Victory Won 17-20:6 I. The Fall of 'Babylon II. The Induction of the King III. The Reign
	GLORY: CHRIST AND THE NEW HEAVEN AND NEW EARTH 20:7-22	
	The Last of Evil 20:7-15 I. The Loosing of Satan War Defeat II. The Great Assize The Books Destiny	The Ultimate Glory 21, 22 I. Inclusive The New Heaven and Earth The Metropolis The Test Inclusion Exclusion II. Particular The City Government Grace Glory

We began by saying that the Old Testament gives a revelation of human need, and that in the New we have the revelation of the divine supply. We have now to complete our work with a general survey of the Book of Revelation, the Book of the Apocalypse. That is an anglicized form of the Greek word translated "revelation," which means taking the veil off, or unveiling. There is no book in the Bible I have read more often or pondered more carefully, but also no book concerning which I would be less willing to give a final and dogmatic interpretation. It is in many ways the final book in the Biblical literature, not because it happens to be bound at the end of the Bible as the last book; but because it is a book of culmination, of consummation. Its light flashes supremely into the future. I would remind you that the very first sentence of the book gives us its subject: *the unveiling of Jesus Christ.* So we have in the Bible a survey of the processes of consummation, and in this last book the consummation itself.

To sum up, the Book of Revelation has for its movement the unveiling of Jesus Christ, not of beasts or dragons, of serpents or evil things—though they are all there, all clearly seen; but they are all seen in the light that shines in the unveiling of Jesus Christ. That, to me, is a very important matter in the study of this book. In passing, it should be noted that it is the only book in the Bible which opens with the pronunciation of a blessing upon those who study it.

The book falls into three parts. We have a revelation of Christ in His grace as we see Him in His person; then in His Church walking amid the candlesticks, and holding in His right hand the stars; and lastly we have a picture of Christ in relation to the kingdoms of the world, a revelation of His government. And the final movement in that section which begins at Chapter 17, and ends in Chapter 20 records the fall of Babylon. Babylon has crumbled into dust, fallen.

Turning to the first chapter, the Lord is there presented as the faithful Witness, i.e. the final Prophet; the First-born of the dead, the victorious Priest; and the Ruler of the kings of the earth, the ultimate King. John tells us later in that chapter that he saw "One like unto the Son of man." We are reminded that John knew Him and lived with Him. He had often looked upon that face and laid his head on that bosom. "The Son of man" was our Lord's favorite designation of Himself. Eighty-five times He is thus spoken of, and eighty-three of them are from His own lips. It is a title which links Him Closely with humanity.

The Letters to the Seven Churches follow. They are full of interest, and again their purpose is to unveil Jesus Christ. He is seen in His personal glory in the midst of them. The seven stars represent the ministers, the lamp-stands are the Churches, and the Lord in the midst speaks to His Churches. His messages show intimate knowledge, severe condemnation, and comforting commendation. Three things are common to each letter: "I know"; "I will"; and, "He that hath an ear let him hear what the Spirit saith to the churches." Would to God that all our Churches would hear that voice and begin to obey it. We listen too much to leaders and do not take time to listen to the Spirit of God.

Chapter 4 takes us into the throne room of the universe, where is centered all authority and all power. In the right hand of Him that sat upon the throne was a book, the book for earthly government and the carrying out of the divine program on the earth level. It was no wonder that John wept. Probably we feel the same when we realize that no one seems equal to the vast task of carrying out the government of the world. But there is Someone who is able. He belongs to heaven and earth and is Master of all the underworld. As John turned to look for the majestic lion who he was assured would be able to open the book, he saw—not a lion—but "a lamb standing as though it had been slain." Into that pierced hand the roll was placed. He alone was worthy to carry forth the government of human affairs.

From Chapter 6 on through the following chapters, whatever is recorded there is of happenings after the breaking of a seal, a seal that is only broken by the pierced hand. Amid conflict and chaos He is governing. The final movement in that section, which begins at Chapter 17 and ends in Chapter 20, records the fall of Babylon. The great foreshowing is that the kingdoms of the world are become the Kingdom of our Lord and of His Christ. Many different views are held regarding the interpretation of these chapters. The chief mistake any person can make is to think that his view is the only one that is right.

In the last section of that earlier part of the book we have the story of the introduction of the king, and then a declaration of a period of a thousand years. That period is generally spoken of as the millennium. I am not saying it is wrong, but I do sometimes regard it as a piece of overemphasis which is placed upon the meaning and its value. Six times over in that section that same phrase occurs, "the thousand years." Now let it be said that one cannot know details of those thousand years, but it remains an assertion. Details are not declared, in fact the statement covers only a few sentences. That period is most evidently an interlude. It is not the ending of things, it is at that section that we are especially to look. In Chapter 20 from verse 7 to verse 15, there is a very mysterious paragraph. It is a paragraph that tells us that beyond the thousand years Satan is to be loosed. During that period of the thousand years he is not to be: he is confined, imprisoned. But at the end of the thousand years he is to be loosed for a season. Then comes a brief and pregnant sentence. Being loosed, he gathers together the nations. There are the names, Gog and Magog. I know some people who, profess to know exactly who they are. I have no means of deciding. I do not think that God has revealed to us or intended us to know who are meant, but they are the nations. Evidently the period of the thousand years has been a period of perfect rule suppressing evil, and at the Close of the period, evil is to be manifested again. Satan is loosed and gathers together the nations against the saints, and against the Kingdom of Christ: and he gathers them together in order to their full and final defeat. During that long interim period evil has been suppressed, but suppressed and held down. It is to be manifested again on this earth, but its manifestation will lead to its immediate and full and final defeat. It is a passage characterized by mystery—details are not given—and yet it is perfectly clear that these things will be.

There follows immediately an account of the great assize, and the great white throne about which we have heard very much all our lives. Many sermons have been preached on the great white throne. Some, I have no doubt were admirable in many ways, and yet I think they may have been misunderstood. But here is the great assize. And remember, the great white throne is not the judgment seat before which we, as Christians, are to appear. In the New Testament we read we must all appear before the judgment seat of Christ, but we cannot—if we are intelligent—take that text and preach from it to the ungodly. The judgment seat of Christ is the judgment seat before which we shall appear for the testing of our service and our works. It shall try us as by fire, and the worthless things shall be destroyed by the clear burning of His eyes, and gold and silver and precious stones will be purified for their final setting in the Kingdom of God. This is the judgment seat of Christ.

"And I saw a great white throne, and him that sat upon it, from whose face the earth and the heaven fled away." You will notice how that assize is conducted. The books were opened—not "the book"—and the dead were judged out of the books, not out of "the book." And at the great assize the books will be opened recording deeds, and no book is to be opened which will have in it those names written in the Lambs book of life. The judgment is for those whose names are not written in that book and whose deeds are recorded in "the books." That is part of this great chapter.

Next come to the vision of the ultimate glory. It begins with the declaration: "I saw a new heaven and a new earth." Think now of where we started. "In the beginning God created the heaven and the earth." We are getting to the end of our study, and what about that end? "I saw a new heaven and a new earth." Everything of divine purpose lay in that great creative potentiality. But we have seen everything ruined, we have seen the processes of human life, and the conduct of history through the long ages and on beyond the ruin. But the end is here now: "I saw a new heaven and a new earth." And in the processes of reading we find how it is brought about. Listen! "Behold, I make all things new." And from that point on are given the visions of the ultimate glory, the new heaven and the new earth. That vision is focused upon the city and the city is the metropolis of that new heaven and that new earth. Could there be anything more wonderful than that description when one reads the account of that city, that metropolis of the new earth? It is an international city. The nations bring their glory and their honor into it. The nations were not destroyed in the ultimate. Is it not very important to remember that? Don't we sometimes think that every nationality will end when the ultimate victory comes? There is no reason whatever to think so. We generally find that people who think nationality will end, think that every nationality will be submerged into the nation to which they belong. It is not so. Each nation has its own deposit, each nation has its own value, in that new Kingdom every nation will have its part; not in any competition with other nations, but for the sole purpose of cooperation with other nations. The gates are wide open; it is a redeemed city. As we approach it and look at the gates, inscribed on them there are twelve names—the names of the Twelve Tribes of the Children of Israel. Go back to the Old Testament and read what Jacob thought of those Twelve Tribes, but there they are. The city is for redeemed and ransomed humanity. Perhaps you have taken your stand by the gates. I imagine looking at the foundation upon which are set the names of the twelve apostles: men of the same nature, men of like passions with ourselves—failing, blundering, redeemed men.

It goes without saying that this holy city of the poetic description which we have here is a city of ineffable beauty. As we read the account we see the glory of the city very largely consists of the nature of things that are *not* there. What do I find? Certain conditions are excluded. We know them all. I simply name them, and trust to your imagination: fear; death; mourning; crying; pain. Certain conditions of character are excluded: the fearful; the unbelieving; the abominable. It is no place for them. There is conduct which is excluded: murder; fornication; sorcery; idolatry; lying. These things are not there. If we go further on we find other things mentioned. There shall be no night there; night is the opportunity of evil. The unclean shall not be there; all uncleanness is the occasion of evil. Nothing that makes a lie is in that city. And there is no curse.

Look around over our world today. Nay, let us look into our own hearts. All the things that spoil and blight are absent from that ultimate order, the order of the full glory and victory of our Lord and Master. We are not given a list of things included, but all the opposites—of which evil is the negative—are included. We may cover all in Johns three great words, and apply them to that city: Light, and Life, and Love. In that city, Love will be the inspiration of everything; and Light in which it is possible to carry out the things inspired; and Life, the energy enabling us to carry out these selfsame things. That city, which is the metropolis of the new order, reveals it in perfect government based on grace and showing in glory. But we have not reached that city yet. We have not seen it, except as we have seen it created from afar, and our revelation of God's supply ends with the picture of that order. Finally, come to the Epilogue of the book, to the final words of Jesus in which the values of the book are declared. It begins with the declarations made as to Himself, and summarizes all we have been trying to see; and the last declaration is, "Behold, I come quickly"—which does not mean "soon," but means in the fullness of time, at the right moment. This is the final word. There are also the final words of John, in which he is in perfect agreement; and the great boundaries, the unveiling of Jesus Christ, and the unveiling of the ultimate glory. That is the great Consummation.

Here is portrayed the fulfillment of the purpose of God when He put man in a garden. A city is always near a garden. There is nothing in London that has not come out of a garden. Think that out, and see if it is possible to suggest anything! I am talking about material London, and I say it all came out of a garden. And God put man in a garden in order that out of the garden he might develop and arrive at the city which should be the metropolis of the perfect order. And man failed, and man has been trying to build a city ever since. That very great man, Bismarck, once said, "All great cities are always great sores upon the body politic." And so they have been, and so they are still. And yet the passion for the city is deeply ingrained in human nature. Side by side with all the blundering and human abortions that man has produced and called a city, there has been this movement toward the ultimate city. Abram left Ur for a city whose Builder and Maker was God. One of the prophets puts into the lips of God these words, and when he did so the walls of Jerusalem lay in ruins, its gates burned by fire—and yet God is speaking, and He says, "Her walls are ever before me." He has never lost sight of her walls. He has never lost sight of His great purpose.

This was the most significant thing which Luke wrote about Jesus when he said, "He stedfastly set his face to go up to the city." To go up to Jerusalem.

Here is the picture of what it meant. Abraham never arrived, he never saw it perfectly, but God saw it. God always saw it. Christ saw it with great and perfect clarity, and set His face to go to the city which was hostile to Him and which he had condemned, moving from the hostility of the ruin toward the building of the city of the established and ultimate order.

In Revelation is the answer to the first part of that prayer the Church has been praying for over 1900 years, "Our Father which art in heaven, Hallowed be thy name. Thy kingdom come. Thy will be done in earth, as it is in heaven." There is the picture of the hour when that prayer will be perfectly answered. Then the Consummation. It is the final supply, the marvelous supply, the working out toward the Consummation. Oh! Tennyson was right:

> One God, one law, one element,
> And one far-off divine event,
> To which the whole creation moves.

And we have been glancing at it in these studies. May I again quote Tennyson:

> Yet I doubt not through the ages one increasing
> purpose runs,
> And the thoughts of men are widened with the
> process of the suns.

Jesus shall reign!

ABOUT CROSSREACH PUBLICATIONS

Thank you for choosing <u>CrossReach Publications</u>.

Hope. Inspiration. Trust.

These three words sum up the philosophy of why CrossReach Publications exist. To creating inspiration for the present thus inspiring hope for the future, through trusted authors from previous generations.

We are *non-denominational* and *non-sectarian*. We appreciate and respect what every part of the body brings to the table and believe everyone has the right to study and come to their own conclusions. We aim to help facilitate that end.

We aspire to excellence. If we have not met your standards please contact us and let us know. We want you to feel satisfied with your product. Something for everyone. We publish quality books both in presentation and content from a wide variety of authors who span various doctrinal positions and traditions, on a wide variety of Christian topics that will teach, encourage, challenge, inspire and equip.

We're a family-based home-business. A husband and wife team raising 8 kids. If you have any questions or comments about our publications email us at:

<u>CrossReach@outlook.com</u>

Don't forget you can follow us on <u>Facebook</u> and <u>Twitter</u>, (links are on the copyright page above) to keep up to date on our newest titles and deals.

BESTSELLING TITLES FROM CROSSREACH²

A. W. TOZER

How to Be Filled with the Holy Spirit
A. W. Tozer

Before we deal with the question of how to be filled with the Holy Spirit, there are some matters which first have to be settled. As believers you have to get them out of the way, and right here is where the difficulty arises. I have been afraid that my listeners might have gotten the idea somewhere that I had a how-to-be-filled-with-the-Spirit-in-five-easy-lessons doctrine, which I could give you. If you can have any such vague ideas as that, I can only stand before you and say, "I am sorry"; because it isn't true; I can't give you such a course. There are some things, I say, that you have to get out of the way, settled.

What We Are In Christ
E. W. Kenyon

I was surprised to find that the expressions "in Christ," "in whom," and "in Him" occur more than 130 times in the New Testament. This is the heart of the Revelation of Redemption given to Paul. Here is the secret of faith—faith that conquers, faith that moves mountains. Here is the secret of the Spirit's guiding us into all reality. The heart craves intimacy with the Lord Jesus and with the Father. This craving can now be satisfied.

Ephesians 1:7: "In whom we have our redemption through his blood, the remission of our trespasses according to the riches of his grace."

It is not a beggarly Redemption, but a real liberty in Christ that we have now. It is a Redemption by the God Who could say, "Let there be lights in the firmament of heaven," and cause the whole starry heavens to leap into being in a single instant. It is Omnipotence beyond human reason. This is where philosophy has never left a footprint.

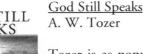

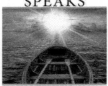

God Still Speaks
A. W. Tozer

Tozer is as popular today as when he was living on the earth. He is respected right across the spectrum of Christianity, in circles that would disagree sharply with him doctrinally. Why is this? A. W. Tozer was a man who knew the voice of God. He shared this experience with every true child of God. With all those who are called by the grace of God to share in the mystical union that is possible with Him through His Son Jesus.

Tozer fought against much dryness and formality in his day. Considered a mighty man of God by most Evangelicals today, he was unconventional in his approach to spirituality and had no qualms about consulting everyone from Catholic Saints to German Protestant mystics for inspiration on how to experience God more fully.

Tozer, just like his Master, doesn't fit neatly into our theological boxes. He was a man after God's own heart and was willing to break the rules (man-made ones that is) to get there.

Here are two writings by Tozer that touch on the heart of this goal. Revelation is Not Enough and The Speaking Voice. A bonus chapter The Menace of the Religious Movie is included.

This is meat to sink your spiritual teeth into. Tozer's writings will show you the way to satisfy your spiritual hunger.

THE TWO BABYLONS

The Two Babylons
Alexander Hislop

Fully Illustrated High Res. Images. Complete and Unabridged.
Expanded Seventh Edition. This is the first and only seventh edition available in a modern digital edition. Nothing is left out! New material not found in the first six editions!!! Available in eBook and paperback edition exclusively from CrossReach Publications.

"In his work on "The Two Babylons" Dr. Hislop has proven conclusively that all the idolatrous systems of the nations had their origin in what was founded by that mighty Rebel, the beginning of whose kingdom was Babel (Gen. 10:10)."—A. W. Pink, The Antichrist (1923) There is this great difference between the works of men and the works of God, that the same minute and searching investigation, which displays the defects and imperfections of the one, brings out also the beauties of the other. If the most finely polished needle on which the art of man has been expended be subjected to a microscope, many inequalities, much roughness and clumsiness, will be seen. But if the microscope be brought to bear on the flowers of the field, no such result appears. Instead of their beauty diminishing, new beauties and still more delicate, that have escaped the naked eye, are forthwith discovered; beauties that make us appreciate, in a way which otherwise we could have had little conception of, the full force of the Lord's saying, "Consider the lilies of the field,

² Buy from <u>CrossReach Publications</u> for quality and price. We have a full selection of titles in print and eBook. All available on the Amazon and Createspace stores. You can see our full selection just by searching for CrossReach Publications in the search bar!

how they grow; they toil not, neither do they spin: and yet I say unto you, That even Solomon, in all his glory, was not arrayed like one of these." The same law appears also in comparing the Word of God and the most finished productions of men. There are spots and blemishes in the most admired productions of human genius. But the more the Scriptures are searched, the more minutely they are studied, the more their perfection appears; new beauties are brought into light every day; and the discoveries of science, the researches of the learned, and the labours of infidels, all alike conspire to illustrate the wonderful harmony of all the parts, and the Divine beauty that clothes the whole. If this be the case with Scripture in general, it is especially the case with prophetic Scripture. As every spoke in the wheel of Providence revolves, the prophetic symbols start into still more bold and beautiful relief. This is very strikingly the case with the prophetic language that forms the groundwork and corner-stone of the present work. There never has been any difficulty in the mind of any enlightened Protestant in identifying the woman "sitting on seven mountains," and having on her forehead the name written, "Mystery, Babylon the Great," with the Roman apostacy.

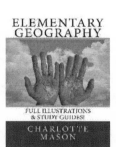

Elementary Geography
Charlotte Mason

This little book is confined to very simple "reading lessons upon the Form and Motions of the Earth, the Points of the Compass, the Meaning of a Map: Definitions."
It is hoped that these reading lessons may afford intelligent teaching, even in the hands of a young teacher.
Children should go through the book twice, and should, after the second reading, be able to answer any of the questions from memory.

Claiming Our Rights
E. W. Kenyon

There is no excuse for the spiritual weakness and poverty of the Family of God when the wealth of Grace and Love of our great Father with His power and wisdom are all at our disposal. We are not coming to the Father as a tramp coming to the door begging for food; we come as sons not only claiming our legal rights but claiming the natural rights of a child that is begotten in love. No one can hinder us or question our right of approach to our Father. Satan has Legal Rights over the sinner that God cannot dispute or challenge. He can sell them as slaves; he owns them, body, soul and spirit. But the moment we are born again... receive Eternal Life, the nature of God,—his legal dominion ends.

Christ is the Legal Head of the New Creation, or Family of God, and all the Authority that was given Him, He has given us: (Matthew 28:18), "All authority in heaven," the seat of authority, and "on earth," the place of execution of authority. He is "head over all things," the highest authority in the Universe, for the benefit of the Church which is His body.

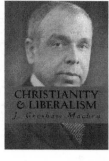

Christianity and Liberalism
J. Gresham Machen

The purpose of this book is not to decide the religious issue of the present day, but merely to present the issue as sharply and clearly as possible, in order that the reader may be aided in deciding it for himself. Presenting an issue sharply is indeed by no means a popular business at the present time; there are many who prefer to fight their intellectual battles in what Dr. Francis L. Patton has aptly called a "condition of low visibility." Clear-cut definition of terms in religious matters, bold facing of the logical implications of religious views, is by many persons regarded as an impious proceeding. May it not discourage contribution to mission boards? May it not hinder the progress of consolidation, and produce a poor showing in columns of Church statistics? But with such persons we cannot possibly bring ourselves to agree. Light may seem at times to be an impertinent intruder, but it is always beneficial in the end. The type of religion which rejoices in the pious sound of traditional phrases, regardless of their meanings, or shrinks from "controversial" matters, will never stand amid the shocks of life. In the sphere of religion, as in other spheres, the things about which men are agreed are apt to be the things that are least worth holding; the really important things are the things about which men will fight.

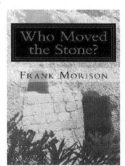

Who Moved the Stone?
Frank Morison

This study is in some ways so unusual and provocative that the writer thinks it desirable to state here very briefly how the book came to take its present form.
In one sense it could have taken no other, for it is essentially a confession, the inner story of a man who originally set out to write one kind of book and found himself compelled by the sheer force of circumstances to write another.
It is not that the facts themselves altered, for they are recorded imperishably in the monuments and in the pages of human history. But the interpretation to be put upon the facts underwent a change. Somehow the perspective shifted—not suddenly, as in a flash of insight or inspiration, but slowly, almost imperceptibly, by the very stubbornness of the facts themselves.

The book as it was originally planned was left high and dry, like those Thames barges when the great river goes out to meet the incoming sea. The writer discovered one day that not only could he no longer write the book as he had once conceived it, but that he would not if he could.

To tell the story of that change, and to give the reasons for it, is the main purpose of the following pages.

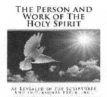

The Person and Work of the Holy Spirit
R. A. Torey

BEFORE one can correctly understand the work of the Holy Spirit, he must first of all know the Spirit Himself. A frequent source of error and fanaticism about the work of the Holy Spirit is the attempt to study and understand His work without first of all coming to know Him as a Person.

It is of the highest importance from the standpoint of worship that we decide whether the Holy Spirit is a Divine Person, worthy to receive our adoration, our faith, our love, and our entire surrender to Himself, or whether it is simply an influence emanating from God or a power or an illumination that God imparts to us. If the Holy Spirit is a person, and a Divine Person, and we do not know Him as such, then we are robbing a Divine Being of the worship and the faith and the love and the surrender to Himself which are His due.

In His Steps
Charles M. Sheldon

The sermon story, In His Steps, or "What Would Jesus Do?" was first written in the winter of 1896, and read by the author, a chapter at a time, to his Sunday evening congregation in the Central Congregational Church, Topeka, Kansas. It was then printed as a serial in The Advance (Chicago), and its reception by the readers of that paper was such that the publishers of The Advance made arrangements for its appearance in book form. It was their desire, in which the author heartily joined, that the story might reach as many readers as possible, hence succeeding editions of paper-covered volumes at a price within the reach of nearly all readers.

The story has been warmly and thoughtfully welcomed by Endeavor societies, temperance organizations, and Y. M. C. A. 's. It is the earnest prayer of the author that the book may go its way with a great blessing to the churches for the quickening of Christian discipleship, and the hastening of the Master's kingdom on earth.

Made in the USA
Columbia, SC
12 November 2017